# Strength Training

## National Strength and Conditioning Association

NSCA

## Lee E. Brown
### *Editor*

**Library of Congress Cataloging-in-Publication**

Strength training / National Strength and Conditioning Association
(NSCA) ; Lee E. Brown, editor.
    p. cm.
 Includes bibliographical references and index.
 ISBN-13: 978-0-7360-6059-2 (soft cover)
 ISBN-10: 0-7360-6059-6 (soft cover)
 1.  Physical education and training. 2.  Muscle strength. 3.  Physical
fitness--Physiological aspects. I. Brown, Lee E., 1956- II. National
Strength & Conditioning Association (U.S.)
 GV711.5.S775 2007
 613.7'13--dc22                                      2006024623

 ISBN-10: 0-7360-6059-6
 ISBN-13: 978-0-7360-6059-2

Copyright © 2007 by the National Strength and Conditioning Association

The Web addresses cited in this text were current as of August 2006, unless otherwise noted.

**Developmental Editor:** Julie Rhoda; **Assistant Editors:** Carla Zych and Cory Weber; **Copyeditor:** Patrick Connelly; **Proofreader:** Kathy Bennett; **Indexer:** Nan Badgett; **Permission Manager:** Dalene Reeder; **Graphic Designer:** Nancy Rasmus; **Graphic Artist:** Kim McFarland; **Photo Managers:** Dan Wendt and Laura Fitch; **Cover Designer:** Keith Blomberg; **Photographer (cover):** Royalty Free/Corbis; **Photographer (interior):** Photo on page 1 (and like thumbnails on pp. i and iv) © Jumpfoto; photo on page 161 (and like thumbnails on pp. i and v) and page 275 (and like thumbnails on pp. i and v) © Getty Images; all other photos by Dan Wendt, unless otherwise noted; **Art Managers:** Kareema McLendon-Foster and Kelly Hendren; **Illustrators:** Argosy, Jason McAlexander, Kareema McLendon-Foster, and Mic Greenberg; **Printer:** United Graphics

We thank the National Strength and Conditioning Association in Colorado Springs, Colorado, and LifeFitness, Inc. in Franklin Park, Illinois, for assistance in providing the locations for the photo shoots for this book.

Human Kinetics books are available at special discounts for bulk purchase. Special editions or book excerpts can also be created to specification. For details, contact the Special Sales Manager at Human Kinetics.

Printed in the United States of America            10  9  8  7  6  5  4  3

**Human Kinetics**
Web site: www.HumanKinetics.com

*United States:* Human Kinetics
P.O. Box 5076
Champaign, IL 61825-5076
800-747-4457
e-mail: humank@hkusa.com

*Canada:* Human Kinetics
475 Devonshire Road, Unit 100
Windsor, ON N8Y 2L5
800-465-7301 (in Canada only)
e-mail: info@hkcanada.com

*Europe:* Human Kinetics
107 Bradford Road
Stanningley
Leeds LS28 6AT, United Kingdom
+44 (0)113 255 5665
e-mail: hk@hkeurope.com

*Australia:* Human Kinetics
57A Price Avenue
Lower Mitcham, South Australia 5062
08 8372 0999
e-mail: info@hkaustralia.com

*New Zealand:* Human Kinetics
Division of Sports Distributors NZ Ltd.
P.O. Box 300 226 Albany
North Shore City, Auckland
0064 9 448 1207
e-mail: info@humankinetics.co.nz

# Strength Training

# Contents

# PART III  Exercise Technique

# PART IV  Sample Programs

# Preface

We are pleased you have chosen this book for your strength training needs. Our purpose is to provide you with information on strength training that is supported by the latest scientific research. Each chapter is written by an expert in the field. This entire book fills a need for a science-based examination of strength training for those who want to know the best way to build strength. The information herein is supported by the National Strength and Conditioning Association (NSCA), a worldwide authority on strength and conditioning.

We have organized the book in a way that will facilitate your progress in understanding and building a complete strength training program. In part I, you will benefit from a detailed explanation of the scientific foundation of strength. You will find a description of muscle anatomy as well as information on how you can maximize your training program by identifying training variables. Part II provides information on assessing your strength and power and interpreting the results of such tests. It also covers ways to prevent injury while strength training so that you can correctly design your workout schedule. The heart of this book is part III, which presents comprehensive exercise techniques through pictures and instructions for all major muscles in the upper body, lower body, and core. Part III concludes with a section on explosive power training movements. In part IV, sample programs are provided for beginners through advanced strength trainers as well as for youth and seniors.

We hope you will find the unique features of this book (such as detailed photos of the start and midpoint of each exercise and the sample training programs) helpful in your search for knowledge on strength training to help you attain your fitness goals.

# PART I

# The Origin of Strength

This part of the book focuses on the science of strength and its foundation. First you need to understand how muscles work and develop in order to plan your strength training program. Chapters 1 through 4 introduce you to many fundamental aspects of muscle physiology, various forms of program design, and proper nutrition for enhancing muscle growth.

Chapter 1, "Muscle Anatomy 101," discusses the various types of muscles and their function as well as muscular contraction and recruitment. This information will allow you to choose exercises targeted for specific body parts as well as to understand the benefits of different types of movements such as pushing and pulling exercises.

Chapter 2, "How Muscle Grows," lays the physiological foundation of the muscular adaptation process. This information is important when you are designing your strength training program because it will guide you in choosing the correct exercises and rest intervals according to your training needs.

Chapter 3, "Types of Muscle Training," introduces the program variables included in a resistance training regimen. It also presents various types of training programs and modalities so you can choose the right workout for you. Finally, it makes recommendations for your training program as they relate to your purpose for exercising.

Chapter 4, "Nutrition for Muscle Development," describes your body's metabolism, how it works, and how you can maximize your efforts to enhance your strength. It further illustrates how food and water interact in your body to provide fuel for maximum muscle development.

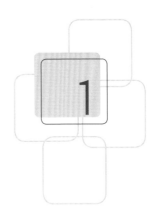

# Muscle Anatomy 101

William J. Kraemer and Jakob L. Vingren

Understanding the basic anatomy of the body is fundamental to knowing how the body works. The general architecture of the skeletal muscles as a whole—as well as the specific composition of individual muscles—determines how each muscle functions. Many of the training principles described throughout this book are based on this knowledge; thus, learning some basic anatomy will help you better understand these training principles and how to use them in strength training.

About 40 percent of the body's tissues are made up of skeletal muscle (based on mass). Skeletal muscles are the muscles that are attached to bones and produce movement across joints. These muscles are discussed throughout this chapter. We start at the smallest anatomical level of the muscle—the proteins that make up each muscle fiber—and gradually expand on each structure to show how they all come together to make an intact, functioning muscle. We include an overview of the muscle anatomy of the human body along with the functions of the major muscle groups.

This chapter also covers how a muscle is stimulated by the nervous system. As you will see, this is ultimately important in strength training—since only those muscles that are stimulated to exercise will be trained and thus developed. In addition, we explain the principles of how different resistance loads stimulate different amounts of muscle (because of the activation of different types of muscle fibers in the muscle). Finally, we cover different types of muscle action and how these actions, along with the structures of the muscle, affect force and power production.

# Muscle Organization

The smallest contractile unit in the muscle is called a *sarcomere*. The sarcomere is made up of many different proteins; the two most important proteins in a sarcomere are *actin* and *myosin*, which produce contractions of the muscle. A *myofibril* is made up of many sarcomeres, and groups of myofibrils make up a single muscle fiber, also called a *muscle cell*. The muscle fibers are grouped together into bundles, and these bundles of muscle fibers make up the intact muscle. As you can see in figure 1.1, surrounding each of the structures—the muscle fiber, the bundles of muscle fibers, and the intact muscle itself—are different types of connective tissue called *fascia*, which help all of the muscle proteins stay together and create very stable structures. The connective tissue found in muscle is what allows for the elastic component in muscle. Just as a rubber band stretches and then recoils, so too can the connective tissue stretch and recoil, adding greater force to the muscle contraction. This is a part of the *stretch–shortening cycle* of the muscle, which consists of an eccentric elongation followed by a rapid concentric shortening of the muscle. The reason that plyometric training, such as bounding exercises or depth jumps, is so effective in improving muscular power is that it trains this elastic component in muscle (i.e., the stretch–shortening cycle).

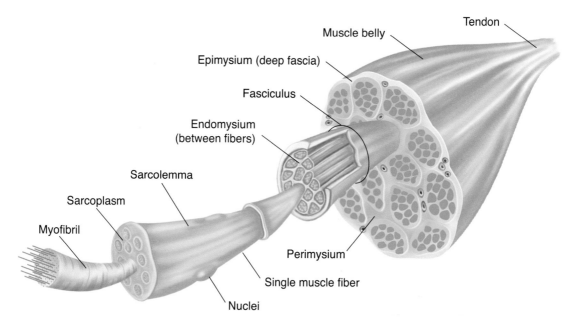

**Figure 1.1** Tendons attach the muscles to the bones allowing muscles to cause movement. The intact whole muscle is made up of bundles of muscle fibers, each with a connective tissue sheath surrounding it. A muscle fiber is made up of myofibrils, which contain many different contractile proteins. The key contractile proteins in the myofibrils of the muscle are actin and myosin.

Reprinted, by permission, from National Strength and Conditioning Association, 2000, *Essentials of strength training and conditioning*, 2nd ed. (Champaign, IL: Human Kinetics), 4.

# Sarcomere

The sarcomere is the basic contractile unit of skeletal muscle, and all force produced in human movement starts with the fundamental interactions of actin and myosin within this small element of the muscle. A sarcomere runs from one Z line to the next Z line and is the smallest functional unit in the muscle that can shorten. Each sarcomere contains several distinct light and dark areas. These areas give skeletal muscle a striped or striated appearance when examined under a special microscope (figure 1.2); because of this striation, skeletal muscle is also

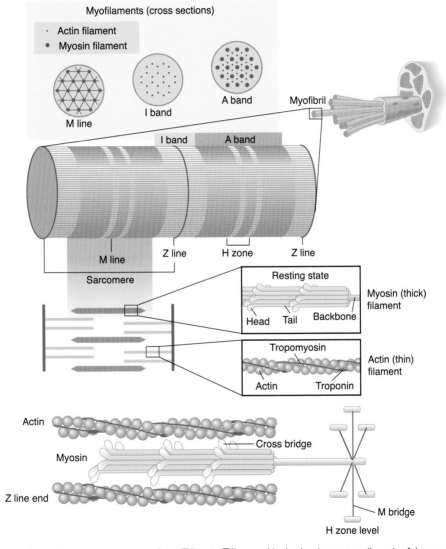

**Figure 1.2** The sarcomere runs from Z line to Z line and is the basic contractile unit of the muscle. The interactions of the actin and myosin create force production that causes the muscle to contract.

Reprinted, by permission, from National Strength and Conditioning Association, 2000, *Essentials of strength training and conditioning*, 2nd ed. (Champaign, IL: Human Kinetics), 6.

called *striated muscle*. These light and dark areas reflect the arrangement of the actin and myosin filaments. The light areas represent the H zone, which contains no actin and only a small amount of myosin, and the I bands, which are at the ends of the sarcomere and contain only actin filaments. The dark areas, which represent the A bands, contain both actin and myosin filaments in an overlapping region. Sarcomeres are "attached" to each other longitudinally at the Z line to form a myofibril. Many myofibrils stacked parallel to each other make up a muscle fiber (refer back to figure 1.1).

Contraction essentially shortens the sarcomere—the myosin protein is stationary, and cross bridges coming from the myosin filaments pull the actin filaments together from opposing directions, causing the actin to move over the myosin. This process, called the *sliding filament theory*, was first described in the 1950s by two scientists, Professors Hugh Esmor Huxley and Emmeline Jean Hanson. Force is produced through these interactions of the actin and myosin. We discuss this in more detail when we describe muscle contraction (pages 11 to 17).

## Muscle Fibers

Skeletal muscle is made up of thousands of muscle fibers ranging in length from about 3 to 9 centimeters (1.9 to 3.5 in.); in shorter muscles, such as the biceps, some fibers run all the way from the origin to the insertion. Connective tissue binds the muscle fibers and blood vessels in place, and nerves run through this tissue. Muscle fibers are unique in that they are individual cells with multiple nuclei that contain the DNA material of the cell. This provides the muscle fiber with greater potential for both repair and hypertrophy via protein synthesis, because each nucleus "regulates" only a small section of the cell.

Muscle fibers come in two basic types: Type I, slow-twitch fibers, and Type II, fast-twitch fibers; in addition, each of these types has various subtypes that we do not discuss in this chapter (see Fleck and Kraemer 2004 for a complete review). Type I fibers have a high oxidative capacity (high aerobic capability) and are made for endurance, with lower contractile force capabilities. Type II fibers, on the other hand, have a high glycolytic capacity and are made for strength and power, with high contractile force capabilities. The percentage of Type I and Type II muscle fibers in the body varies for each person. These percentages mainly depend on hereditary factors and only to a small extent on training adaptations. In addition, different muscles within the body have different percentages of Type I and Type II muscle fibers. No differences in fiber type have been observed between men and women; however, men generally have more numerous and larger muscle fibers than women.

Different athletes also have different fiber type profiles that explain in part their unique abilities in a given event or sport. For example, elite endurance athletes have higher percentages of Type I muscle fibers in their legs, while elite weightlifters and powerlifters have higher percentages of Type II muscle fibers throughout their bodies. This difference in muscle fiber composition is mainly because of the genetic predispositions of these athletes—these athletes were able to excel at their respective sport partly because of the fiber types they were born with. Although training may cause a small change in fiber type composition, the changes are mainly from one subgroup of fiber to another. A person cannot change his or her inherent fiber type through training; that is, a person cannot change Type I muscle fibers to Type II muscle fibers. Regardless of whether the athlete trains for strength or endurance, the fiber type change appears to go strictly in the direction of increasing the oxidative capacity of the fibers. For example, Type IIX fibers (fast-twitch glycolytic) are converted to Type IIA fibers (fast-twitch oxidative-glycolytic) through either resistance or endurance training. It may seem counterintuitive that resistance training will make muscle fibers more oxidative; however, the resistance training per se may not be making the fibers more oxidative as much as restoring the fibers from an untrained state to a more conditioned and functional state. The magnitude of this transformation, however, will not be sufficient to create the fiber type compositions seen in elite athletes unless the genetic predisposition is already present in the individual.

Figure 1.3 shows how these different fibers are classified under a microscope using staining or coloring of the muscle fibers to differentiate between Type I and Type II fibers. Depending on the fiber type makeup, each person

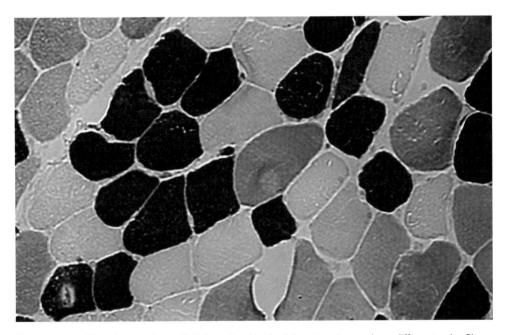

**Figure 1.3**  Muscles can be artificially stained in the laboratory to produce different color fibers in order to classify what percentage of Type I and Type II muscle fibers exist in the muscle. In this picture, Type I muscle fibers are black, and Type II muscle fibers are light gray (Type IIA) and dark gray (Type IIX).

Reprinted, from J. Wilmore and D. Costill, 2004, *Physiology of sport and exercise*, 2nd ed. (Champaign, IL: Human Kinetics), 39. By permission of D. Costill.

has different genetically determined strength, power, and endurance capabilities. Since Type I fibers cannot be converted to Type II fibers (and vice versa) through training, a person cannot develop a training program to change the overall fiber type composition. However, as you will see later in this chapter, altering training loads and movement speeds changes the involvement of the muscle fiber types.

## Motor Units

The basis of muscle stimulation starts with the motor unit—a motor neuron and all the muscle fibers it stimulates. A motor unit is composed of either all Type I (slow-twitch) or all Type II (fast-twitch) muscle fibers.

The muscle fibers in a motor unit are not all located adjacent to each other but are spread out in the muscle in *microbundles* of about 3 to 15 fibers. Thus, adjacent muscle fibers do not necessarily belong to the same motor unit. Because of how the fibers of a motor unit are spread out within a muscle, when a motor unit is activated, fibers are activated throughout the whole muscle. If fibers of a motor unit were all adjacent to each other, activating that motor unit would appear to stimulate only one segment of the muscle. When a muscle moves, those motor units that are not activated (and their associated muscle fibers) do not generate force; they only move passively through the range of motion as the muscle moves to follow the activated motor units.

The size of the motor units within a muscle varies, as does the number of fibers in a motor unit within different muscles. In the muscles of the eye, as few as 10 fibers may make up a motor unit, whereas 450 or more fibers may be included in a motor unit of the quadriceps.

# Muscles of the Body

The body contains more than 600 skeletal muscles varying in size, shape, and use (figure 1.4, *a* and *b*). The major purpose of skeletal muscles is to provide force to move the joints of the body in the different directions or planes that they are designed to move in. Many joints, such as knee and finger joints, are hinge joints that can only be moved in one plane—they can extend and flex. Other joints, such as the hip and shoulder joints, are ball-and-socket joints that can move in all planes—extend, flex, adduct, and abduct—as well as rotate. Each joint generally has one or more muscles for each of the movements it can perform. These muscles or muscle groups are usually paired so that they have opposite functions to each other; if one causes flexion of the joint, the other causes extension. This arrangement is required because muscles can only produce an active shortening and not a lengthening of themselves. Thus, two muscles or muscle groups with opposite functions are required for each dimension or plane that a joint can move in.

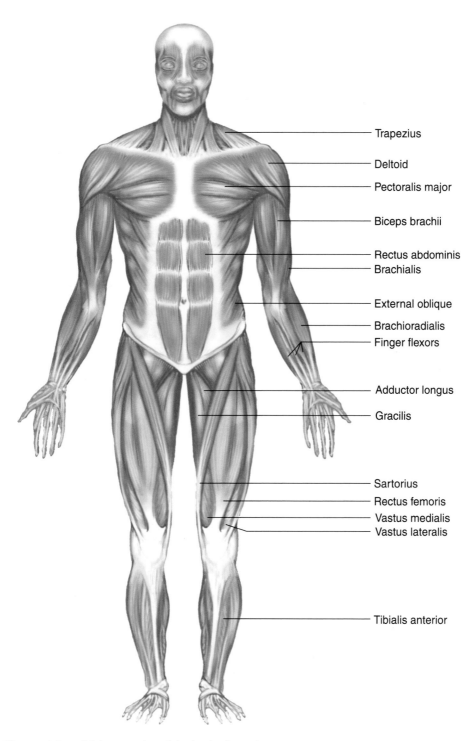

**Figure 1.4a** Major muscles of the body; front view.

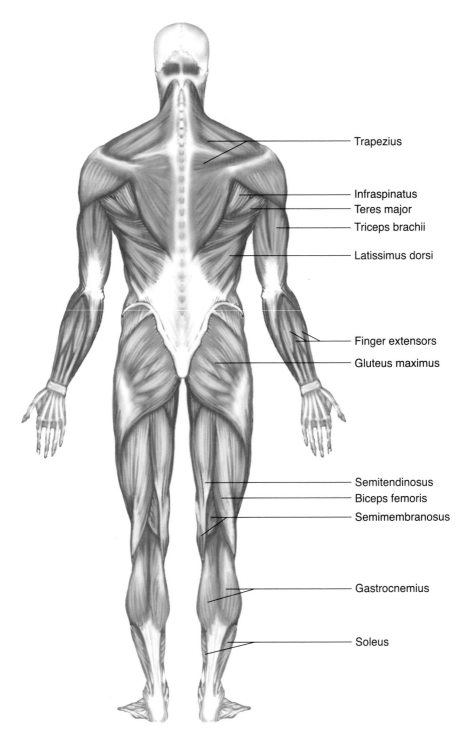

**Figure 1.4b** Major muscles of the body; back view.

Reprinted, by permission, from National Strength and Conditioning Association, 2000, *Essentials of strength training and conditioning*, 2nd ed. (Champaign, IL: Human Kinetics), 29.

The muscles that are the primary movers of a joint in one direction are called the *agonists* for that movement, and muscles that assist in that movement are called *synergists*. Muscles that can oppose a movement are called *antagonists* to that movement. For example, the biceps brachii and the brachialis are the agonists during an arm curl; the brachioradialis is a synergist, whereas the triceps brachii is an antagonist to the movement.

A muscle is usually connected to the bones it acts on via two different kinds of attachment sites. One site is called the *origin* of the muscle. The origin can be either a small distinct site on a bone or a large area covering most of the length of the bone. The origin is generally on the bone closest to the core of the body. The other attachment site for the muscle is called the *insertion*. This end of the muscle is usually connected to a tendon that spans the joint on which the muscle functions. A muscle can have more than one origin or insertion, and in such cases, the muscle is divided into different segments called *heads*. This allows the muscle to fine-tune its function (when heads function on the same joint but at slightly different angles), or to span more than one joint while still affecting these joints independently of each other. The triceps brachii, for instance, has three heads that all function across the elbow joint, whereas only two of its heads function across the shoulder joint.

Figure 1.4, *a* and *b*, and table 1.1, *a* and *b*, present the major muscles of the human body that are involved in resistance exercise. Note that some muscles consist of several heads, or segments, that attach on different sites on the body, and that some muscles span more than one joint. These features give the muscles added function. The quadriceps, for example, does not only extend the knee; one of its heads (medial) also keeps the kneecap (patella) in place during leg extensions (see page 224), and another head (long) is involved in movements of the hip.

# Muscle Contraction

The Huxley sliding filament theory (see Huxley 2004 for a complete review) is an explanation of how the muscle fibers can produce force. This all happens at the level of the sarcomere through the interactions of the major structural proteins of the sarcomere (figure 1.2).

As discussed early in the chapter, in the relaxed state, the muscle has a striated appearance. When muscle is in the contracted (fully shortened) state, there are still striations of the muscle tissue, but they have a different pattern. This change in the striation pattern occurs because of the sliding of the actin over the myosin protein filaments. The actins are anchored to the Z line at each end of the sarcomere. Upon muscle contraction, the A bands maintain their length, but the I bands shorten, pulling the Z lines closer together. This causes the H zone to diminish as actin filaments slide into it and give it a darker appearance. The I bands become shorter as the Z lines move closer to the ends of the myosin filaments.

**Table 1.1***a*    **The Major Muscles in the Body, Along With Their Origin, Insertion, and Function**

| Name of muscle | Origin | Insertion | Function |
|---|---|---|---|
| Abductors (tensor fasciae latae, gluteus medius, gluteus minimus) | Ilium | Femur | Moves hip sideways away from body |
| Adductors (includes adductor longus, adductor brevis, adductor magnus muscles) | Pubis | Femur | Moves leg back and across body sideways |
| Biceps brachii | Scapula | Radius and ulna | Flexes elbow and moves forearm |
| Brachialis | Humerus and septum | Coronoid process and ulna | Flexes elbow |
| Brachioradialis | Humerus and septum | Radius | Flexes and rotates elbow |
| Deltoids | Clavicle, deltoid tuberosity, acromion, and scapula | Deltoid tuberosity (humerus) | Raises and rotates arm in all directions |
| Erector spinae | Sacrum and ilium | Upper thoracic vertebrae | Extends spine and trunk back |
| Gastrocnemius (calf muscle) | Femur, lower leg, back | Calcaneum (by Achilles tendon) | Raises heel when leg is straight |
| Gluteus maximus | Ilium | Femur | Moves hips forward |
| Hamstrings (made of 3 muscles): 1. Biceps femoris 2. Semitendinosus 3. Semimembranosus | 1. Ischium 2. Ischium 3. Ischium | 1. Fibula and femur 2. Tibia 3. Tibia | 1. Bends knee 2. Bends knee 3. Bends knee |
| Iliopsoas | Ilium, sacrum, thoracic and lumbar vertebrae | Femur | Moves hips backward |
| Latissimus dorsi | Lower thoracic, lumbar vertebrae and sacrum | Humerus | Moves shoulders and arms back to body |
| Pectoralis major and minor | Sternum | Humerus | Moves humerus (arm) to chest |
| Quadriceps (made of 4 muscles): 1. Rectus femoris 2. Vastus lateralis 3. Vastus medialis 4. Vastus intermedius | 1. Ilium 2. Femur 3. Femur 4. Femur | 1. Tibia (patella tendon) 2. Tibia (patella tendon) 3. Tibia (patella tendon) 4. Tibia (patella tendon) | 1. Extends leg out 2. Extends knee 3. Extends knee 4. Extends knee |

| Name of muscle | Origin | Insertion | Function |
|---|---|---|---|
| Rectus abdominis | Costal cartilages, medial inferior costal | Margin and xiphoid | Brings trunk forward, and aids expiration |
| Rhomboids | Upper thoracic vertebrae | Scapula | Pulls back scapula (shoulder blade) |
| Soleus (calf muscles) | Tibia and fibula | Calcaneum (by Achilles tendon) | Raises heel when leg is bent |
| Tibialis anterior | Tibia | Metatarsal #1 (big toe) | Raises front of foot |
| Trapezius | Starts at base of skull; ends at last thoracic vertebra | Scapula and clavicle elevation | Elevates and lowers pectoral girdle; also moves scapula toward the spine |
| Triceps brachii | Scapula and humerus | Olecranon process (elbow) | Extends forearm |

## Table 1.1*b*  **Major Resistance Exercises and the Muscles They Involve**

| Exercise | Muscles used |
|---|---|
| Bench press, page 176 | Pectoralis major, anterior deltoid, triceps |
| Incline bench press, page 180 | Pectoralis major, anterior deltoid, triceps |
| Dumbbell biceps curl, page 204 | Biceps, brachialis |
| Machine triceps extension, page 203 | Triceps |
| Standing military press, page 166 | Deltoids, triceps |
| Lat pulldown, page 191 | Latissimus dorsi, pectoralis major, biceps |
| Seated cable row, page 194 | Latissimus dorsi, teres major, biceps |
| Barbell shrug, page 165 | Trapezius |
| Sit-up, page 232 | Rectus abdominis, obliques |
| Back squat, page 214 | Quadriceps, gluteus, adductor magnus, gastrocnemius, hamstrings |
| Leg extension, page 224 | Quadriceps |
| Seated leg curl, page 223 | Hamstrings, gluteal |
| Leg press, page 216 | Quadriceps, gluteus, hamstrings |
| Standing calf raise, page 227 | Gastrocnemius, soleus |
| Machine back extension, page 249 | Erector spinae |

The muscles are listed in order of their involvement in the exercise. Only the agonists and major synergists to each exercise are listed.

When the sarcomere relaxes and returns to its original length, the H zone and I bands return to their original size and appearance (figure 1.5, *a* through *d*).

The neural signals involved in muscle contraction converge in the *zoma*, the body of the alpha motor neuron located in the spinal cord. This neuron can be stimulated (or inhibited) from the central nervous system and from sensory and reflex neurons. If the sum of the stimuli is sufficient to create an electric signal

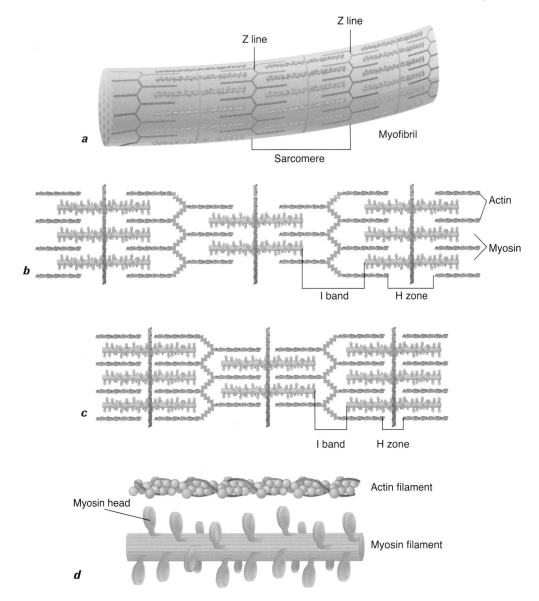

**Figure 1.5** As a muscle contracts, the Z lines move closer together, the width of the I bands decreases, the width of the H zones decreases, but there is no change in the width of the A band. Conversely, as a muscle is stretched, the width of the I bands and H zones increases, but there is still no change in the width of the A band.

(depolarization) in the zoma, this signal (action potential) then propagates along the axon of the efferent motor neuron to the neuromuscular junction. Here the signal causes the release of acetylcholine (ACh) from the nerve ending, and the ACh subsequently travels across the junction to the outer membrane of the muscle fiber (sarcolemma). When ACh reaches the sarcolemma, it attaches to ACh receptors, causing a depolarization of the sarcolemma; the signal has now reached the muscle fiber. The signal then rapidly spreads throughout the surface of the muscle fiber. This ionic current triggers the release of calcium ions ($Ca^{++}$) from the sarcoplasmic reticulum into the interior fluid of the muscle fiber. The sarcoplasmic reticulum is a membranous structure that surrounds each muscle fiber and acts as a storage space for $Ca^{++}$. The released $Ca^{++}$ binds to the troponin molecule; this triggers a change in the arrangement of troponin and tropomyosin so that the active sites on the actin become exposed, allowing binding of the myosin cross bridges. This phase is referred to as the *excitation-coupling* phase of the contraction process (figure 1.6).

Since Huxley originally proposed the sliding filament theory over 40 years ago, a great deal more has been discovered about how the protein filaments of muscle interact. At rest, the projections, or cross bridges, of the myosin filaments can touch the actin filaments, but they cannot interact to cause muscle shortening.

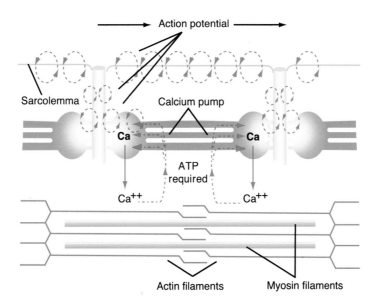

**Figure 1.6**   As the signal for contraction (action potential) spreads across the surface (sarcolemma) of the muscle fiber, the signal causes the release of $Ca^{++}$ from the sarcoplasmic reticulum (SR). To pump $Ca^{++}$ back into the SR following a contraction, adenosine triphosphate (ATP) is required.

This is because the actin filaments have active sites that the myosin cross bridges must bind to in order to cause shortening. At rest, however, the active sites are covered by troponin and tropomyosin, two regulatory proteins that are associated with the actin filament (figure 1.7).

Once the myosin cross bridge attaches to an active site on actin, *contraction* (shortening) of the sarcomere can take place. The binding between the myosin cross bridge and actin results in the head of the myosin swiveling forward or collapsing, causing the actin to slide over the myosin. This then results in the sarcomere shortening. (The swivel movement of the head of the myosin is often referred to as the *power stroke*.) At this point, the movement stops, and the myosin cross bridge remains attached to the actin. For further shortening to occur, the cross bridge must first detach from the actin, swivel back, and then attach to another active site on the actin filament—a site that is closer to the Z line than the site to which it was previously attached.

Detachment from the actin is caused by the binding of an adenosine triphosphate (ATP) molecule to the cross bridge. The ATP molecule is then hydrolyzed to adenosine diphosphate (ADP), causing the cross bridge to swivel back (cock) into its original position. At this point, one cross bridge cycle has been completed (figure 1.8). If the active sites on the actin are still exposed, the cross bridge can bind to a new active site closer to the Z line, and the sarcomere can shorten further. The energy for this cocking of the myosin cross bridge, which is the only energy-requiring step in the cross bridge cycle, is provided by the breakdown of ATP by an enzyme called myosin adenosine triphosphatase (ATPase) that is located on the myosin cross bridge. Thus, as for many cellular activities, ATP is

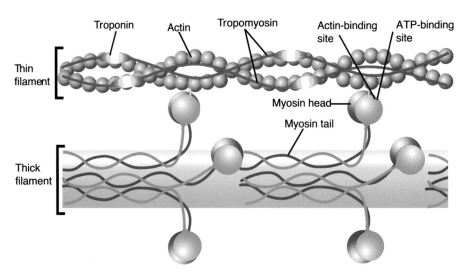

**Figure 1.7**   At rest, the active sites on actin are covered by troponin and tropomyosin. As $Ca^{++}$ binds to troponin, the troponin and tropomyosin proteins move, thereby exposing the active sites on the actin filament and allowing the binding with the myosin heads to occur.

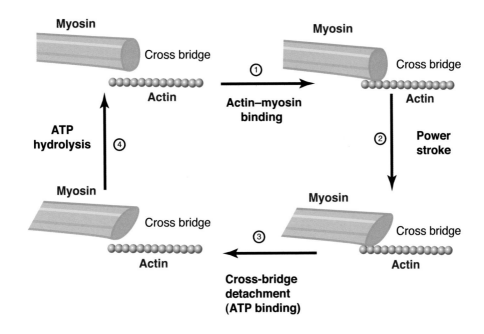

**Figure 1.8**    The cross bridge cycle. (1) The cross bridge attaches to the active site on the actin. (2) The power stroke moves actin over the myosin. (3) ATP attaches to the cross bridge, which then detaches from the active site on the actin. (4) ATP is hydrolyzed by ATPase in the cross bridge, and the cross bridge cocks back to its starting position. If a new active site on the actin is available, the cross bridge will attach to the site, and the cycle can continue. (For a more detailed schematic of myosin heads, see figure 1.7.)

the only energy source used directly for muscle contractions. The process of breaking contact with one active site and binding to another is called *recharging*. This cyclical process (referred to as the *ratchet theory*) is repeated until the sarcomere has shortened as much as possible, no more ATP is available, or relaxation of the muscle takes place.

*Relaxation* of the muscle occurs when the impulse (or signal) from the motor neuron ends. Without a continuous stream of signals from the motor neuron, the release of $Ca^{++}$ stops, and the $Ca^{++}$ already released is actively pumped back into storage within the sarcoplasmic reticulum. As for the cross bridge cycle, this pump mechanism requires energy from the breakdown of ATP to function. Thus, ATP is required for both contraction and relaxation of the muscle fiber. As $Ca^{++}$ is removed, the troponin and tropomyosin assume their original position covering the active sites on the actin. The cross bridges of the myosin filament now have no place to attach to on the actin in order to pull it over the myosin. With relaxation, cross bridge activity of the muscle stops, and the muscle will remain in the shortened state unless pulled to a lengthened position by gravity or an outside force. Muscles are only able to actively shorten; there is no mechanism within the muscle to actively cause a lengthening of that muscle to occur.

# Whole Muscle Design

The overall design of the muscle plays an important role in its function because it influences the force and velocity of contractions. In general, the more sarcomeres arranged in series (producing a longer muscle), the faster the velocity of the muscle contraction. This is because each sarcomere has a maximal contraction velocity; when sarcomeres are arranged in series, their contraction velocities become additive and the overall contraction velocity of the muscle increases. An additional benefit to sarcomeres being arranged in series is that they can achieve a fast overall velocity of contraction while staying close to their optimal length–tension relationship (the length of the sarcomere at which it produces maximal force).

In contrast to velocity, the force of contraction increases as more sarcomeres are arranged parallel to each other (producing a wider muscle). Each sarcomere has a maximal force production capability; when sarcomeres are arranged parallel to each other, their force outputs become additive. In this manner, large force can be produced without a large change in the length of the muscle, again potentially keeping the individual sarcomere close to its optimal length–tension relationship.

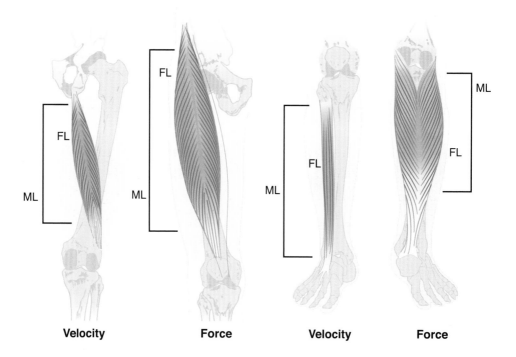

**Velocity**    **Force**    **Velocity**    **Force**

**Figure 1.9**   Pennation angle, muscle fiber length (FL), and muscle length (ML) for muscles with either high-force or high-velocity functions. Relatively long muscle fibers make the muscle well suited for high-velocity movements; relatively short fibers arranged in parallel make the muscle well suited for high-force movements.

Another important aspect of whole muscle design is pennation (figure 1.9). Pennation is the angle between the muscle fiber orientation and the direction in which the overall muscle force is directed during contraction. A greater angle of pennation allows for more sarcomeres in parallel to be packed into the space between the origin and insertion of a given muscle, thus increasing the potential force production of that muscle. Pennation does have a drawback; as the angle of pennation increases, the resultant force that a given muscle fiber relays to the tendon is reduced. However, the angle of pennation must be greater than approximately 30 degrees before the additional increase in force from packing in more muscle fibers is lost. ■

# Muscle Recruitment

One of the most important concepts to understand regarding muscle physiology and strength training is how muscle is recruited or stimulated. This is because muscle fibers that are not recruited in an exercise will not gain any of the benefits from that exercise.

## Size Principle

The body uses several different mechanisms to recruit individual motor units from the available pool in order to produce very specific amounts of force. This is accomplished by varying the amount of electrical stimulus required to reach the threshold of activation for an individual motor unit.

The *size principle* states that motor units are recruited from the smallest to the largest based on the force demands placed on the muscle. Each muscle contains a different number of muscle fibers and motor units. The smaller—or what are called *low-threshold* (low electrical stimulus needed for activation)—motor units are recruited first (figure 1.10). Low-threshold motor units are predominantly composed of Type I fibers. Then motor units with progressively higher thresholds are recruited based on the increasing demands of the activity. The higher-threshold motor units are composed predominantly of Type II fibers.

Heavier resistances, such as those used in lifts that a person can only perform for 3 to 5 repetitions—called a 3 to 5 *repetition maximum* (RM)—require the recruitment of motor units with a higher threshold than those required for a lighter resistance (e.g., 12 to 15RM). However, lifting heavier resistances will (according to the size principle) start with the recruitment of low-threshold motor units first (Type I) and progressively move up the line until enough motor units are recruited to produce the needed force. This process of recruiting progressively larger motor units is very rapid. Since only the motor units that are recruited benefit from the training, this principle has important implications for training programs. If only a low resistance (e.g., 12 to 15RM) is used, then the largest motor units will not be recruited and thus will not benefit. Therefore, to maximize strength gains from

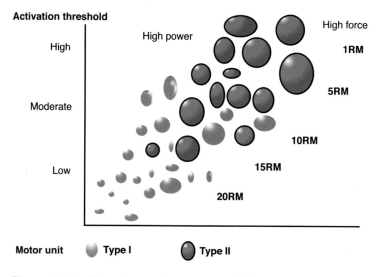

**Figure 1.10**   Recruitment of motor units (alpha motor neuron and the associated muscle fibers—depicted as circles) occurs based on size. Small motor units are recruited first, going up to larger motor units that produce high force and power. Some people do not have many fast-twitch, or Type II, motor units; also, if not stimulated with resistance exercise, these motor units can be lost with age. The force requirement needed to stimulate motor units varies.

a resistance training program, high resistance (1 to 5RM) must also be used to stimulate adaptation in the largest motor units.

The size of the motor units within a muscle varies such that motor units with fewer fibers, in keeping with the size principle, are recruited first. This selective activation of motor units and the difference in size of motor units allow for *graded force production*—and thus, more precise control of the amount of force that the whole muscle can generate. This in turn allows for more precise control of body movements.

## All-or-None Law

Another important concept is the *all-or-none law*, which states that when a specific motor unit reaches its threshold level for activation, all of the muscle fibers in that motor unit are activated fully. If the threshold is not reached, then none of the muscle fibers in that motor unit is activated. Although this holds true for individual motor units within a muscle, whole muscles, such as the biceps, are not governed by the all-or-none law.

The fact that motor units follow the all-or-none law is one reason why a muscle can vary the amount of force it produces. The more motor units stimulated within a muscle, the more force that muscle produces. In other words, if one motor unit in a muscle is activated, that muscle produces only a very small amount of force. If several motor units are activated, the muscle produces more force. If all of the

## Protective Mechanisms: Muscle Spindles and Golgi Tendon Organs

The muscle employs two neural mechanisms or reflexes to protect itself from acute damage; one protects against the muscle becoming overstretched, and the other protects the muscle from tearing itself from its tendon.

Muscle spindles—sets of specialized muscle fibers wrapped with sensory nerves—are located between the regular muscle fibers within the muscle. Since the muscle spindles are attached to the regular muscle fibers, they can sense when the muscle is being rapidly stretched. This signal is sent directly to the spinal cord where it can trigger a signal in the muscle's motor neurons, causing the muscle to reflexively contract. In this manner, the muscle spindle monitors the lengthening of the muscle and helps to prevent the muscle from being overstretched. This mechanism, however, only protects the muscle during fast stretches; if the muscle is stretched slowly, the muscle spindles will not be stimulated to send a signal to the spinal cord.

The Golgi tendon organs are not located in the muscle itself; however, they do play an important role in protecting the muscle from being torn from its tendon. As the name suggests, the actual location of the Golgi tendon organ is in the tendon near where the muscle fibers and tendon intersect. The Golgi tendon organ senses tension in the tendon and operates much like a strain gauge. When the Golgi tendon organ is stimulated by high tension in the tendon, it sends a signal to the spinal cord to inhibit the contraction of the muscles to which the tendon is attached (agonists) and to excite the muscle on the opposite side of the joint (antagonist). Experts have speculated that this reflex can be diminished with training, and that the inhibition of this reflex may play a role in the strength gains seen with resistance training. ■

motor units in a muscle are activated, maximal force is produced by the muscle. This method of varying the force produced by a muscle is called *multiple motor unit summation*.

## Muscle Activation and Strength Training

Periodization of training (see chapter 3) is based on the principles stated previously—that different loads (light, moderate, or heavy) or power requirements recruit different types and numbers of motor units. On a light training day, you would allow some muscle fibers to rest by recruiting fewer of them than on a heavy training day. For example, if your maximal lift (1RM) for one dumbbell biceps curl is 100 pounds (45.4 kg), then 10 pounds (4.5 kg) of resistance represents only about 10 percent of your maximal strength in the biceps curl exercise. Performing 15 repetitions of the dumbbell biceps curl with 10 pounds (see page 204) would activate

© Human Kinetics

only a small number of your motor units in the biceps. Conversely, performing a 100-pound biceps arm curl would require all of the available motor units.

Only the motor units that are actively recruited during an exercise produce force and subsequently are subject to the adaptations from the exercise. Therefore, which motor units your body recruits is fundamentally important to the effectiveness of a resistance exercise program. Activated motor units stay stimulated for a period of time following their use, which is important for subsequent muscle contractions. Repeated stimulation can continue to increase force production up to muscle failure. In resistance exercise, it is the load—typically the amount of weight lifted—that determines how many motor units are recruited. Heavier loads recruit more motor units than lighter loads. Additionally, high power outputs (moderate force produced at very high velocities), such as Olympic-style weightlifting, recruit different motor units than just heavy loads; there are specialized high-power motor units that are recruited only during high-power muscle contractions.

Exceptions to the size principle may occur in movements at a very high velocity (ballistic) and movements with high power outputs using highly trained movement patterns. In the animal world, these movements might be represented by escape or catching movements (e.g., a cat's paw flick); in human sporting activities, they could be represented in the action of a baseball pitcher throwing a fastball. In such movements, rather than the muscle first recruiting low-threshold (Type I) motor units, high-threshold (Type II) motor units are recruited first in order to allow faster movement. In these exceptions, the Type I motor units are skipped over—thus, not slowing down the activity—so that the Type II motor units can be recruited first. This process appears to be facilitated by inhibiting activation of the Type I motor units, making it easier to go directly to the Type II motor units. However, how this exception to the size principle applies to training humans for such movements remains unclear.

The size principle's order of recruitment ensures that low-threshold motor units are predominantly recruited to perform lower-intensity, long-duration (endurance) activities, whereas the higher-threshold motor units are only used to produce higher levels of force or power. This helps to delay fatigue during submaximal muscle actions because the high activation threshold for the highly fatigable Type II motor units is not reached unless high levels of force or power are needed; instead, mainly the lower-threshold, fatigue-resistible Type I motor units are recruited. Higher-threshold motor units will only be recruited when enough total work has been performed to dramatically reduce the glycogen stores in the lower-threshold motor units. However, with resistance exercise, this has not typically been observed because the activity does not tend to significantly reduce muscle glycogen stores. When the force production needs are low to moderate, motor units can be alternately recruited to meet the force demands (asynchronous recruitment). This means that a motor unit may be recruited during most of the first repetition of a set with a light weight and then not (or only minimally) recruited during the second repetition. This ability to rest motor units when submaximal force is needed also helps to delay fatigue. When velocities are very slow and loads are very light—as in "super-slow" training—this type of recruitment may predominate during the exercise, leaving many muscle fibers not stimulated and thus primarily promoting endurance.

The neurons of the higher-threshold motor units recover more quickly (i.e., become available for reactivation faster) than the neurons of the lower-threshold motor units following a contraction. This allows the higher-threshold motor units to be activated quicker in repeated actions than the lower-threshold motor units. So, although the high-threshold Type II motor units fatigue quickly, the ability of their neuron to recover quickly makes them ideal for repeated high-force, short-duration activities.

Recruitment order is important from a practical standpoint for several reasons. First, in order to recruit the Type II fibers and thus achieve a training effect in these fibers, the exercise must be characterized by heavy loading or demands for high power output. Second, the order of recruitment is fixed for many movements, including resistance exercise; if the body position is changed, however, the order of recruitment can also change and different muscle fibers can be recruited. For multifunctional muscles, such as the quadriceps, the order of recruitment can change from one movement or exercise to another. The magnitude of recruitment of different portions of the quadriceps also varies among different types of leg exercises (e.g., in a leg press, page 216 versus a squat, pages 212 and 214) and from one isolated quadriceps exercise to another. Likewise, the magnitude of recruitment of different abdominal muscles is different from one abdominal exercise to another. Variation in the recruitment order and magnitude of recruitment of different muscles may be one of the factors responsible for strength gains being specific to a particular exercise. The variation in recruitment order provides some evidence to support the belief (held by many strength coaches) that to completely develop a particular muscle, it must be exercised using several different movement angles or exercises.

Not every person has the same complement of motor units available to him or her. Thus, not every person has the same strength potential. This, along with differences in the total number of muscle fibers available, allows for differences in force and power capabilities from individual to individual. These differences in the number of muscle fibers and fiber type composition are largely determined by genetics; however, the fiber type composition can be changed slightly by various forms of endurance and resistance training as well as by detraining. The latter is especially seen with aging, where some people may have only low-threshold motor units made up predominantly of Type I muscle fibers, thus limiting their power and force production capabilities. The type, number, and size of muscle fibers in the motor unit dictate the functional abilities of that individual motor unit and eventually the functional abilities of the whole muscle.

# Types of Muscle Actions

Muscles can perform a number of different types of actions, including concentric, eccentric, and isometric actions (figure 1.11).

Normally, when a weight is lifted (i.e., the muscle produces more force than the resistance it is trying to move), the muscles involved are shortening while producing force. This is called a *concentric* muscle action. Because shortening occurs during a concentric muscle action, the use of the word *contraction* for this type of muscle action is appropriate.

When a weight is lowered in a controlled manner (i.e., the resistance is greater than the force that the muscle is producing), the muscles involved are lengthening while producing force. This is called an *eccentric* muscle action. Muscles can only pull or lengthen in a controlled manner; they cannot push against the bones that they are attached to. In most exercises, gravity will pull the weight back to the starting position. To control the weight as it returns to the starting position, the muscles must lengthen in a controlled manner or the weight will fall.

If no movement of a joint takes place but a muscle is activated and developing force (i.e., the force produced by the muscle equals the resistance), the action is called an *isometric* or *static* muscle action. This can occur when a weight is held stationary or the weight is too heavy to lift any higher. Some muscles, such as the postural muscles of the spine, primarily perform isometric muscle actions; they act to stabilize the upper body during most lifts.

The maximal force that a muscle can produce changes throughout the range of motion and is a function of the architecture of the muscle and the joint angle. This relationship is described by the *strength curve* for the muscle. The "sticking point" of an exercise is often related to a low point on the strength curve.

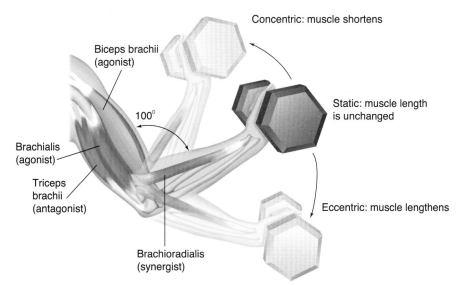

Concentric: muscle shortens

Biceps brachii
(agonist)

100°

Static: muscle length
is unchanged

Brachialis
(agonist)

Triceps
brachii
(antagonist)

Eccentric: muscle lengthens

Brachioradialis
(synergist)

**Figure 1.11**    Concentric, eccentric, and isometric muscle action. The arrow indicates the direction of the movement.

Reprinted, by permission, from J. Wilmore and D. Costill, 2004, *Physiology of sport and exercise*, 2nd ed. (Champaign, IL: Human Kinetics), 53.

The ascending curve is characterized by the ability to produce greater and greater force over the range of motion. This is the most common curve for exercise movements. Exercises such as the bench press, squat, shoulder press, and leg press follow this strength curve. Rubber band resistance also matches this curve best.

Descending curves are less common but are seen in movements that are performed at unusual angles. The leg curl (page 223) is one example of an exercise where the most force that can be exerted is at the beginning of the range of motion.

A bell curve represents exercises where the highest force that can be produced over the range of motion occurs somewhere in the middle of the curve. The biceps curl is a great example of an exercise that follows this strength curve.

Let's briefly cover how some different types of resistance training use these muscle actions and strength curves. More information on each of these types of lifting can be found in chapter 6.

**Free weights** such as barbells and dumbbells require the use of both concentric and eccentric muscle actions. This type of training is also considered "free-form" exercise because there is no set path for the bar movement and this must be controlled by the user. Thus, assistance and support provided by the prime mover or core muscles are vital when using this type of equipment.

**Stack plate machines** such as Universal or Nautilus weight machines are considered "fixed-form" exercise because the movement pattern is for the most part dictated by the machine itself. Both concentric and eccentric muscle actions are part of the repetition. Because there is less need for balance and stability, more weight can often be lifted when using these machines than in a free weight exercise. However, the stabilizing muscles get less training than during free weight lifts because of the machines guiding the movement.

**Rubber band resistance** is unique in that it produces a classic resistance that goes from little or no resistance to increasingly difficult resistance as the rubber or elastic polymers stretch to their limits of length. In addition, the return resistance follows a different pattern back to the starting position. This direction-dependent behavior of the rubber band is called *hysteresis*. In other words, the elastic resistance is directly related to an ascending strength curve where the person can exert continually increasing force production over the range of motion. If the band is not set up properly, little or no resistance is often observed during the first 10 to 30 degrees of a range of motion. Rubber band resistance has both the concentric and eccentric components of a repetition, but proper setup is vital to allow this to happen optimally across the entire range of motion.

**Isokinetic movements** refer to when the velocity of the movement of a joint is held constant. This muscle action can be either concentric or eccentric and is usually performed using a computerized device that controls the speed. No specific resistance is used; the load is determined solely by how much force the person produces. Although no specific resistance is used, the force produced by the muscles involved can be measured. Isokinetic movements are most often used for research testing purposes and in rehabilitation settings.

**Pneumatic resistance**, developed by the Keiser Corporation (Fresno, CA), eliminates the dependence on gravity and the momentum associated with iron weight, thus allowing the ability to train at any speed with a consistent concentric and eccentric resistance. This resistance system trains both the force and speed component of a movement, thereby providing the means to help develop the explosive power needed for certain movements (e.g., upper body movements and knee extensions) in competitive sport.

**Hydraulic resistance** uses the concentric muscle action only, and the equipment involves moving a piston in and out of a fluid cylinder under pressure. Thus, you push out and pull in when performing an exercise. No eccentric loading is available in this type of lifting, which has been popularized in many "women-only" fitness clubs. The lack of the eccentric loading in this type of resistance makes it less efficient, with double the reps needed in order to gain the same effects as a normal concentric-eccentric repetition.

## Length–Tension (Force) Curve

The length–tension (force) curve demonstrates that there is an optimal length at which muscle fibers can generate their maximal force (figure 1.12). The total amount of force developed depends on the total number of myosin cross bridges interacting with active sites on the actin. At the optimal length, there is the potential for maximal cross bridge interaction and thus maximal force. Below this optimal length, less tension is developed during muscle fiber activation because with excessive shortening an overlap of actin filaments occurs; as a result, the actin filaments interfere with each other's ability to interact with the myosin cross bridges. The

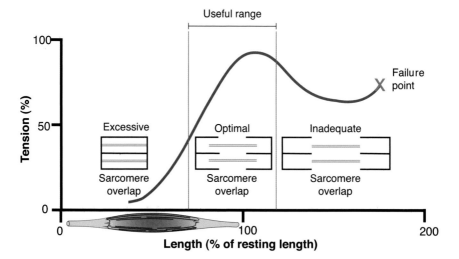

**Figure 1.12** The relationship between the length of the sarcomere and the sarcomere's tension (force) production capability. Optimal force production capability is achieved when all myosin cross bridges are opposed by an active actin filament and there is no overlap of actin filaments.

reduction in cross bridge interaction with the active sites on the actin results in a smaller potential for force and power development.

At lengths greater than optimal, there is less and less overlap of the actin and myosin filaments, resulting in fewer cross bridges attaching to the active sites on the actin; the cross bridges close to the center of the myosin filament will not have an actin site across from them to attach to. Thus, if the sarcomere's length is greater than optimal, less force and power can be developed.

The length–tension curve shows that the muscle's capacity for force development changes throughout a particular movement. In addition, the curve indicates that some prestretch of the muscle before the initiation of a contraction will increase the amount of force generated. Too much prestretch, however, will actually decrease the total amount of force developed. This is especially important during isometric muscle actions; for the maximal force to be produced, the length of the muscle must correspond to the optimal point on the length–tension curve.

## Force–Velocity Curve

As the velocity of movement increases, the force a muscle is able to produce concentrically (while shortening) decreases (figure 1.13). This is empirically true. If an athlete is asked to bench press the maximal amount of weight possible (1RM), the weight will move very slowly. But if the athlete is asked to bench press half of his or her 1RM, the bar moves at a faster velocity. Maximal velocity of shortening occurs when no resistance (weight) is being moved or lifted. It is determined by the maximal rate at which cross bridges can attach to and detach from the active sites on the actin. The force–velocity curve is important when examining various

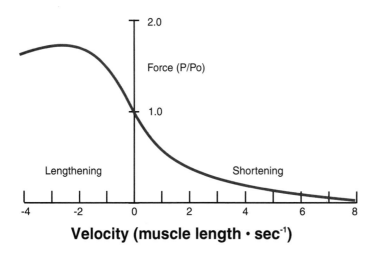

**Figure 1.13**  The relationship between the velocity of the muscle action and the muscle's force production capability. The faster the velocity of a concentric muscle action, the lower the force production capability. For an eccentric muscle action, the opposite is true—the faster the velocity, the higher the force production capability.

forms of weight training, such as isokinetic training (see page 121) where the velocity of the movement is controlled, but the resistance is not, as well as other types of training (e.g., using free weights and variable resistance machines; see chapter 6).

In contrast to concentric muscle actions, increases in the velocity of movement actually increase the force that a muscle can develop eccentrically (lengthening). This is thought to be caused by the elastic component of the muscle, though the actual explanation for such a response remains unclear. It is interesting to note that eccentric force at even low velocities is higher than the highest concentric force or isometric force. Such high force development when using maximal eccentric muscle actions has been related to muscle damage in untrained people. However, it has been demonstrated that muscle exposed to repeated eccentric actions can adapt by strengthening part of the connective tissue so that the damage per training session is reduced in subsequent training sessions. At the percentages of 1RM normally used for resistance training, eccentric force is not maximal. Thus, the eccentric portion of the repetition may not be optimal in terms of strength gains. New methods and equipment that allow higher loads to be applied only during the eccentric phase of a lift are being developed (see chapter 3 for a discussion of these).

Understanding the basic structures of muscle allows you to better understand the primary elements affected by a resistance training program. These muscle structures begin with the smallest organizational parts and build into a system allowing human movement. Progression resistance training enhances the muscular system by making it stronger and more powerful, and it conditions the large tissue mass, which is important not only in sport but in fighting the effects of aging. Health is in part related to appropriate muscle fitness, and only with proper weight training can muscle become healthy and fit.

# How Muscle Grows

William J. Kraemer and Barry A. Spiering

A strong relationship exists between the size of a muscle and its strength; in general, a bigger muscle is a stronger muscle. Adhering to a resistance training program stimulates the muscle to enhance its size by increasing the amount of contractile proteins. Subsequently, this adaptation permits more actin–myosin cross bridges to be formed during muscle activation, which allows the muscle to produce greater force. To fully appreciate the origin of strength, you must grasp the underlying principles of muscle growth, that is, how muscle size increases.

Increases in muscle size are due to a number of factors, each of which contributes to the end result of muscle growth. A muscle can grow in two ways:

1. by hypertrophy, which means an increase in the size of individual muscle fibers, and

2. by hyperplasia, which means increased number of muscle fibers.

Hypertrophy is the primary means of muscle growth. The existence of hyperplasia in humans is controversial, and if it does occur, it likely contributes very little to muscle growth (less than 5 percent). Therefore, in this book we will focus on hypertrophy.

One common method of enhancing muscle growth is by participating in a resistance training program. In addition to increasing muscle size, resistance training improves muscle strength and bone health, and it can improve athletic performance. The benefits of resistance training are important for both men and women to help them stay healthy and to offset the natural aging process, which

© Jumpfoto

can lead to loss of muscle mass (sarcopenia) and bone mass (osteoporosis), and subsequent disability.

Muscle growth is a healthy process that provides many physical benefits. Too often, people (frequently women) do not engage in resistance training because they are afraid it will make them "too big." This unfounded fear can prevent them from obtaining the full benefits of a strength training program. Not only do women have fewer muscle fibers than men, especially in the upper body, but additionally, the primary anabolic (muscle-building) hormone—testosterone—is dramatically lower in women than in men. Therefore, women rarely develop overly large (or "manly") muscles without the use of anabolic drugs. With a well-designed resistance training program, women typically see an increase in the muscle size with a corresponding decrease in body fat, resulting in smaller dimensions and improved muscle definition. For men, the increase in muscle size depends on proper training and nutrition, and the upper limits of size are related to genetics.

In this chapter, we discuss muscle growth in a natural environment. The extreme muscle size seen in bodybuilders using anabolic drugs is beyond the typical result of a healthy sport- or fitness-based resistance training program (and outside the scope of this chapter).

# Foundation for Muscle Growth

Two essential principles form the basis for muscle growth. First, muscle must be stimulated to increase its size. In this context, the most prolific stimulus for muscle growth is a well-designed resistance exercise program. Second, increasing muscle size requires energy, and this energy comes from a well-balanced diet that provides adequate calories. If either of these principles is ignored, muscle simply will not adapt. The basic paradigm for how muscle grows can be seen in figure 2.1. It shows how the foundation for muscle growth is a proper resistance training stimulus along with a sound nutritional diet. As discussed in greater detail in chapter 4, nutritional intake is vital for optimal muscle development. The body needs the basic building blocks (carbohydrate, protein, and fat) to repair and remodel muscle. Thus, everyday dietary patterns, the timing of nutrient intake around the workout, along with proper sleep and a healthy lifestyle, all contribute to the effectiveness of muscle repair and, therefore, its growth.

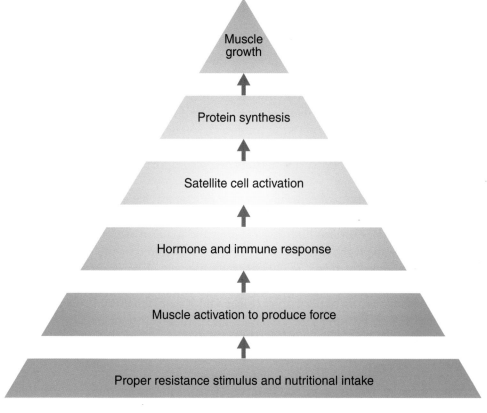

**Figure 2.1**   Paradigm of muscle growth. Muscle growth begins with a solid foundation consisting of a proper resistance exercise stimulus and adequate nutritional intake.

## Neural Adaptations to Strength Training

Neural adaptations, along with increased muscle size, are important for enhanced muscle strength. During the first few weeks of a strength training program, there is a dramatic increase in strength. However, there is very little change in muscle size during this initial phase. This early increase in strength is due primarily to improved neural function.

Neural adaptations that accompany resistance training include increased activation of agonist muscles (prime movers) and synergists, reduced activation of antagonistic muscle groups, improved inter-muscle group coordination, and improved rate of force development. Ultimately, these changes improve the expression of muscle strength and power. ■

## Muscle Stimulus

Let's briefly examine the need for a proper resistance training stimulus for optimal muscle growth. (Specific types of muscle training are discussed in detail in chapter 3.) Many important attributes are required for a well-designed resistance training program. For example, you must consider muscle actions (concentric and eccentric; see chapter 1), exercise intensity and volume, and rest intervals between sets and sessions.

Work at the National Aeronautic Space Administration (NASA) by Dr. Gary Dudley's laboratory in the early 1990s demonstrated the importance of performing both concentric and eccentric muscle actions for increasing muscle size and strength (Dudley et al. 1991; Hather et al. 1991). These studies found that when only concentric muscle actions were used in the weightlifting regimen, twice the work had to be performed to get the same training effects as when eccentric actions were included. Clearly, eccentric actions are an important part of a resistance training program.

Although various types of resistance training programs have been shown to elicit muscular hypertrophy, certain ranges of exercise intensity and volume appear to be optimal. Briefly, exercise intensity denotes the load, or weight, used during a lift; exercise volume is the number of repetitions multiplied by the number of sets. Generally, moderate to heavy loads (70 to 85 percent of maximal strength for a given lift) and high volume (8 to 12 repetitions for three or four sets) are recommended for maximizing hypertrophy (Fleck and Kraemer 2004). Programs using these intensities and volumes for each exercise stimulate greater acute increases in naturally occurring anabolic hormones than higher-load, lower-volume regimens do (i.e., programs that emphasize gains in muscular strength; Kraemer et al. 1990; Kraemer et al. 1991).

The amount of rest between each exercise set also affects the muscles' responses to resistance exercise. Short rest periods (one to two minutes) used in accordance with moderate to high intensity and volume elicit greater acute responses of anabolic hormones than programs using very heavy loads and longer rest periods

© Eyewire/Photodisc/Getty Images

(three minutes; Kraemer et al. 1990; Kraemer et al. 1991). Shorter rest periods are associated with greater metabolic stress (e.g., higher levels of lactic acid in the blood), and metabolic stress is a stimulus for hormone release. The hormonal response is important because naturally occurring anabolic hormones stimulate muscle protein synthesis and increased muscle size. Therefore, relatively short (one- to two-minute) rest periods are recommended for optimizing long-term gains in muscle size.

Whether you have a personal trainer or you design your own resistance training program, you must keep these three issues—muscle actions, exercise intensity and volume, and length of rest periods—in mind when trying to stimulate muscle growth. Important concepts for designing resistance training programs are discussed in more detail in chapter 3.

# Muscle Metabolism

To understand the importance of nutrition for muscle growth, it is important to introduce the fundamental principles of muscle metabolism. Adenosine triphosphate (ATP) (see chapter 1, pages 16 to 17) is the ultimate source of energy for contraction. However, only a very small amount of ATP can be stored within muscle (only enough to fuel approximately two seconds of muscle contraction). Therefore, muscle must metabolize various substrates (made up of what we consume in carbohydrate, proteins, and fats) to continuously regenerate ATP.

Muscle metabolic pathways function on a continuum and range from pathways that provide ATP very quickly, but with a small overall capacity, to pathways that produce ATP relatively slowly, but with a larger capacity. At the onset of exercise, the first pathway activated is the ATP-creatine phosphate (ATP-CP) pathway. As ATP is degraded, a phosphate group is removed from CP and transferred to adenosine diphosphate (ADP) to regenerate ATP. Although this pathway can produce energy very quickly, its capacity is limited to enough ATP for approximately six seconds of muscle contraction (e.g., enough energy to sprint 40 yards [37 meters]).

As exercise progresses in duration to greater than six seconds, an increasing amount of energy is derived from anaerobic glycolysis. *Anaerobic* means that this reaction can occur without oxygen; *glycolysis* means splitting (metabolizing) glucose. Anaerobic glycolysis produces energy quickly; however, because oxygen is not involved, lactic acid is produced, which may inhibit energy metabolism if it is not adequately buffered.

Exercise of relatively low intensity and long duration relies primarily on oxidative metabolism. Oxidative metabolism occurs in the muscle mitochondria and is capable of producing greater ATP than anaerobic metabolic pathways. The substrates for oxidative metabolism can be glucose, fat, or protein. However, very little protein is oxidized during exercise.

Metabolic pathways are active at all times on the continuum. However, the intensity and duration of the exercise determine which pathway will provide most of the ATP for contraction (e.g., a 100-meter sprint relies primarily on ATP-CP and anaerobic glycolysis, while a marathon relies primarily on oxidation of fats and glucose).

Because muscles metabolize glucose, fats, and protein during exercise, it is important after an exercise session to ingest adequate nutrients to replenish muscle substrates and promote repair. Perhaps the most important fuel for continued exercise is muscle glycogen. When muscle glycogen is low, exercise intensity is dramatically reduced and, ultimately, exercise must be ceased. Additionally, following exercise, muscle must synthesize proteins to repair damage and produce new enzymes; therefore, it is important to consume adequate carbohydrate and protein.

# Process of Muscle Growth

The first necessary step for increasing muscle size is for motor units to be activated. Clearly, if a specific muscle is not stimulated to produce force, then it will not respond and adapt to the stimulus. To activate a muscle fiber, you must apply adequate exercise intensity.

As we discussed in chapter 1, the activation of motor units follows the *size principle*. You can see a simple example of the size principle and its role in muscle growth by comparing endurance training, which typically uses low-intensity and high-volume exercises, to strength training, which tends to use high-intensity and low-volume exercises. Resistance training is a more prolific stimulus for muscle fiber growth than endurance training because resistance exercise provides the high-intensity stimulus necessary to recruit Type II (fast-twitch) fibers, which are more capable of increasing their size than Type I fibers. In other words, to stimulate muscles to grow, they have to be activated—and to activate the necessary motor units, a relatively heavy load must be used.

© Human Kinetics

Upon activation, muscle fibers produce force, which ultimately allows movement of the human body. As you learned in chapter 1, if the muscle produces more force than the resistance it is trying to move, this is called a *concentric* (shortening) muscle action; if the resistance is greater than the force that the muscle is creating, the muscle performs an *eccentric* (lengthening) muscle action (see page 24).

The production of muscular force sends a host of signals to all organ systems of the body. These systems, in turn, support the muscle's ability to produce force and contribute to recovery and growth of muscle. For example, the cardiovascular system pumps blood to the muscle to provide oxygen and nutrients and to remove waste products; the endocrine system produces hormones that aid in force production (e.g., epinephrine, also known as *adrenaline*) and hormones that stimulate muscle growth (e.g., testosterone, growth hormone, and insulin-like growth factors); and the immune system provides signals to help coordinate the tissue repair process. In the next sections, we look more specifically at the hormonal and immune system responses to muscle activation and resistance training, and we examine how these responses activate satellite cells to effect muscle growth.

## Hormonal Response to Muscle Contraction

As stated previously, the endocrine system releases hormones during and following muscular force production. Hormones such as epinephrine help the muscles to produce force. Other hormones in the body—such as testosterone, growth hormone (GH), and insulin-like growth factor (IGF-I)—stimulate muscle protein synthesis by sending signals to the muscle to regenerate and grow. Resistance exercise naturally (i.e., without the use of drugs) increases the concentration of anabolic (muscle-growing) hormones in the blood during and approximately one hour after exercising, allowing your body to rebuild and add muscle during that time.

Testosterone, which is produced primarily in the testes in men and in the adrenal glands in women, is secreted into the blood during resistance exercise and for up to an hour afterward. On reaching the exercising muscle, testosterone passes through the muscle's membrane to inside the muscle cell and binds to one of many testosterone-specific receptors (known as *androgen receptors*). (It is not known if there is a difference between men and women in the number of these receptors or if the number of receptors changes with training.) Once this binding occurs, testosterone sends a signal to the cell's nucleus to increase protein synthesis (i.e., make new proteins), causing the cell to get larger.

Muscular force production also stimulates the release of growth hormone (GH) from the pituitary gland (a small gland within the brain). The hormone then travels through the bloodstream and stimulates the production of insulin-like growth factor (IGF-I) in the liver and in the muscles. IGF-I can then bind to a receptor on the outer membrane of the muscle cell and send a "signal" to the muscle cell nucleus to increase the production of proteins.

A critical function of both IGF-I and testosterone is to activate a group of cells called *satellite cells*, which we discuss in detail later in this chapter.

You can maximize the hormonal response to exercise—and, over time, the increase in muscle size—by paying attention to the structure of your resistance training program. In general, the hormonal response to exercise is greatest when using high exercise volume (three or four sets of 6 to 12 repetitions for each exercise), heavy loads (greater than 80 percent of maximal strength), short rest periods (one to two minutes between sets), and exercises that target large muscle mass (squats, deadlifts, power cleans, and so forth). (For a review of the hormonal responses and adaptations to resistance exercise, see Kraemer and Ratamess 2005.) It may be helpful to keep in mind that the hormonal response to exercise is generally correlated to the amount of metabolic stress. Therefore, workouts that are structured using high volume and intensity, short rest periods, and that use large muscle mass will maximize the body's natural capacity to stimulate muscle growth.

The significance of the relationship between an increase in the anabolic hormones circulating in the bloodstream and gains in muscle strength was demonstrated in a clever experiment performed by a group of scientists in Denmark (Hansen et al. 2001). First, the scientists tested the arm strength of a group of subjects and, subsequently, divided the subjects into two groups: One group trained only their arms (A group), and the other group trained their arms and their legs (AL group). Both groups spent the same amount of time training their arms; however, the AL group performed additional leg exercises to increase the concentration of circulating anabolic hormones—that is, testosterone and growth hormone (as already mentioned, the amount of anabolic hormones in the blood will increase more if a large amount of muscle is exercised). At the end of the experiment, the scientists found that the A group increased their arm strength by 9 percent, while the AL group increased their arm strength by 37 percent! This study clearly shows the

importance of recruiting a large muscle mass during resistance exercise, because doing so causes a large increase in anabolic hormones and a greater increase in strength.

## Muscle Damage and the Immune Response

During concentric and, in particular, eccentric muscle actions, microscopic muscle damage occurs. This muscle damage consists of a disruption of sarcomeres and membranes, which leads to inflammation and swelling that contribute to the soreness that can be felt for up to several days after a workout; however, the damage also provides an important stimulus for muscle growth and therefore is necessary for increasing muscle size.

When muscles are damaged, an immune response follows. Immune cells (for example, white blood cells) cause an increase in blood flow to the injured area, resulting in cell swelling. In turn, the increase in blood flow brings oxygen and nutrients to the area and helps remove the waste products. Also, similar to the hormonal response produced by resistance training, the immune response signals activation of satellite cells. This process helps muscles repair themselves and grow.

## Role of Satellite Cells

Before getting into the specifics about how satellite cells contribute to muscle growth, let's first consider a concept called the *myonuclear domain theory*. As discussed in chapter 1, unlike most cells in the body, which have only one nucleus, muscle cells have many nuclei. The myonuclear domain theory proposes that each nucleus of a muscle cell is responsible for controlling the functioning of a finite volume of cytoplasm—the cell material outside of the nucleus. In other words, a nucleus can "regulate" only a certain amount of muscle tissue. So, if a muscle is stimulated to increase its size through the hormonal and immune responses, the muscle must have a corresponding increase in the number of nuclei to regulate the increase in cytoplasm. Therefore, as the muscle grows, the number of nuclei must also increase. How does a muscle increase its number of nuclei? That's where satellite cells come into play.

As previously mentioned, one of the primary functions of the hormonal and immune responses to resistance exercise is to activate satellite cells. These cells are similar to stem cells in that they are undifferentiated, meaning they are neither muscle cells nor any other specific type of cell, though they have the capacity to become muscle cells. They are named *satellite cells* because they are located at the periphery of muscle cells. Normally, satellite cells are quiescent (or inactive). However, when muscle is damaged, the hormonal and immune responses activate the satellite cells, causing them to proliferate (increase in number) and, finally, to differentiate (to become incorporated into the muscle fiber and actually become part of the muscle cell).

Once the satellite cells fuse to the muscle fiber, they donate their nuclei. This is critical because by increasing its number of nuclei, the muscle fiber (and therefore the muscle) now has an increased capacity for growth. These new nuclei then produce more proteins that cause the muscle to grow (figure 2.2). In addition, these satellite cells can regenerate in number so that the next time the muscle is injured, they can continue to contribute to its repair. (For further review of muscle satellite cells, see Hawke 2005.)

The importance of satellite cells for muscle growth has been clearly shown by scientists in Sweden (Kadi and Thornell 2000). These scientists studied a group of females as they performed 10 weeks of resistance training. Before and after

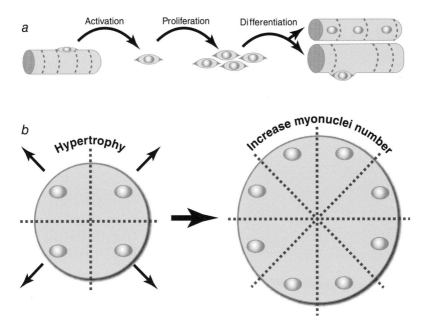

**Figure 2.2**   The role of satellite cells in muscle growth. *(a)* When a muscle fiber is damaged during resistance exercise, quiescent satellite cells are activated, causing them to proliferate and differentiate. If damage is relatively minor, as is usually the case following resistance exercise, the satellite cells will fuse to the muscle fiber and donate their nucleus (bottom fiber). This process helps to repair the muscle and allows for growth. However, if there is severe muscle damage, which is rare following resistance exercise, the satellite cells will fuse to one another and generate a new fiber (top fiber). *(b)* The myonuclear domain theory suggests that nuclei can only "manage" a finite amount of cytoplasm. Therefore, if a muscle is stimulated to grow, the muscle must increase its number of nuclei to "manage" the increase in cytoplasm. The increase in nuclei is donated by satellite cells. Note that each nucleus "manages" the same volume of cytoplasm before and after muscle growth.

Reprinted, by permission, from T.J. Hawke, 2005, "Muscle stem cells and exercise training," *Exercise and Sport Sciences Reviews* 66: 63-68.

the training protocol, the scientists took small muscle samples from the women's trapezius (upper back) muscle. The women had a 36 percent increase in the cross-sectional area of muscle fibers at the end of 10 weeks. The hypertrophy of muscle fibers was accompanied by an approximately 70 percent increase in the number of myonuclei and a 46 percent increase in the number of satellite cells. The number of myonuclei was positively correlated to the number of satellite cells, indicating that a muscle with an increased concentration of myonuclei contains a correspondingly higher number of satellite cells. The scientists suggested that the acquisition of additional myonuclei appears to be required to support the enlargement of multinucleated muscle cells following 10 weeks of strength training. The number of myonuclei dictates how big a muscle fiber can become. The number is a *limiting* factor in muscle size development. Nuclear domains, or the amount or area of protein that can be managed by a given myonucleus, have genetic limits and dictate the upper limits of protein accretion.

## Protein Synthesis

Upon completion of resistance exercise, the acute increase in anabolic hormones within a muscle stimulates the myonuclei to increase protein synthesis. More specifically, the nuclei increase production of the contractile proteins actin and myosin within the existing sarcomere. Increased quantity of contractile proteins means two things:

1. An increase in the size of the muscle
2. An increase in the force-generating capacity of the muscle

Or, more succinctly, increased protein synthesis means a bigger, stronger muscle.

Proteins are molecules made of amino acids. Therefore, to synthesize proteins, amino acids are transported across the cell membrane and into the skeletal muscle. By increasing your amino acid intake after resistance exercise, you can increase the availability of amino acids to assist in protein synthesis; this underscores the need for an adequate diet. In total, muscle protein synthesis following resistance exercise depends highly on amino acid availability, timing of the intake of nutritional amino acid (the sooner after exercise the better), hormonal regulation (insulin, GH, testosterone, and IGF-I, mechanical stress, and cellular hydration. The take-home message is this: To maximize protein synthesis, you should eat a meal soon after exercise. This meal should contain adequate carbohydrate (to stimulate insulin) and protein (to increase amino acid availability).

In the long run, muscle hypertrophy is the result of an overall increase in protein synthesis, a decrease in protein degradation (catabolism), or a combination of both. Scientists examined protein synthesis and degradation for 48 hours after a single bout of resistance exercise (Phillips et al. 1997). They found that while protein synthesis was elevated by 112, 65, and 34 percent, respectively at 3, 24, and 48 hours postexercise, protein breakdown rate was elevated by only 31, 18, and 1 percent at these same time points. The difference between protein synthesis and breakdown indicated that muscle protein synthesis was 23 to 48 percent higher over the 48-hour postexercise time period, indicating that resistance exercise is indeed a potent stimulus for muscle protein synthesis.

## Fiber Size Increases

The coordinated responses of the endocrine system, the immune system, and the satellite cells lead to an increase in protein synthesis and, ultimately, an increase in muscle fiber size. This increase in the cross-sectional area of existing muscle fibers is attributed to an increased number of actin and myosin filaments and the addition of sarcomeres within existing muscle fibers.

You can easily see the increase in muscle fiber size by examining a group of muscle fibers under a microscope after they have been stained. Figure 2.3 shows two pictures of a muscle sample obtained from a woman's vastus lateralis (quadriceps muscle): *(a)* before and *(b)* after an eight-week heavy resistance training program. The fibers are cut in cross section; the dark fibers are Type I muscle fibers, and the white fibers are Type II fibers. It is obvious that this woman increased the size of all of her muscle fibers with heavy resistance training, especially the Type II (fast-twitch) muscle fibers, in just eight weeks of training.

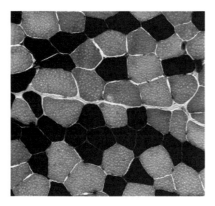
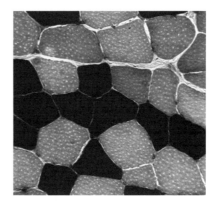

a    b

**Figure 2.3**  These micrographs are from a biopsy sample from the thigh muscle that was obtained and then stained in the laboratory to demonstrate both the type and size changes that occur with training. It is easy to see that the posttraining fibers are larger than the pretraining fibers (following eight weeks of heavy resistance training). Such increases in muscle fiber hypertrophy contribute to hypertrophy of the whole muscle if enough muscle fibers are recruited in the muscle through proper loading.

Courtesy of Dr. Kraemer's Laboratory.

Logically, increases in the size of individual muscle fibers can lead to increased size of the entire muscle group. However, a significant number of fibers need to hypertrophy to see such a response for the whole muscle (figure 2.4, *a* and *b*).

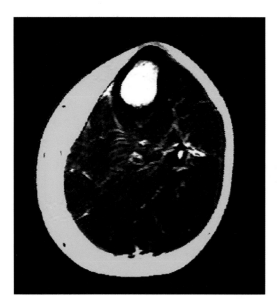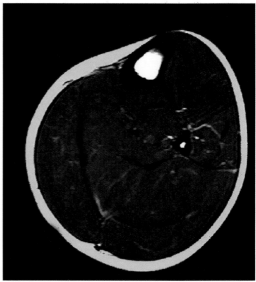

**Figure 2.4**    A magnetic resonance image of the upper arm of a woman before and after six months of periodized resistance training. Notice the increase in lean tissue mass of the arm and the reduction of fat around the muscle. Whole muscle hypertrophy is a result of hypertrophy of each individual muscle fiber.

Courtesy of Dr. Kraemer's Laboratory.

# Changes in Muscle Fiber Type

Although the focus of this chapter is to address the increased size of muscle (a quantitative issue), we should also note that there are some qualitative changes in the muscle as well. Work by Dr. Robert Staron's laboratory has been crucial in our understanding of the changes in muscle fiber type that occur with exercise.

As discussed in chapter 1, human muscles can be generally classified as Type I or Type II. Type II fibers are often further subclassified into Type IIA or Type IIX; however, many "hybrid" fibers exist in between each of these fiber type classifications—for example, there are fiber types that exist between Type I and Type IIA, between Type IIA and Type IIX, and so forth. Therefore, fiber types should be considered to exist on a "continuum," not just as finite classifications. For simplicity's sake, though, we stick to the major fiber types.

With the initiation of a heavy resistance training program, changes in the types of muscle proteins (e.g., myosin-heavy chains) start to take place within a couple of workouts (Staron et al. 1994). In general, resistance training will stimulate a transition of Type II fibers. It appears that as soon as Type IIX muscle fibers are stimulated, they start a process of transformation toward the Type IIA profile by changing the quality of proteins. However, it is doubtful that muscle fibers transform from Type II to Type I, or vice versa, under normal training conditions. ∎

© Jumpfoto

## Hyperplasia

Although we have discussed hypertrophy as the primary means of increasing muscle size, muscle fiber hyperplasia—an increase in the number of muscle fibers—is also a possible mechanism for increasing the size of muscle. The concept of hyperplasia following resistance training has not been directly proven in humans because of methodological difficulties (e.g., the whole muscle cannot be taken out for examination), but it has been shown in response to various exercise protocols in birds and mammals.

Though limited data support hyperplasia in humans, there are indications that hyperplasia occurs following resistance training. However, because of conflicting results, this topic remains controversial. Hyperplasia may not be the primary adaptation of most muscle fibers, but it might represent a modification in response to resistance training that is possible when certain muscle fibers have reached a theoretical "upper limit" in cell size. Nevertheless, the bottom line is that if hyperplasia does occur, it likely only accounts for a small portion (e.g., 5 percent) of the increase in muscle size.

The foundation of muscle growth is a well-designed resistance training program and solid nutritional habits. Based on this foundation, the process of muscle growth can occur. The first step in this process is the activation of muscle fibers to produce force. During repeated efforts to produce force, especially those that include eccentric muscle actions, microscopic muscle damage occurs. Muscle damage then stimulates hormone and immune responses, which, in turn, signal satellite cells to activate, proliferate, and differentiate in order to become a part of the damaged muscle fiber. This step is crucial because the satellite cells donate their nuclei to the muscle fiber, which supports increased protein synthesis and continued growth. In addition to activating satellite cells, anabolic hormones (particularly testosterone and insulin-like growth factors) stimulate the muscle's nuclei to increase synthesis of contractile proteins (actin and myosin). By increasing the amount of contractile proteins, the individual muscle fiber becomes bigger and stronger. If enough fibers are stimulated to hypertrophy by a proper resistance exercise regimen, then an increase in size will be noted at the level of the whole muscle as well.

As you can see, the process of muscle growth is well coordinated and supported by several physiological systems. Now that you have an understanding of how muscle grows, you can begin to appreciate the origin of strength.

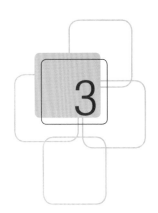

# Types of Muscle Training

William J. Kraemer, Disa L. Hatfield, and Steven J. Fleck

The world of strength training has seen hundreds of different types of training programs introduced in muscle magazines, by fitness and health clubs, by champion lifters, by fitness experts, and in TV infomercials. Designing a resistance training program is ultimately a very individual process, and the needs of the individual are paramount to the program characteristics (Fleck and Kraemer 2004). A program for a person wishing to increase maximal strength will differ greatly from a program for a person wishing to increase muscular endurance. Aside from the outcome goals, a program design must also take into account individual differences such as training experience, time allotted to train, the facilities available for training, and any special needs the person may have. In addition to addressing individual needs, the underlying principles that are the foundation of any effective muscle training program are as follows:

1. Specificity of training—Only those muscles that are trained will adapt and change in response to a resistance training program.
2. GAS principle—Han Seyle's *general adaptation syndrome* (GAS) refers to the three stages of adaptation: (1) the "alarm stage" caused by the onset of physiological stress (i.e., training); (2) the resistance stage in which the body begins to adapt to the demands; and (3) the exhaustion stage, which occurs with overtraining.
3. SAID principle—*Specific adaptations to imposed demands* (SAID) relate to the fact that the adaptation will be specific to the characteristics of the workout used.

4. Variation in training—No program can be used without changing the exercise stimulus over time. Periodized training is the major concept related to constructing the optimal training and recovery program.

5. Prioritization of training—It is difficult to train for all aspects of strength fitness. Thus, within a periodized training program, you need to focus or prioritize training goals over each training cycle.

In this chapter, you will learn how these principles are integral to designing an effective resistance training program. In addition, this chapter outlines how to manipulate variables of a resistance training program to affect the outcomes, such as muscular hypertrophy, strength, and local muscular endurance.

# Acute Training Variables

Any sound resistance training program is made up of several variables—what exercises are chosen, the order in which the exercises are performed, the intensity or load of the exercise, the number of repetitions and sets of the exercise, and how much rest you take between exercises. We call these *acute program variables* because they are the variables that you can change within a single workout and that will determine the outcome of training over the long term. Moreover, you can evaluate any workout by examining the choices you made for the acute program variables (Fleck and Kraemer 2004) and noting how these choices affect the training adaptations that may be associated with a resistance training program. In addition, the acute program variables are what allow you to create different types of workouts.

Understanding the factors that go into creating the "exercise stimulus" is crucial to designing an effective training program. Creating an effective exercise stimulus starts by first deciding what direction you want the training to go in—to increase force production, power, hypertrophy, and so forth. From there, the next step is to develop a single training session directed at these specific trainable characteristics. The acute program variables describe the choices you can make in a single workout. The changes in the choices you make for each variable over time dictate the progression of your training program.

## Choice of Exercises

The exercises you choose should reflect the areas of the body and the biomechanical characteristics of these areas that you want to target for improvement. The number of possible exercises that target specific joint angles is almost as limitless as the body's functional movements that these exercises help improve. When choosing which exercises to do, remember that muscle tissue that is not activated does not benefit from resistance training; therefore, you should first determine what

© Jumpfoto

you want to get out of a resistance training program and then select exercises that stress the muscles and joint angles you want to target.

Exercises can be designated as primary exercises and assistance exercises. Primary exercises are the exercises that train the muscles called the *prime movers* (typically major muscle groups), such as the leg press (page 216), the bench press (page 176), hang clean (page 262), and so forth. Assistance exercises are those that train predominantly one muscle group that aids in the movement produced by the prime movers. The triceps pushdown (page 202) and dumbbell biceps curl (page 204) are two examples of assistance exercises.

Exercises can also be classified as structural (i.e., involving multiple joints) or body part specific (i.e., involving an isolated joint; see figure 3.1, *a* and *b*). Structural exercises include those whole body lifts that require the coordinated action of several muscle groups. The power clean (page 252), deadlift (page 222), and squat (pages 212, 214) are good examples of structural whole body exercises. Other structural exercises don't involve the whole body, but do involve multiple joints or muscles. For example, the bench press (page 176) involves movement of both the elbow and shoulder joints. Some other examples of multiple-joint exercises are the lat pulldown (page 191), the standing military press (page 166), and the leg press (page 216). Isolation exercises are body-part-specific exercises that isolate single muscle groups. The dumbbell biceps curl (page 204), leg extension (page 224), seated leg curl (page 223), and many other assistance exercises are good examples of isolation exercises.

**Figure 3.1**    Some exercises, such as the *(a)* front squat, work multiple joints with the movement while others, such as the *(b)* biceps curl, move just one joint.

Structural or multiple-joint exercises require neural coordination among muscles and promote the coordinated use of movements that involve multiple joints and multiple muscle groups. It has recently been shown that multijoint exercises require a longer initial learning or neural phase compared to single-joint exercises. Many times, structural exercises involve advanced lifting techniques (e.g., power clean; see page 252) that require additional coaching of exercise technique beyond simple movement patterns. Structural and multiple-joint exercises are especially important to include in a program when whole body strength movements are required for a particular target activity. Most sports and functional activities in everyday life (e.g., climbing stairs) depend on structural multijoint movements. In all sports, whole body strength and power movements are the basis for success in running and jumping activities (as well as in making a tackle in American football, taking down an opponent in wrestling, and hitting a baseball). The time economy achieved with multiple-joint exercises is also an important consideration for an individual or team with a limited amount of time per training session. The benefits of multijoint exercises (in terms of muscle tissue activated, hormonal response, and metabolic demands) far outweigh those of single-joint exercises, and for best results, most workouts should revolve around these multijoint exercises.

# Order of Exercises

The order in which you perform your exercises can be an important variable that affects the quality of the workout, especially if you are lifting heavy loads (see the discussion on intensity in the next section). Most experts believe that exercising the larger muscle groups first provides a superior training stimulus to all of the muscles involved. This is thought to be true because exercising more and larger muscle groups stimulates greater neural, metabolic, endocrine, and circulatory responses, which potentially augments the training of subsequent muscles later in the workout. Thus, more complex multijoint exercises (e.g., squats; see pages 212, 214) should be performed initially, followed by the less complex single-joint exercises (e.g., dumbbell biceps curls; see page 204). Another rationale for sequencing the multiple-joint exercises before the single-joint exercises is that the exercises performed in the beginning of the workout require the greatest amount of muscle mass and energy for optimal performance. Thus, these sequencing strategies focus on attaining a greater training effect for the exercises involving large muscle groups. If structural exercises are performed early in the workout, you can use more resistance to do them since your muscles are not yet fatigued.

Most important, exercise order needs to correspond with specific training goals. A few general methods for sequencing exercises (for training sessions targeting either multiple or single muscle groups) include the following:

- Targeting large muscle groups before small muscle groups
- Performing multiple-joint exercises before single-joint exercises
- Alternating push and pull exercises for total body sessions (see page 142)
- Alternating upper and lower body exercises for total body sessions
- Performing exercises for a person's weaker points (priorities) before exercises for the person's stronger points
- Performing Olympic lifts before basic strength and single-joint exercises
- Performing power exercises before other exercise types
- Performing more intense exercises before less intense ones (particularly when performing several exercises consecutively for the same muscle group)

One final consideration for exercise order is the fitness level of the person and his or her experience in resistance training. Training sessions must be designed so that they are not too stressful for the individual, especially a beginner.

# Intensity or Resistance

The amount of resistance used for a specific exercise is one of the key factors in any resistance training program. It is the major stimulus related to changes in strength and local muscular endurance.

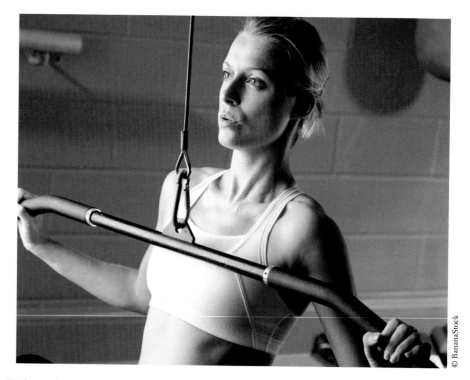

© BananaStock

When designing a resistance training program, you need to choose a resistance for each exercise. One of the easiest methods for determining the right resistance for an exercise is to determine your repetition maximums (RM)—the specific resistance that only allows you to perform a specific number of repetitions. Typically, to determine RM, you can choose a single training RM target (such as 10RM) or choose an RM target training zone (a range such as 3 to 5RM); you then perform each exercise at different resistances until you meet this target. As your strength level changes over time for each lift, you can adjust the resistance so that you continue to hit your specified RM target or zone. Going to failure on every repetition can be stressful on the joints, but for optimal results, you should make sure that the resistance you use places you within a targeted group of reps (e.g., the resistance allows you to lift the weight for only 4 or 5 repetitions compared to 14 or 15 repetitions—the training outcome for these two resistances is quite different).

Another method of determining resistance for an exercise involves using a percentage of the 1-repetition max (1RM) for a lift—the maximal amount of weight you can lift in just one repetition (e.g., 70 or 85 percent of the 1RM). For example, if your 1RM for an exercise is 100 pounds (45.4 kg), lifting 80 percent of the 1RM would mean lifting 80 pounds (36.3 kg). This method requires that you regularly evaluate your maximal strength in the various lifts so that you can adjust the resistance appropriately as you get stronger. If you do not test your 1RM each week, especially when beginning a program, the resistance represented by the percentage of 1RM that you use in training will decrease; as a result, the training intensity will be reduced. From a practical perspective, using a percentage of 1RM as the resistance for many exercises may not be an efficient method because of the amount of testing time required. Use of an RM target or RM target zone allows you to change resistances as necessary during training in order to stay at the RM target or within the RM target zone you've chosen.

Like the other acute variables, the loading intensity a person chooses depends on his or her goals and training status (i.e., whether the person is a trained athlete versus a sedentary individual). The intensity of the loading (as a percentage of 1RM) affects the repetition continuum—the number of repetitions that a person can perform at a given load or intensity. It is ultimately the number of repetitions that you can perform at a given intensity that determines the effects of training on strength development (Hoeger et al. 1990). If an athlete lifting a specific percentage of the 1RM can lift only a specific number of repetitions, then lifting fewer repetitions without changing the resistance would mean the athlete is using different motor units to perform the exercise. For instance, a low-intensity, high-repetition scheme would effectively activate the Type I muscle fibers (those more suited to endurance) but would not adequately activate the Type II muscle fibers (the predominant muscle fibers responsible for maximal strength and hypertrophy gains). Thus, if you want to maximize strength gains, you should lift heavier loads (and therefore fewer repetitions). If muscular endurance is the goal, you should use a lighter load, which in turn allows a greater number of repetitions.

## Volume

Total exercise volume (sets × repetitions × weight) is a vital concept of training progression. Using a program with a constant volume may lead you to feel stale in your training and may cause you to discontinue it. Ultimately, varying the training volume through periodization (which enables you to use different exercise stimuli over long-term training periods) is an important way to provide rest and recovery periods. We cover periodization in more detail later in this chapter.

The number of sets is one of the factors in the *volume* of exercise. First, you should note that not all exercises in a training session need to be performed for the same number of sets. In studies examining resistance-trained individuals, multiple-set programs were found to be superior for increasing strength, power, hypertrophy, and high-intensity endurance. These findings have prompted the recommendation from the American College of Sports Medicine (ACSM 2002) to use periodized multiple-set programs when long-term progression (not maintenance) is the goal in any area (strength, endurance, hypertrophy, and so on).

No study, of either trained or untrained individuals, has shown single-set training to be superior to multiple-set training; it appears that both types of programs are effective for increasing strength in untrained subjects during short-term (6- to 12-week) training periods. However, some short-term and all long-term studies support the contention that a training volume greater than one set is needed for progressive physical development and improved performance.

Still, the need for variations—such as using lower volumes of training during some phases of the overall training program—is also critical for continued improvement and to augment training adaptations. The key is to periodize training *volume* rather than just the number of sets, which represents only one factor in a volume and intensity periodization model. This model is covered in greater detail later in this chapter. Each set of an exercise presents a training stimulus to the muscle; thus, once initial fitness has been achieved, performing multiple sets (three to six) with specific rest periods between them that allow for the desired intensity (resistance) is more effective than doing a single set. Some advocates of single-set programs believe that a muscle or muscle group can only perform maximal exercise for a single set; however, research has not shown this to be true.

The optimal number of exercises for a given resistance training goal has not been studied. Typically, the total number of sets spanning all exercises done is used to calculate total exercise volume. However, the type of exercises chosen (multijoint and structural exercises versus single-joint movements) should be considered when calculating volume. Furthermore, the calculation of volume is body-part specific. Thus the appropriate volume for lower body and upper body exercises should be determined separately from one another and calculated based upon need.

## Rest Periods Between Sets and Exercises

A major topic of study over the past 10 years has been aimed at understanding the influence that rest periods have on the stress of the workout and the amount of resistance that can be used. Rest periods between sets and exercises determine the magnitude of ATP-PC energy source resynthesis and the concentrations of lactate in the blood (see chapter 2). The length of the rest period can significantly alter the metabolic, hormonal, and cardiovascular responses to an acute bout of resistance exercise, as well as the performance of subsequent sets.

For advanced training that emphasizes increasing absolute strength or power, rest periods of at least three to five minutes are recommended for structural exercises (e.g., squats, power cleans, deadlifts) using maximal or near maximal loads; less rest (one minute or less) may be needed for exercises involving smaller muscle mass or single-joint movements (ACSM 2002). The reason these advanced lifters need so much rest is that they are often lifting resistances that are closer to their genetic potential; this intensity necessitates that they maximize their recovery of energy stores for the next lift. For novice to intermediate lifting, two to three minutes of rest may suffice for structural lifts because the intensity at this level of resistance training appears to be less stressful to the neuromuscular system.

On the other hand, stressing the glycolytic and ATP-PC energy systems may enhance muscle hypertrophy; thus, less rest between sets appears to be effective if training to increase muscle size (e.g., for bodybuilding). And varying the amount of rest between sets (sometimes a little, sometimes a lot) may be effective if the goal is to optimize both strength and size. From a practical standpoint, research demonstrates that short-rest programs (exercises using rest periods of one minute or less) can cause greater psychological anxiety and fatigue. This might be related to the greater discomfort, muscle fatigue, and higher metabolic demands of such programs. Although the psychological demands are higher, the changes in mood states do not constitute abnormal psychological changes and may be a part of the arousal process before a demanding workout.

# Muscle Training Programs

You can find literally hundreds of different methods of strength training muscle. However, very few of these have stood the test of time or the scrutiny of scientific research. Of all of these programs, periodization has emerged as the preferred approach to optimizing many types of training, including resistance training.

## Periodization Training

Periodized resistance training has been shown to be superior to constant training methods (Fleck and Kraemer 2004). Periodization training allows for the use of many different types of workouts, training programs, and modalities. In essence, it calls for varying the training stimulus (intensity or volume) over determined periods of time to allow for a proper progression in the exercise stress and planned periods of rest.

© SportsChrome/Monte Isom

Periodization training evolved from a principle of resistance training called *progressive resistance training* or *overload*. The principle was coined by Dr. Thomas Delorme, an army physician working with physical rehabilitation of soldiers in the 1940s. It was born from the SAID principle (specific adaptations to imposed demands), and it refers to the need to gradually increase the amount of physical stress placed on the body in order to continually stimulate adaptations.

Delorme's principle was originally based on a 10RM set and then percentages of that load. From there, to increase the stress, he manipulated any combination of the acute variables (such as increasing the resistance load, volume, and frequency of training and decreasing the rest time between sets) to allow the adaptations to occur.

Most of the approaches that Delorme tried were linear in nature and therefore hit plateaus very quickly. Over the decades, training methods evolved to using periodization to ensure steady improvements in performance, provide for recovery, and avoid staleness. Thus, the case for periodized training was made as athletes looked to further improve their fitness levels for competition.

Strength athletes initially relied on the *classical periodization model*, also called *linear periodization*. The concept of linear periodization as we know it is attributed to the work of Eastern Bloc sports programs in the early 1950s. It came about through trial and error and through mathematical modeling of how champion athletes trained, as coaches tried to optimize sports performance (figure 3.2). The coaches noticed that decreasing the *volume* and increasing the *intensity* (in this case, defined as a percentage of near maximal effort) in the weeks leading up to a competition elevated performance. The classic linear periodization programs were developed for strength and power athletes peaking for one particular contest at the end of a year, such as world championships or Olympics.

These early periodization models were built around one competitive season broken into four phases: preparation, first transition (end of preseason), competition, and second transition (off-season). The length of time of each phase depended on the length of the competition season, the mode of training, and individual differences of the athletes. The preparation phase involved increasing strength and muscle mass. Exercise volume was high in this phase, and intensity was low. In the first transition phase, volume decreased as intensity increased, and the goals were to optimize muscular power and increase skill proficiency. The competition phase was also referred to as *peaking*. The characteristics of the competition phase differed depending on the sport; however, training during this time was always sport specific, or designed based on the demands of competition. The off-season was spent performing activities that would aid in recovery and rehabilitation, but not lead to complete detraining.

The four phases are still applicable today when evaluating a classical periodization model; however, in Western literature you often see the following terminology used: *mesocycle*, *microcycle*, and *macrocycle*. A *mesocycle* refers to a small number of training sessions in which the goal (e.g., power) is the same. One or two weeks within any one particular phase would be considered a mesocycle. A *microcycle* is a run of mesocycles, and it is analogous to an individual phase as defined by the classical periodization model. A *macrocycle* includes all four phases of the classical model.

## *Linear Periodization*

Linear periodization often uses progressive overload within its phases, which calls for gradual and linear increases in the load or volume (depending on the goals of the athlete) lifted from week to week within a microcycle. The basic idea that a person wants to lift more weight from week to week seems inherently correct;

© Getty Images

**Figure 3.2** Olympic lifter, Vasiliy Alexyev. His training was a product of early classical periodization.

however, we know now that progressive overload (in its simple form) is not the most effective method for enhancing performance over a long period of time. The most notable downfall is the tendency of the athlete's progress or improvement to plateau in various phases of the cycles after a few macrocycles.

In linear periodization, the aim in each mesocycle is to attempt to increase the body's muscle hypertrophy and strength toward the theoretical genetic maximum. Thus, the theoretical basis for a linear method of periodization consists of developing muscle hypertrophy followed by improved nerve function and strength. This is repeated again and again with each mesocycle, and within each phase, loading would progressively increase from workout to workout (see table 3.1).

Table 3.1  **A Typical Periodization Format for a Training Program**

|  | Preparation phase (4 weeks) | First transition (4 weeks) | Competition phase (4 weeks) | Second transition (off-season) (4 weeks) |
|---|---|---|---|---|
| Goal | Muscle growth (hypertrophy) | Maximal strength and power | Peak | Recovery (light physical activity) |
| Reps | 8-10 | 4-6 | 1-3 | 12-15 |
| Sets | 4-5 | 3-4 | 3-5 | 3-5 |
| Intensity | Low | Moderate | Very high | Low |
| Volume | High-moderate | Moderate | Low | Low |

You can see in table 3.1 that there is some variation within each microcycle because of the range of repetitions for each cycle. Still, the general trend for the 16-week program is a steady linear increase in the intensity.

The volume of the linear periodization program will also vary. The program starts with a higher initial volume, and as the intensity of the program increases, the volume gradually decreases. The drop-off between the intensity and volume of exercise can become less as the athlete becomes stronger and can tolerate higher volumes of exercise during the heavy and very heavy microcycles. For beginners, linear periodization can be very helpful for allowing an individual to get used to the training stress, because it starts off with relatively light weights and higher volume.

The linear periodization program may also be designed based on RM target training zones (see table 3.2).

Table 3.2  **A Linear Periodized Program Using Repetition Training Zones (each cycle is 4 weeks long)**

| Microcycle | Repetition training zones |
|---|---|
| 1 | 3-5 sets of 12-15RM |
| 2 | 4-5 sets of 8-10RM |
| 3 | 3-4 sets of 4-6RM |
| 4 | 3-5 sets of 1-3RM |

You must be very careful not to progress too quickly to high volumes of heavy weights. Pushing too hard can lead to injury or overuse strain, and it can also pave the way to overtraining syndrome, all of which can compromise progress for months. Although it takes a great deal of excessive work to produce such an overtraining effect, young and highly motivated trainees can easily make the mistake out of sheer desire to make gains and see progress in their training. To ensure that you avoid progressing too quickly, you can first do 6 to 12 weeks of a *general preparation phase* to get ready for a more formalized program. This phase would involve using light weights, learning the exercises, and progressing to the starting RM percentage range that will be used in a program.

In any periodized training program, the purpose of the high volume of exercise in the early microcycles (often called the *off-season* training for a given sport) is to promote the muscle hypertrophy needed to eventually enhance strength in the later phases of training (toward peaking). Thus, the late cycles of training are linked to the early cycles, and these cycles enhance each other because strength gains are related to size changes in the muscle. Programs designed for attempting to gain strength without the needed muscle tissue are limited in their potential.

The increases in the intensity of the periodized program then start to develop the needed nervous system adaptations for enhanced motor unit recruitment. Heavier weights demand high-threshold motor units to become involved in the force production process. With the associated increase in muscle protein in the muscles from the earlier cycles of training, force production of the motor units is further enhanced. Here again you can see how different parts of the 16-week program integrate and build on one another.

## Nonlinear Periodization

Periodization has evolved beyond the linear method, and more modern forms can be manipulated to meet the special needs of particular athletes. Within the past decade, *nonlinear periodization* (sometimes referred to as *undulating periodization*) has replaced the classical, linear approach for most athletes. Rather than sequentially increasing or decreasing the volume and intensity, nonlinear periodization calls for more frequent changes—weekly and sometimes daily—to maintain variation in the training stimulus. Recent research comparing it to linear periodization has shown that making more frequent variations to a program elicits greater gains in as little as 15 weeks. Nonlinear periodization is thought to be superior because the constant variations of the acute variables demand constant physiological adaptations to take place (as opposed to a gradual increase in intensity or volume that causes plateaus in gains to occur).

Another important aspect of nonlinear periodization is the volume and intensity of the assistance exercise. The primary exercises are typically periodized, but with the nonlinear approach, you can also use a two-cycle program to vary the exercises involving small muscle groups. For example, in the triceps pushdown (page 202), you could rotate between the moderate (8 to 10RM) and the heavy (4 to 6RM) cycle intensities. This would provide the hypertrophy needed for isolated muscles of a joint but also provide the strength needed to support heavier workouts of the large muscle groups.

Individual differences in schedule or competitive demands are also of great consideration when designing this type of program. Different from the linear programs, in the nonlinear approach, you can train both for increases in muscle size (hypertrophy) and for making gains in neural aspects of strength within the same 7- to 14-day period of the longer mesocycle. This may be more conducive to many individuals' schedules, especially when competition, travel, or other schedule conflicts make the traditional linear method difficult to adhere to.

In this approach, workouts rotate among very heavy, heavy, moderate, and light training sessions. If you were to miss a workout, you would just perform that workout on the next day and continue with the rotation. Rather than letting a certain number of weeks dictate the length of a mesocycle, a mesocycle is completed when a certain number of workouts are completed (e.g., 48).

Table 3.3 provides an example of a nonlinear periodized training program over a 16-week mesocycle for the lower body muscles. You will notice that the variation in training is much greater within each week than in a linear program, ranging from 1RM sets to 12RM sets. You can also add a power training day in which loads may be from 30 to 45 percent of 1RM and release of the mass being lifted is allowed if no deceleration exists with the movement of the joints (e.g., as in bench press throws or squat jumps). Variations such as this may also be considered a "down" day in which the physiological stress of the workout is not high (because of the lack of the eccentric portion of the lift), thus allowing the athlete more recovery time.

Table 3.3 **Example of a Nonlinear or Undulating Form of Progression in Resistance Training**

|  | Week 1 | Week 2 | Week 3 | Week 4 | Week 5 |
|---|---|---|---|---|---|
| **Day 1** | 82% × 3 × 3 | 87% × 2 × 3 | 75% × 6 × 3 | 85% × 3 × 3 | 90% × 1 × 3 |
| **Day 2** | 60% × 8 × 3 | 50% × 3 × 9 | 53% × 12 × 3 | 62% × 8 × 2 | 55% × 5 × 5 |
| **Day 3** | Optional day: active rest and recovery or very light assistance work | | | | |

Read table as intensity (as a percentage of 1RM) × repetitions × number of sets.

Table 3.4 shows a nonlinear program using an RM target training zone for each of the different workouts. In this program, the variation in training is much greater within the week, ranging from 1RM to 15RM. To add variation to the program and allow some recovery from higher-intensity exercise, medicine ball plyometrics and other lower body plyometrics are also performed in this program. You take a break after 12 weeks of training, which would correspond to the second transition phase in the classical periodization model.

Table 3.4 **A Nonlinear Periodized Program Using the RM Training Zone Approach**

| Day | RM training zone |
|---|---|
| Monday | 4 sets of 12-15RM |
| Wednesday | 4 sets of 8-10RM |
| Friday | 3-4 sets of 4-6RM |
| Monday | 4-5 sets of 1-3RM |
| Wednesday | Power day |
| Friday | 2 sets of 12-15RM |

Whether you use a linear or nonlinear periodization program, the overall effects appear to be the same—training both for hypertrophy and neural gains. Any periodized program is superior to a constant training program.

# Other Strength Training Protocols

Although periodization training has become the predominant method of training in both the athletic and fitness worlds, there are still many other forms of training that can be useful in attaining goals and adding variation to the normal routine. Many of these programs are simple to follow, and beginners tend to find some of them (such as circuit training) less intimidating. Furthermore, most of these programs have been shown to elicit gains in short-term training (up to eight weeks), after which periodized training is superior.

## *Circuit Training*

Circuit training gained popularity as strength training machines, such as Universal, Nautilus, Marcy, and Pyramid, became more commonplace in the 1970s. Eight to twelve exercise stations are chosen, and the athlete performs the exercises in a circuit (one after the other), then repeats the circuit one to three times.

Circuit training aims to address cardiovascular endurance as well as local muscular endurance. It also promotes some moderate strength gains. Chapter 7 covers circuit training in more detail.

This type of program is very time efficient when large numbers of people are training, because each piece of equipment is virtually in constant use. It is also very time effective for an individual with only a limited amount of training time.

## *One-Set Program*

Like circuit training, most one-set programs evolved from the machine mythologies of the 1970s and were popularized because of their limited time commitment and inflated claims of efficacy. One-set programs are often performed in a circuit fashion; you perform one set of 8 to 12 repetitions of each exercise to failure.

These programs, also sometimes referred to as *HIT* (high-intensity training), have not been proven to be as effective compared to periodized programs, or even progressive overload programs that use multiple sets (Tan 1999). Nevertheless, they can provide a fast change-up routine in even a nonlinear workout and might be categorized as a one-set circuit workout.

## *Multiple-Set System*

The multiple-set system originally consisted of two or three warm-up sets of increasing resistance followed by several work sets at the same resistance. This training system became popular in the 1940s and was the forerunner of the multiple-set and repetition systems of today. Considerable research has been done to try to determine the optimal resistance and number of repetitions for developing strength using a multiple-set system. For some multijoint exercises, a 5 or 6RM performed for a minimum of three sets appears to be optimal for causing increases in strength.

You can perform a multiple-set system at any desired resistance, and for any number of repetitions and sets, to meet the desired goals of a training program. However, performing a multiple-set system for a long period of time without changing other training variables normally results in plateaus in the strength and power gains. The majority of resistance training systems use some variation of a multiple-set system. If gaining strength and power is the objective of training, you can optimize the multiple-set system by periodizing the training.

## Super Slow System

The super slow system involves performing very slow repetitions ranging from 20 to 60 seconds per repetition. Proponents say that the increased amount of time the muscle is "under tension" enhances its strength development. To date, little data are available to support this theory. The amount of force that a muscle can produce dramatically decreases with time; to move a weight slowly, you have to significantly reduce the resistance you use, which in turn recruits more endurance muscle fibers. Using super slow sets appears to have some potential efficacy in developing slow-velocity muscular endurance.

This system of resistance training is typically used for isolated-joint exercises or machine exercises where the movement can be controlled throughout the range of motion. Usually, super slow sets are performed for only one or two sets in an entire workout. The resistance varies depending on a person's muscular endurance fitness level; therefore, it is not related to the resistance used for a repetition at normal speed. As the time of the repetition increases, the amount of resistance that can be lifted decreases. Thus, each point in the range of motion receives less than an optimal strength stimulus.

## Pyramid or Triangle Routine

Popularized by powerlifters, the pyramid method of resistance training uses a gradual increase in resistance (and thus a decrease in the repetitions) with each set of a single exercise. Once you perform a very low number of repetitions (1 to 5), you then decrease the resistance and increase the number of repetitions in increments until you reach your starting point. An example of this would be performing a 10RM, 8RM, 6RM, 4RM, 2RM, 4RM, 6RM, 8RM, and 10RM with the resistance set to allow only the listed number of repetitions. This method is often performed as a half pyramid (e.g., only going up to a specific resistance, such as the peak 2RM set in the previous example). The heavier the resistance, the longer the rest you need. Therefore, this type of program is very time intensive, and it is typically only used for two or three exercises in a workout. Pyramid routines are discussed in more detail in chapter 7.

## *Super Setting*

Arising from bodybuilding training, *super setting* is a term used to describe alternating two exercises for two different target muscle groups. These muscle groups can be opposing groups (e.g., biceps and triceps) or groups at different joints (e.g., quadriceps and deltoids). Scant data exist on the efficacy of using super sets, yet many programs use various types of super sets to maximize the metabolic intensity (i.e., to improve the hormonal profile for specific gains such as hypertrophy) of a body part being trained (e.g., biceps and triceps). Proponents hypothesize that super setting ensures that all the muscles of a particular joint are exercised, thus allowing symmetry of size to be maintained among the muscles around a joint. Super setting may be created in a number of ways. Here are two examples:

1. Biceps curl 10RM, triceps pushdown 10RM. Repeat three times with no rest between exercises.
2. Lat pulldown 10RM, seated cable row 10RM, bent-over rows 10RM. Rest one minute between each exercise. Repeat three times.

The first example focuses on two opposing muscle groups, using the push-pull approach (see page 142). The second example concentrates on one particular body part (in this case, the back muscles). Many times super sets are placed within a workout, or at the end of a workout, when local muscular endurance and definition are the primary goals of the program. With the short rest periods, this type of workout protocol can be very demanding. Again, it is commonly used by bodybuilders seeking to stimulate definition and to burn fat. Super sets are discussed in more detail in chapter 7.

© Jumpfoto

## Negative Resistance Training

For most resistance exercises, the *negative* or eccentric portion of the repetition is lowering the weight. During this phase, the muscles involved are actively lengthening so that you can lower the resistance in a controlled manner. Conversely, the lifting of the resistance during the repetition of an exercise is called the *positive* or concentric portion.

A person is normally able to handle more weight in the lowering phase of a repetition than in the actual lifting or positive portion of the repetition; negative resistance training involves lowering more weight than you can lift in the concentric phase of the repetition. You can perform this type of training by having spotters help you raise the weight and then lowering it alone. You can also perform negative resistance training on some resistance training machines by lifting the weight with both arms or legs and then lowering the resistance with only one arm or leg. On some machines, it is possible to lift the weight with both the arms and legs and then lower the weight using just the arms or the legs. You must be sure to use proper exercise technique and safety spotting techniques whenever performing heavy negative resistance training.

Advocates of negative training believe that using more resistance during the negative portion of the exercise results in greater increases in strength. However, studies using 120 percent of the concentric (positive) 1RM for negative training have not resulted in greater gains in strength than "normal" training with concentric repetitions. Only limited data are available concerning the optimal eccentric resistances for particular muscle groups. Ranges of 105 to 140 percent of the concentric 1RM have been proposed, but such resistances may depend on whether a machine or free weights are being used. Machines reduce the amount of balance required and the involvement of assistance muscles; thus, heavier eccentric (negative) resistances may be possible. It has been shown that a repetition that uses a heavier eccentric resistance (105 percent of the concentric 1RM) immediately before the concentric phase of the repetition results in achieving a heavier concentric 1RM. Eccentric training may enhance the neural facilitation of the concentric movement. Further study will be needed to determine if such training affects gains in strength. For free weights, 105 to 110 percent of the concentric 1RM probably represents the upper limit of effective eccentric resistances for most exercise movements.

## Split Routine System

Many bodybuilders use a split routine system. Bodybuilders perform many exercises for the same body part to encourage hypertrophy. Because this is a time-consuming process, not all parts of the body can be exercised in a single training session. Solving this predicament has led to training various body parts on alternate days—or a split routine. A typical split routine system entails training the arms, the legs, and the abdomen on Monday, Wednesday, and Friday, and training the chest, the shoulders, and the back on Tuesday, Thursday, and Saturday. This system helps minimize the time spent per session, but it means training six days a week.

You can develop variations of a split routine system so that training sessions take place four or five days per week. Even though training sessions are still quite frequent, this allows sufficient recovery of muscle groups between training sessions because body parts are not trained on successive days. The split routine system allows you to maintain a higher intensity of training for a particular body part or group of exercises; these higher intensities would not be possible if the four to six training sessions were combined into two or three longer sessions. Maintaining a higher intensity (heavier resistances) should result in greater gains in strength. In a study of highly strength-trained athletes (i.e., college football players), short-term (10-week) strength gains in the bench press and squat exercises depended on increased use of assistance exercises. Split routines allow you to pay more attention to the assistance exercises needed to enhance strength development.

## Forced Repetition System

Forced repetitions are an extension of the exhaustion set system and the cheat system used by some powerlifters. After you have performed a set to exhaustion, your training partners assist you by lifting the resistance just enough to allow you to lift three or four additional repetitions. You can easily use this system with many exercises after you have performed a set to exhaustion. This system forces the muscle, which is partially fatigued, to continue to produce force. This may benefit those attempting to increase local muscular endurance.

Take care when using this system because it can easily cause muscular soreness. Because the forced repetitions are being performed under conditions of fatigue, you must concentrate on lift technique and never give up during a movement. The spotters need to be extremely attentive and capable of lifting the weight if exercise technique is lost by the lifter. The efficacy of forced repetitions to increase strength remains unclear.

## Functional Isometrics

The functional isometrics system attempts to take advantage of the joint angle specificity of strength gains from isometric training. Usually performed in a power cage, the pins are often placed at the sticking point of the exercise being performed. However, functional isometrics can also be performed by a partner holding a weight at a certain angle, or by both individuals pushing against one another. Functional isometrics entail performing a dynamic contraction for 4 to 6 inches (10.2 to 15.2 cm) of a movement; at that point, the resistance hits the pins in a power rack. You then continue to attempt to lift the resistance with maximal effort for five to seven seconds.

The objective of this system is to use joint angle specificity to cause increases in strength at the weakest point within the range of motion. The maximal resistance for any exercise is determined by the amount of resistance that can be moved through the sticking point or weakest point in that movement. The use of functional isometrics in conjunction with normal resistance training (i.e., dynamic and constant) has been shown to cause significantly greater increases in 1RM for the bench press than normal resistance training alone.

Many powerlifters use this system without a power rack during the last repetition in a heavy set (e.g., 1 to 6RM). They attempt to perform as much of a repetition as possible, and when they cannot move the weight, they continue to produce force isometrically for five to seven seconds at the exact angle where the sticking point occurs. This type of training does require very attentive spotters. To optimize this training, you must know where the sticking point is within the range of motion. These sticking points can change with training. This system is appropriate when the major goal of the program is to increase 1RM capabilities for a particular exercise.

## Rest-Pause System

The rest-pause system involves using near maximal resistances (1RM) for multiple repetitions. This is made possible by taking a 10- to 15-second rest between repetitions. For example, you may perform one repetition of an exercise with 250 pounds (113.4 kg), which is near the 1RM for the exercise. You put the weight down and rest for 10 to 15 seconds, and then perform another repetition with 250 pounds. You repeat this four or five times. If you cannot perform a complete repetition, spotters lend just enough assistance to allow completion of the four or five repetitions. You perform only one set of an exercise, but you may perform two or three exercises per muscle group in the same training session. The goal of this system is to use the maximal resistance possible; proponents of the system believe that this allows for the greatest possible gains in strength.

## Priority System

The priority system is a concept that can be applied to virtually all types of resistance training programs. This system involves using an exercise order in which those exercises that apply to the major goals for the training program are performed first; this way you can perform these exercises with maximal resistances or intensity. If you perform the high-priority exercises or training late in the training session, fatigue may prevent you from using maximal resistances or intensity. This may limit your adaptation to the training.

For example, a bodybuilder's weakest muscle group in terms of definition and hypertrophy may be the quadriceps group. Using the priority concept, this bodybuilder would perform exercises for the quadriceps group at the beginning of a training session. A basketball coach may decide that a power forward's biggest weakness is lack of upper body strength, which results in being pushed around under the boards. Therefore, this player would perform major upper body exercises at the beginning of the training session. A football player may want to develop strength and power in the thighs, hips, and lower back; therefore, this player would perform heavy hang cleans and squats in the beginning of the workout.

## Complex, Concurrent, Contrast, or Cross-Training

Complex, concurrent, contrast, or cross-training have all been used to describe the necessity of training all three energetic pathways concurrently. This is necessary for several sports that rely on a range of different metabolic pathways, such as speed-strength, muscular endurance, or power. Depending on the requirements of the individual training, concurrent training goals may or may not conflict with each other. For instance, it has been shown that aerobic training can affect maximal strength gains. Aerobic training up to a specific threshold appears to have no effect on strength gains (a threshold of around 75 percent of heart rate maximum for 20 to 30 minutes, two or three times per week), but anything more than that can negatively affect strength gains. Although heavy resistance training, such that a strength athlete or bodybuilder performs, may lead to muscular adaptations that would normally be disadvantageous to an aerobic athlete, studies have shown that strength training does not impair maximal oxygen consumption.

Concurrent training may be mutually beneficial to different goals. For instance, it has been shown that concurrent strength and power training increases measures of power, such as throwing velocity and vertical jump height. Often, these two variables are trained together in one workout (sometimes called the *contrast method*). By alternating heavy loads with lighter loads performed at maximal speed, you can develop both maximal strength and power.

This type of training fits very well into a periodized scheme of training. Once you have established your goals, you can develop the meso- and microcycles for obtaining the primary objectives. Secondary objectives can then be added to the existing program to make a complete and well-rounded training program. For instance, speed and power may be the primary goals of a football running back, but maximal strength may be a secondary objective. Thus, the contrast method would work well for this athlete.

# Training Modalities

It is clear from the many methods of training that there are also many different tools to train with (i.e., free weights, machines, medicine balls, and so on). All of these tools fit into a specific modality of training, and all have inherent strengths and weaknesses. For instance, many power athletes use both free weights and medicine balls or plyometric training. In addition, even powerlifters will use some machine training as a supplement to their free weight training.

## Constant External Resistance Devices

With constant external resistance devices, the absolute load does not change during the course of the exercise. These devices include barbells, dumbbells, medicine balls, and other freestanding objects that do not require a pulley or lever to move.

The primary drawback of these devices is that they do not correct for the increase in musculoskeletal leverage during a movement. Thus, the "top end" or lockout of a movement may be easier than the initial portion of the concentric motion. However, these devices also require other muscles to act as stabilizers during a particular lift, thus increasing the total amount of physiological work the body must do to perform the exercise. Secondary benefits of using such devices are that the range of motion is not limited and that any exercise can be adapted to account for individual differences, such as a person's size or physical capabilities. Furthermore, these devices can easily be adapted to fit within the scope of an individual's functional movements (mimicking an individual's sport-specific or everyday movements) and allow for progression (i.e., in weight, range of motion, and modality) as skill capabilities improve.

© Jumpfoto

## Variable Resistance Devices

Variable resistance devices include most resistance exercise machines, cable systems, and rubber tubing. These devices are characterized by a change in load somewhere in the range of motion. For instance, machine levers are designed to increase the absolute load at the point in the range of motion where the musculoskeletal system is at a mechanical advantage. Rubber devices such as bands and surgical tubing have become popular because they offer more resistance at the top end of a movement. Although it may be advantageous to overload the musculoskeletal system throughout the whole range of motion (for instance, to increase lockout strength in the bench press exercise), there are some notable disadvantages to using machines to strength train:

1. Machines are not always designed to fit the proportions of all individuals. People who are taller or shorter than the norm, those with special physical considerations, and obese people often cannot use machines with ease.

2. Machines use a fixed range of motion; thus, the individual must conform to the movement limitations of the machine. Often, these movements do not mimic functional or athletic movements.

3. Most machines isolate a muscle or muscle group, thus negating the need for other muscles to act as assistant movers and stabilizers.

4. The misconception of the extra safety that machines provide may lead you to not pay attention to the exercise. It is still possible to become injured when using machines.

Despite these drawbacks, variable resistance devices are still a good tool for training. They do isolate particular muscle groups, which may be necessary in the case of an injury or a special physical need (such as vertigo problems). These devices are also useful for beginners because they are perceived to be less intimidating. However, for mid-level and advanced lifters and athletes, machines and other variable resistance devices should be used only as a supplement to training; the benefits of constant resistance devices (i.e., free weights) far outweigh the benefits of variable resistance devices.

## Static Resistance Devices

Static contraction devices are rarely used. These are devices in which a person pulls or pushes against an immovable apparatus for isometric exercises. Isometric contraction is not practical for most sports or for everyday functioning. However, as discussed on page 64, pushing a barbell against the safety racks, or using a wall or partner for an isometric contraction, is occasionally used to overcome a sticking point in a range of motion.

## Plyometric Training

Plyometric training is a popular form of training for speed, power, and starting strength. The term *stretch–shortening cycle exercises* is starting to replace the term *plyometrics*, and it describes this type of resistance exercise more accurately.

The stretch–shortening cycle (SSC) refers to a natural part of most movements; the cycle is a sequence of eccentric, isometric, and concentric actions. It is characterized by an eccentric motion leading into a ballistic concentric motion. For example, in the bench press exercise, if you were to start the lift from your chest, you would use an isometric and then a concentric action only. However, if you were to start the lift with the bar at arm's length, you would use an eccentric, then isometric, then concentric action. Depending on the length of the isometric action, the concentric portion of the lift can be much easier because of the SSC (i.e., the longer you isometrically hold the weight before the concentric action, the larger the decrement in the SSC and therefore the more difficult the concentric portion of the lift will be).

Bounding, leaping, and medicine ball throws are common plyometric or stretch-shortening cycle exercises (figure 3.3). The key to plyometric training is using the SSC to allow for an enhanced concentric contraction because of the preactivation during the eccentric action. Thus, the speed of the eccentric muscle action is vital to the concentric repetition. The ability of the SSC to increase power output depends on load and time and the ability of the muscle to induce a force-enhancing prestretch of the muscle.

**Figure 3.3**   Passing a medicine ball takes advantage of the stretch–shortening cycle to help increase your power output.

When the sequence of eccentric to concentric actions is performed quickly, the muscle is stretched slightly before the concentric action. The slight stretching stores elastic energy. This elastic energy is added to the force of a normal concentric action, which is one of the reasons commonly given that a more forcible concentric action results after a stretch–shortening cycle. The other common explanation for a more forcible concentric action after an SSC is a reflex that results in quicker recruitment of muscle fibers or recruitment of more muscle fibers involved in the movement.

It is easy to demonstrate how an SSC results in a more powerful concentric action. Perform a normal vertical jump (a countermovement jump). During this type of jump, you bend at the knees and hips (eccentric action), then quickly reverse direction and jump (isometric followed by concentric action). A countermovement jump involves an SSC. Now perform a jump by bending at the knees and hips, stopping for three to five seconds in the bent knee and hip position, and then jumping. This is called a *noncountermovement jump*; it does not involve an SSC and results in a jump that is not as high as a countermovement jump (a jump involving an SSC). You can also demonstrate the effect of a stretch–shortening cycle by throwing a ball for distance with a normal overhand throwing motion. Then throw a ball for distance without a windup—starting from the end of the windup position (no stretch–shortening cycle). The normal throwing motion will result in a throw of greater distance.

# Training Recommendations

To design an effective training program, you must perform a needs analysis. Such an analysis can help you determine what type of training modality is best for you (free weights versus machines versus plyometrics), what exercises to select, what energy pathways you want to use in your training, how to manipulate the acute variables of training, and how to work around existing injuries and prevent future ones.

Chapter 7 provides more guidelines for determining your workout goals and building your program from those, but briefly, the following are some general recommendations for achieving specific goals with resistance training during a peaking portion of a macrocycle.

**Maximal strength.** You can achieve maximal strength best by using heavy loads (above 85 percent of 1RM) for low repetitions, with long rest periods between sets. For advanced lifters, a split routine is best for achieving these goals, so that workouts are spread over four to six days per week. Elite Olympic weight-lifters are known to use two workouts per day, thus increasing the frequency and overall volume of training. You should lift for each muscle group two or three days per week, organized in a periodized manner. Multiple-joint exercises with free weights should make up the primary exercises, with machines and single-joint movements being used as complements.

**Muscular hypertrophy.** For muscular hypertrophy, exercises that use both concentric and eccentric muscle actions are best. Use moderate loading (70 to 85 percent of 1RM) for 8 to 12 repetitions per set, with one to three sets per exercise. Advanced lifters, such as bodybuilders, may increase the load and the number of sets, and they may decrease the rest time (one to two minutes between sets). Like training for maximal strength, both single- and multiple-joint exercises should be included. Keep frequency similar to when training for maximal strength, with each major muscle group being worked one to three days per week, depending on training status.

**Muscular power.** When training for muscular power, velocity of the movement is very important. You can generate optimal power using 30 to 60 percent of 1RM. The number of repetitions should be from 3 to 6 (and not performed to failure). Frequency and rest time between sets are similar to that for hypertrophy and strength. Also note that you can enhance power development through concurrent training for maximal strength. You should plan power training in a periodized fashion, paying attention to developing maximal strength along with power. When training for maximal power, you can use a variety of training modalities—such as plyometric exercises (e.g., depth jumps and bounding), medicine ball throws, resistive running devices (e.g., parachutes), and free weights.

**Local muscular endurance.** Local muscular endurance is best trained using lighter loads for higher repetitions (15 to 25). Keep rest time between sets

© SportsChrome/Monte Isom

short—one to two minutes for sets with higher repetitions, under one minute for sets with moderate repetitions. Frequency and exercise selection are similar to when training for muscular hypertrophy and strength.

■□■■

You can use many different methods to train muscle, and the program you design should be specific to your goals for training. The potential for creating a new resistance training program appears almost infinite.

With the manipulation of acute program variables, it is easy to design many distinctly different programs. Any resistance training program should address the needs of the individual or the event for which the individual is being trained. Popular or faddish training systems should be evaluated in terms of their acute program variables and their ability to address the needs of an individual or sport. The choice of which training system or systems to use depends on the goals of the program, time constraints, and how the goals of the resistance training program relate to the goals of the entire fitness program. A major goal of any program is to bring about physiological adaptations while providing the needed rest and recovery to avoid overtraining.

# Nutrition for Muscle Development

William J. Kraemer, Maren S. Fragala, and Jeff S. Volek

A proper, balanced, and sufficient diet is essential to building muscular strength and allowing the intense training necessary to produce gains in muscle strength and size. It is estimated that 2,300 to 3,500 calories are required to build one pound (.5 kg) of muscle.

The ultimate goals of proper nutritional intake during resistance training are to maximize protein synthesis, minimize protein degradation, and restore muscle fuel stores. This is achieved by creating an environment in the body that promotes the development of tissues, including muscle and bone. Creating this environment involves ensuring the availability of enzymes (which are catalysts for biochemical reactions) and amino acids (which are the building components of muscle). As you learned in chapter 2, it also requires hormonal actions to signal and facilitate the building of muscle, as well as the necessary exercise intensity to stimulate the growth and development of protein. Protein synthesis requires ATP (adenosine triphosphate), the body's energy source for muscular contraction. This energy source is available in limited supplies in the body's stores, and you need to replenish these supplies from the foods you eat.

For anyone undertaking weight training, nutrition can influence both the workout intensity and the recovery process between training sessions, which in turn affects the intensity of the following exercise session. Consuming the proper proportion of nutrients at critical times around any single resistance training session is necessary to optimize the postworkout recovery process in the muscle—and therefore to maximize muscle strength gains. Without adequate energy stores in the muscle, the muscle may not be able to generate adequate force during a

© SportsChrome/Monte Isom

muscular contraction when called on to do so. Furthermore, without adequate availability of amino acids, protein synthesis and recovery after training may be compromised.

In this chapter, we review some of the basics of muscle metabolism as they relate to nutritional intake, as well as the role of hormones in that metabolism. We discuss the different macronutrients, micronutrients, and supplements and how these—and the timing of their intake—affect the gains brought on by resistance training.

# Muscle Metabolism

Muscle proteins are constantly undergoing remodeling through physical and chemical processes. This is referred to as *muscle metabolism*, which encompasses the building or synthesis (anabolism), the maintenance, and the breakdown (catabolism) or degradation of protein for energy.

Protein synthesis occurs when energy demands are adequate to support the stimulus created for muscle growth. When energy requirements are not adequate, protein degradation can occur to produce energy. Protein, because of its important roles in the body, is generally spared as a source of energy production, and the body primarily relies on carbohydrate or fat to produce energy for exercise, depending on the intensity, duration, and type of training. Carbohydrate is stored in the muscle and liver in the form of glycogen. This glycogen is broken down into glucose molecules and is then metabolized to produce ATP. During longer-duration or lower-intensity training, the body can metabolize fat tissue through a process called *lipolysis* to generate energy.

Protein synthesis needs to be understood in terms of acute versus chronic responses. Acute responses occur in the short time after a single training session, such as changes in the protein balance or glycogen degradation and synthesis. Chronic responses are long-term effects seen from long-term training, such as increases in muscle strength and size. Numerous studies have examined the immediate environmental effects of nutrition and training on the muscle after an acute bout of exercise. However, few have examined the long-term effects on muscle mass and strength. Thus, much of what is known about the acute effects of nutritional practices for strength training—such as glycogen repletion and protein synthesis—is assumed to result in long-term gains in muscle strength and size.

During fasting or in the absence of nutritional intake after training, the muscle is in a state of negative protein balance, indicating that protein degradation exceeds protein synthesis, with little glycogen repletion occurring. Even without training, a positive energy balance or overfeeding results in both increased lean body mass and fat mass. The goal for strength athletes is to maintain a net positive protein balance, meaning that protein synthesis exceeds protein breakdown and the muscle is in an anabolic or muscle-building state. Accordingly, strength athletes want to avoid a net negative protein balance, where muscle protein breakdown exceeds synthesis and the muscle is in a catabolic or "muscle breakdown" state.

## Role of Hormones

Nearly every physiological function in the body is regulated by hormones—chemical messengers that travel via the bloodstream in the body to target tissues (such as muscle). Figure 4.1 provides an overview of the different roles that hormones play. Since resistance exercise dramatically affects hormonal responses in the body—and in part stimulates the development of tissues (including muscle and bone)—you need to understand how these hormones interact with food that is

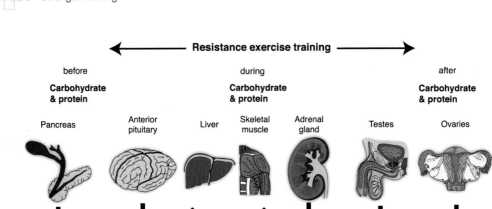

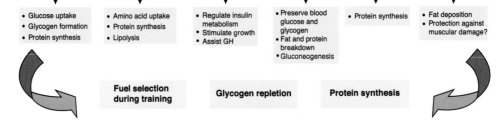

**Figure 4.1** The quantity, quality, and timing of nutrient consumption with regard to resistance training may have important influences on the hormones that regulate fuel selection during training, glycogen repletion, and protein synthesis. This can result in optimal gains in muscle strength and power.

consumed. Hormones play a significant role in metabolic balance. They are largely responsible for the fuel selection, partitioning of nutrients, and gene regulation that ultimately affect body composition and muscle mass.

As you learned in chapter 2, an acute bout of resistance exercise (considering the load, number of sets, number of repetitions, and number and length of rest intervals) creates a stimulus that generates a hormonal response. Muscle contraction triggers a series of mechanical and chemical events in the muscle that signal hormones to regulate enzymes, which in turn regulate the genetic formation of proteins. Exercise increases the blood flow, and thus increases the delivery of hormones and nutrients to the target receptors in the muscle cells. The anabolic environment is enhanced by the exercise stimuli along with the availability of nutrients and hormones. Carbohydrate and protein consumption appears to affect the responses of hormones involved in muscle metabolism—including insulin, testosterone, growth hormone (GH), cortisol, estrogen, and IGF-I—thus affecting muscle protein and glycogen balance. Although the role of insulin in response to exercise and diet is understood, the influence of the other listed hormones remains unclear.

**Insulin** is released from the pancreas in response to high levels of circulating blood glucose. This hormone promotes glucose uptake by the tissues from the blood, glycogen formation, and protein synthesis in the presence of sufficient amino acids (by decreasing catabolism).

**Growth hormone** (GH) is secreted from the anterior pituitary gland (located at the base of the brain) in response to exercise, sleep, stress, and low plasma glucose. It functions metabolically to cause the muscle cells to take up amino acids, leading to an increase in protein synthesis, lipolysis (fat metabolism), and glucose conservation—ultimately increasing muscle and skeletal growth. An increased amount of GH is released in response to exercise, likely contributing to metabolic fuel adaptations during exercise and tissue repair after the exercise. GH levels decrease in response to increased blood glucose from carbohydrate consumption. Contrarily, GH levels rise in response to the hypoglycemia (low blood glucose levels) created after the glucose is taken up from the blood by the body cells in the hours after carbohydrate ingestion. Furthermore, circulating fatty acids inhibit GH secretion. An increased amount of GH is released in response to greater activation of anaerobic glycolysis and lactate formation. Both in men and women, GH levels are elevated in the 30 minutes after resistance training.

**Insulin-like growth factor** (IGF-I) is an anabolic hormone produced in the liver and skeletal muscle in response to the presence of GH in the blood. IGF-I functions to regulate insulin metabolism, stimulate the growth of most body tissues, and assist with the anabolic effects of GH. IGF-I levels are substantially elevated in response to progressive overload resistance exercise, resulting in skeletal muscle hypertrophy. IGF-I does not appear to be immediately affected by metabolic stressors to glucose and insulin (exercise and feeding); IGF-I does appear to regulate glucose during the fasted state.

**Testosterone** is an anabolic (tissue-building) hormone and an androgenic hormone (responsible for masculine characteristics) produced primarily in the male testes, but also in the adrenal glands in both men and women. Testosterone is accordingly present in much larger quantities in men than women. Feeding appears to decrease the postprandial (post meal consumption) circulating levels of testosterone. This effect appears to be influenced by both the macronutrient type and source (as we discuss later in this chapter).

**Estrogen** is a sex hormone produced primarily in the ovaries in the female (males do have small amounts of estrogen produced in the testes) and is responsible for fat deposition and female sex characteristics. Although estrogen is rarely considered an important hormone for muscular development and strength, understanding the role estrogen plays in energy metabolism and protein synthesis is critical to the female athlete. Many researchers avoid studying female athletes because of the difficulty controlling these athletes' monthly hormone fluctuations; in many studies of female hormones and muscle, animal models are used. Nevertheless, estrogen has recently been recognized to have a potential protective effect against skeletal muscle damage, which may have important consequences for female muscular responses to resistance training. Females have been shown to have lower levels of creatine kinase, a marker of muscle damage, when compared to males, suggesting that female muscle may sustain less damage. The mechanisms for this protective effect are not completely understood, but estrogen may play an antioxidant role or a role in the inflammatory response. Some evidence in vitro and in rats indicates that ovarian hormones inhibit muscle protein synthesis. How these findings apply to humans and how they affect nutritional considerations for the female strength athlete are unclear.

© Jumpfoto

**Cortisol** is a steroid hormone (i.e., it can pass through a cell membrane without a receptor to reach the nucleus) produced in the adrenal gland of the kidney in response to exercise, injury, or stress. Cortisol functions to preserve blood glucose and glycogen levels by increasing fat and protein breakdown in the liver, which fuels the production of new glucose (gluconeogenesis). Cortisol also works to break down proteins to provide amino acids for use in repair of tissues and energy production. It promotes the breakdown of protein (by inhibiting protein synthesis) to form amino acids that can be taken up by the liver, stimulating the mobilization of free fatty acids from adipose (fat) tissue, which stimulates the liver enzymes for glucose synthesis; this also blocks the entry of glucose into tissues, encouraging those tissues to use fatty acids as fuel. Since cortisol is related to an increased rate of protein catabolism, it has an inhibiting effect on skeletal muscle hypertrophy. Cortisol levels fluctuate regularly throughout the course of the day. Protein appears to have the greatest stimulatory effect on cortisol levels. Cortisol levels are significantly increased during an acute bout of resistance exercise, in both men and women.

Clearly, adult males and females, both athletic and sedentary, differ in muscle mass. Because muscle hypertrophy results from a positive net muscle protein balance, net muscle protein synthesis in males must exceed the rate in females. Sex hormones (testosterone, estrogen, and progesterone) likely play a role in this gender difference. Testosterone increases muscle protein synthesis. Net muscle protein balance and a lack of anabolic hormones, such as testosterone, in women may limit their gains in muscle strength and size. As mentioned, females also have been shown to have lower creatine kinase (CK) activity, an indicator of muscle damage, after exercise compared to males. This suggests that female muscle may sustain less damage. However, some studies have shown no histological differences in male and female muscle following a damaging protocol, indicating that estrogen may have a membrane-stabilizing effect against peroxidation or breakdown.

Unfortunately, most of the research on nutritional considerations has focused on the male athlete. Whether or not these findings hold true for the female strength athlete is yet to be determined. However, during endurance exercise, men and women have been shown to differ in substrate metabolism, where women tend to metabolize greater amounts of fat than carbohydrate. Whether this difference applies to resistance training and posttraining muscle adaptations is unclear.

# Macronutrients

All three of the major energy-yielding macronutrients, or dietary nutrients, required by the body in large quantities (carbohydrate, fat, and protein) are essential to muscular development. Protein provides amino acids, which are the chief structural material of protein that in turn help protein synthesis. Carbohydrates are the primary energy source to fuel training, and it is their presence in the body that stimulates muscle growth. Fats are essential for maintaining an adequate hormonal environment for muscle development. The quantity and quality of these macronutrients, as well as the timing of when you consume them, affect how the nutrients are used by muscle tissue. When the muscle tissues take up these macronutrients, hormones are released in response. These hormones interact with receptors on target tissues, resulting in gene transcription and translation for protein, fat, and carbohydrate metabolism. In the 24 to 48 hours after resistance exercise, the muscle protein metabolism response occurs. Thus, any meals consumed during this time will affect muscle hypertrophy (i.e., increase muscle size).

## Protein

Muscle is primarily composed of protein (about 22 percent) and water (about 70 percent). (The remaining percentage of muscle composition is glycogen, fat, vitamins, and minerals.) Similar to fat and carbohydrate, protein is made up of carbon, hydrogen, and oxygen. But, unlike fat and carbohydrate, protein contains nitrogen. This molecular difference gives an indication of the metabolic state of muscle tissue. Nitrogen balance is considered the difference between the amount of nitrogen taken in and the amount excreted or lost. When nitrogen supplies do not meet the nitrogen demands, protein tissue is broken down because of catabolism, and nitrogen is lost in the urine (negative nitrogen balance). If more nitrogen is consumed than excreted, you will be in an anabolic or muscle-building state (positive nitrogen balance).

Amino acids, which are the building blocks of protein, contain carbon, hydrogen, oxygen, nitrogen, and in certain cases, sulfur. They are characterized by the presence of a carboxyl group (-COOH) and an amino group ($-NH_2$) attached to the same carbon at the end of the compound. Adequate quantities of amino acids must be available for protein synthesis. At least 20 different amino acids are used to synthesize proteins, each differing by molecular structure, shape, and properties (see table 4.1). Typically, nine amino acids are considered *essential* for adults, mean-

**Table 4.1　Essential and Nonessential Amino Acids**

| Nonessential | | Essential |
|---|---|---|
| Alanine | Glutamine | Isoleucine |
| Asparagine | Gluthathione | Leucine |
| Aspartic acid | Glycine | Lysine |
| Carnitine | Hydroxyproline | Methionine |
| Citrulline | Ornithine | Phenylalanine |
| Cysteine | Proline | Threonine |
| Cystine | Serine | Tryptophan |
| GABA | Taurine | Valine |
| Glutamic acid | Tyrosine | |

At publication it is unclear whether the recently discovered selenocysteine and pyrrolysine are nonessential or essential amino acids.

ing that they must be consumed in the diet because they cannot be synthesized in the body from other precursors—unlike the *nonessential* amino acids, which can be synthesized in the body from the essential amino acids. Additionally, some amino acids, such as histidine and arginine, are considered semiessential because infants and children have a reduced ability to produce them. Furthermore, some amino acids (such as arginine and glutamine) are considered conditionally essential because their requirements are increased during times of catabolic stress.

© Jumpfoto

Proteins are rated by their biological value as complete (high biological value) or incomplete (low biological value) depending on whether or not they contain all of the essential amino acids. Typically, proteins from animal sources (eggs, meat, fish) contain all of the essential amino acids and are thus considered complete. Proteins in grain and vegetable products do not contain all of the amino acids and are considered incomplete. These plant-based foods can be combined to provide all of the amino acids.

Although protein contains about 4 calories per gram of energy, it is not typically considered a primary energy source like carbohydrate and fat. The amino acids, especially the essential amino acids supplied by dietary protein, allow the body to synthesize the proteins it needs for tissues, hormones, and enzymes. In addition, protein is inefficient at providing energy. Protein has a high thermic effect, meaning that for the amount of calories provided per gram of protein (compared to fat or carbohydrate), much of the energy is used for metabolic processes, resulting in a lower energy density.

## How Muscles Use Protein

Intense training increases the rate of both muscle protein synthesis and degradation. The rate of muscle protein synthesis exceeds the rate of protein degradation, resulting in net protein accretion, or growth. Research has shown that in the 4 hours after training, muscle protein synthesis activity is 50 percent greater than before training. In the 24 hours after training, muscle protein synthesis activity is 109 percent greater than before training.

Ingesting amino acids through food or supplements before and after exercise stimulates amino acids being transported into skeletal muscle, and therefore, stimulates protein synthesis. In terms of the timing of when you consume amino acids postexercise, similar results have been observed when consumption occurs either one or three hours postexercise. Furthermore, some evidence suggests that consuming amino acids immediately before resistance exercise increases protein synthesis to an even greater extent than consuming them after training. This is possibly because of the increased blood flow to muscle that occurs during training, which then results in increased delivery of amino acid to the muscles. Muscle anabolism occurs whether amino acids are consumed alone or carbohydrate is consumed alone at one and two hours after exercise. However, the greatest anabolic effect is apparent when amino acids and carbohydrate are combined.

High-volume resistance training or overreaching heavy training (that is, when training volumes are higher than normal, but not quite to the point of overtraining) followed by inadequate recovery initially reduces muscle strength and power. These reductions are moderated with amino acid supplementation. Additionally, during periods of energy deficit, such as in a fasted state or after a workout, a high-protein diet has been shown to be effective in increasing lean body mass and strength.

How muscles use protein is also related to why some athletes turn to using steroids, even though they are dangerous and banned from most competitive

© Jumpfoto

sports. The use of steroids appears to lower the protein requirements necessary for nitrogen balance and anabolism; this results from an increased ability to recycle the amino acids from broken-down proteins in order to synthesize new muscle protein. Some evidence suggests that infusion or ingestion of certain amino acids can increase growth hormone (GH) levels, but this effect is variable and attenuated by exercise and high-protein diets.

## Daily Protein Requirements

Some experts believe that a strength athlete requires 1.2 to 1.7 grams of protein per kilogram of body weight a day (.04 to .06 ounces per pound of body weight) to maintain nitrogen balance (an indicator of whole body protein use) and to promote anabolism. Others believe that .8 grams per kilogram (.03 ounces per pound) of body weight per day (requirements for the general population) is sufficient; despite their greater protein demands, strength athletes may have an improved efficiency in their use of amino acids. Generally, a diet composed of 25 to 30 percent protein is recommended for the strength athlete (which is typically greater than .8 grams per kilogram per day). This proportion should allow for adequate amino acids, while also allowing sufficient quantities of carbohydrates and fat to be consumed. Additionally, the type of training and the amount of muscle fibers stimulated during training may influence protein requirements, with higher amounts of protein required when training stimulates a larger amount of muscle fibers.

Essential amino acids are more critical than the nonessential amino acids. Essential amino acids have been shown to be primary regulators of muscle protein synthesis, while nonessential amino acids show little contribution. In particular, branched-chain amino acids (such as leucine) appear to be the most important stimulators of muscle protein synthesis.

## Carbohydrates

Carbohydrate molecules contain carbon, hydrogen, and oxygen, similar to proteins and fats. Like protein, carbohydrates provide 4 calories of energy per gram, but carbohydrates do this much more efficiently than protein. Many foods contain carbohydrates in combination with other macronutrients. Some foods containing primarily carbohydrates are bread, rice, pasta, potatoes, cereals, and crackers.

The carbohydrates you consume are ultimately converted to glucose, a simple sugar that is transported to all body tissues for energy. When this energy isn't used immediately, it is stored in the form of glycogen, a more complex sugar. Glycogen is the major energy source during resistance exercise using moderate repetitions (8 to 12 repetitions), and it is primarily stored in the muscle and the liver, with some amounts found circulating in the bloodstream.

### How Muscles Use Glycogen

The muscles use glycogen by breaking it down into glucose, which is then broken down into ATP (adenosine triphosphate) through a process known as *glycolysis*. About 82 percent of the ATP used during a set of biceps curls taken to the point of failure is derived from glycolysis. Because of its proximity and availability to the mitochondria (the site of aerobic ATP production in the muscle cell), glycogen is readily and quickly available to fuel the muscle during resistance training. Thus, if glycogen stores are low, exercise performance can be impaired.

Glycogen stores are depleted after exercise. Muscle glycogen is depleted by about 30 to 40 percent after resistance exercise, particularly in Type II (fast-twitch, anaerobic) muscle fibers. Furthermore, muscle damage resulting from the eccentric, muscle-lengthening phase of isotonic exercises, such as lowering the weight in a biceps curl, results in a reduced ability of the muscle to store glycogen. This reduced storage capacity is caused by a decreased rate of entry into the muscle cell by insulin.

Since glycogen is the primary fuel for muscle during resistance training, glycogen depletion may inhibit the volume or the intensity of training. Thus, the daily dietary carbohydrate requirement for strength athletes to promote optimal muscle glycogen resynthesis is increased when muscle is damaged. The idea is that you want to replenish those glycogen stores as soon as possible.

Because insulin release is triggered by circulating blood glucose, ingesting carbohydrate leads to elevated insulin levels. Glycogen repletion is faster when carbohydrate is consumed after exercise. Glycogen repletion is similar whether carbohydrates are consumed alone or combined with protein or amino acids; some evidence suggests that certain amino acids can increase insulin secretion, leading to attempts to enhance postexercise glycogen resynthesis and protein anabolism by combining carbohydrates with amino acids. This postexercise consumption of combined carbohydrates and amino acids has been shown to increase glycogen resynthesis after submaximal cycling exercise, likely because of increased insulin secretion, but its effects after resistance training are unknown.

To maximize the effect of insulin, consuming a carbohydrate and protein supplement before and during resistance exercise is recommended; this enables a person to benefit from increased blood flow for amino acid delivery. Carbohydrates appear to be most effective at leading to muscle glycogen repletion when consumed immediately after training (versus two hours after training) at a rate of 1.2 grams per kilogram per hour at 30-minute intervals for four hours. Furthermore, carbohydrates consumed before and during exercise have been shown to attenuate the decrease in muscle glycogen during training and improve the volume and intensity of a second training session within the same day.

Some studies have also shown that supplementation of protein and carbohydrates before, immediately after, or two hours after resistance training enhances the acute GH response and the GH response during late recovery (as compared to a placebo).

Although feeding does not appear to affect total IGFBP-I levels, another protein that travels in the blood and is bound to IGF-I, referred to as *insulin-like growth factor binding protein* (IGFBP-I), appears to contribute to glucose regulation by countering the glucose uptake of free IGF-I. IGFBP-I levels gradually decrease after feeding, and they increase in the three to four hours after feeding. In response to carbohydrate feeding (versus no supplementation) during and after endurance exercise, IGFBP-I levels are reduced. However, these reductions were not correlated to blood glucose levels during feeding, suggesting that factors other than blood glucose and insulin regulate IGFBP-I. These other factors may include liver glycogen depletion, because a high correlation has been observed between liver glycogen and IGFBP-I responses to exercise.

Compared to fasting, consuming nutrients before and after resistance training results in a prolonged decrease in testosterone levels. This is related to either the production, secretion, or metabolic clearance of testosterone. In men, total testosterone levels are acutely increased in response to resistance training; in women, some research shows an elevation but other research shows no change. Carbohydrate and protein supplementation appears to attenuate the testosterone response to exercise. Postexercise feeding leads to increased muscle-specific protein synthesis during recovery that is testosterone dependent. Therefore, it is likely that these observed decrements in circulating testosterone are because of the increased uptake in the skeletal muscle that results in protein synthesis. Furthermore, in response to a glucose tolerance test (where a given amount of glucose is supplied and blood is sampled and evaluated at periods after the consumption of glucose), testosterone levels are significantly decreased.

A carbohydrate solution consumed during exercise has been shown to decrease the acute cortisol response, and it has been shown to increase muscle hypertrophy over 12 weeks of training. Carbohydrate supplementation during exercise may reduce the need for gluconeogenesis during exercise, thus potentially reducing the need for cortisol.

## Daily Carbohydrate Requirements

Ultimately, for the general population, 5 to 6 grams of carbohydrate per kilogram of body weight per day (55 to 60 percent of total calories) is recommended to maintain optimal muscle glycogen stores. Athletes, particularly those with high energy demands, require additional carbohydrates.

Carbohydrates with a high glycemic index are more effective at increasing the rate of glycogen repletion. The glycemic index refers to how quickly carbohydrates are metabolized. It is a numerical rating of how much of a rise in circulating blood sugar is triggered by the consumption of a food. Carbohydrate sources with a high glycemic index, such as fruits and processed sugar, are metabolized quickly. Carbohydrate sources with a low glycemic index, such as starches and cellulose, are metabolized more slowly. *Glycemic load* is another term used when referring to the rise in blood sugar that a specific food causes. Unlike glycemic index, the glycemic load takes into consideration the amount of the food that is consumed. See table 4.2 for some typical glycemic index values.

### Table 4.2   Glycemic Index of Select Foods

| High (GI > 69) | Medium (56 < GI < 69) | Low (GI < 56) |
| --- | --- | --- |
| White bread | Wheat bread | Rye bread |
| Corn flakes | Life cereal | All-Bran cereal |
| Rice cakes | Ice cream | Peanuts |
| Jelly beans | PowerBar | Apple |
| Popcorn | Sweet corn | Milk |
| Pretzels | Baked potato | Baked beans |
| Gatorade | Raisin Bran | Yams |

Glycemic index is a rating of the time and amount that a given food causes a rise in blood sugar in regard to pure glucose, which has a glycemic index of 100.

# Fats

Like carbohydrates, fats are composed of carbon, hydrogen, and oxygen. But fats are the most energy-dense macronutrient, providing about 9 calories per gram. One pound (.5 kg) of body fat contains 3,500 calories of energy.

Dietary fats are often considered "good" or "bad" depending on their effects on blood cholesterol. Saturated fats, derived mainly from animal products (e.g., butter, cheese, ice cream, red meat), and trans fats, found most often in commercially packaged snack foods, are usually considered the bad fats because they elevate blood cholesterol levels. Unsaturated fats, derived from plant sources (such as vegetable oils, nuts, and seeds), are considered the "good" fats because they improve blood lipid profiles. Unsaturated fats include polyunsaturated fats (e.g., sunflower, corn, and soybean oils) and monounsaturated fats (e.g., canola, peanut, and olive oils).

Although dietary fat is required in order to maintain levels of circulating testosterone in the body, a high-fat diet appears to impair the ability to perform exercise at a high intensity compared to a high-carbohydrate diet. Some research has shown that eating a low-fat diet and replacing saturated fat (fat with all chemical bonds filled with hydrogens) with polyunsaturated fat (fat with at least two available bonding sites for hydrogen) may decrease circulating levels by 13 to 20 percent. Testosterone levels have also been shown to be reduced by about 23 to 30 percent in response to high-fat meals in healthy men. On the other hand, another study showed that testosterone levels were not affected after a low-fat meal. Some evidence suggests that the testosterone response after a meal may be influenced by the source of protein and fat and the amount of fat; this evidence indicates that lean meat reduces postprandial testosterone levels to a greater degree than higher-fat or plant sources of fat and protein. Thus, a moderate level of fat (15 to 20 percent of daily energy consumption) with some saturated fat (less than 10 percent) is often recommended for the strength athlete.

# Water

The human body is composed of about 40 to 75 percent water, depending on body composition and age. Water is essential to muscular strength because it constitutes about 70 percent of muscle. Fat is only 20 to 25 percent water, making it a lighter-weight form of energy storage than muscle. The water molecule is an essential link between glucose molecules in glycogen as well as between amino acids in protein. For every gram of carbohydrate stored in the body, 2.7 grams of water are stored. So for every pound (454 grams) of carbohydrate, 3.7 pounds of water are stored. Dehydration of as little as 1.5 percent of body weight has been reported to decrease muscular endurance and 1RM bench press performance.

Without exercise and under normal environmental conditions, a typical adult loses about 2.5 liters of water per day, mostly from urine. However, high temperature and exercise can increase a person's water loss to as much as 7 liters per day. Generally, you should replace water at a rate of 1 to 1.5 milliliters per calorie of energy expended. But, since this is difficult to track, approximately 8 to 16 ounces (237 to 473 milliliters) of water should be consumed per hour before, during, and after training to avoid dehydration.

# Micronutrients

Vitamins and minerals are called *micronutrients* and are essential to facilitate various body functions and biochemical reactions, including muscular contraction. Vitamins are organic substances, meaning that they contain carbon, yet they do not contain calories (energy). They function to trigger reactions in the body. Vitamins are classified into two types: water soluble and fat soluble. Water-soluble vitamins are not able to be stored in the body; these include the B vitamins and vitamin C. Fat-soluble vitamins are stored in the adipose (fat) tissue in the body; these include vitamins A, D, E, and K. Vitamins are only required in small amounts in the body, and they are metabolized, so they must be replaced by what is consumed in the diet. Vitamins play critical roles in energy metabolism and tissue formation. See table 4.3 for a complete list of vitamins and minerals, along with their dietary sources and functions.

Minerals are inorganic substances found in the water and soil in the earth, and they enter our bodies from the foods we eat—from the plants that take up the minerals and the animals that eat the plants. Minerals are all the chemical elements in our body besides carbon, hydrogen, oxygen, and nitrogen. Four percent of our total body weight is composed of 22 minerals. Minerals are classified as macrominerals and microminerals. Macrominerals (major minerals) include calcium, phosphorus, magnesium, sulfur, sodium, potassium, and chloride; these minerals exist in the body in quantities of about 35 to 1,050 grams, depending on mineral and body size. Trace minerals include iron, iodine, fluoride, zinc, selenium, copper, cobalt, chromium, manganese, molybdenum, arsenic, nickel, and vanadium; these exist in the body in quantities of less than a few grams. Both macro- and microminerals are critical to metabolic processes and the synthesis of glycogen, protein, and fat. Although few studies show beneficial effects with vitamin or mineral supplementation above recommended levels, vitamin or mineral deficiencies may impair strength and training. Thus, a multivitamin is often recommended for athletes to ensure that they are consuming adequate amounts and that they have no deficiencies.

Table 4.3    **Vitamins and Minerals**

| Vitamin or mineral | Major dietary source | Major functions |
|---|---|---|
| **Fat-soluble vitamins** | | |
| Vitamin A | Dairy products<br>Liver<br>Carrots<br>Sweet potatoes<br>Green leafy vegetables | Antioxidant to protect cells from oxidation<br>Gene expression |
| Vitamin D | Dairy products<br>Egg yolk<br>Fish oil<br>Sunlight exposure | Promotes absorption and use of calcium and phosphorous |
| Vitamin E | Vegetable oils<br>Nuts<br>Seeds | Antioxidant to protect cells from oxidation |
| Vitamin K | Spinach<br>Eggs<br>Cauliflower<br>Liver | Assists in protein formation (particularly essential to blood clotting) |
| **Water-soluble vitamins** | | |
| Vitamin $B_1$ (Thiamin) | Pork<br>Peanuts<br>Legumes<br>Whole grains | Coenzyme (assists enzymes) in energy metabolism |
| Vitamin $B_2$ (Riboflavin) | Dairy products<br>Meats<br>Enriched grains<br>Beans<br>Green leafy vegetables | Coenzyme in energy metabolism |
| Niacin | Nuts<br>Meats<br>Beans | Coenzyme in energy metabolism |
| Vitamin $B_6$ | Meats<br>Fish<br>Poultry<br>Legumes | Coenzyme in amino acid metabolism |
| Folic acid | Green vegetables<br>Legumes<br>Nuts<br>Grains | Coenzyme in DNA and RNA metabolism |
| Vitamin $B_{12}$ | Animal products | Coenzyme in DNA and RNA metabolism |
| Pantothenic acid | Animal products<br>Whole grains | Coenzyme used in energy metabolism |

*(continued)*

Table 4.3   **Vitamins and Minerals** *(continued)*

| Vitamin or mineral | Major dietary source | Major functions |
|---|---|---|
| Biotin | Meats<br>Whole grains<br>Vegetables | Coenzyme in energy metabolism |
| Vitamin C (Ascorbic acid) | Citrus fruits<br>Broccoli<br>Strawberries<br>Cantaloupe | Antioxidant<br>Improves iron absorption |
| **Macrominerals** | | |
| Calcium | Milk<br>Dark green vegetables<br>Legumes | Muscle contraction<br>Nerve transmission<br>Bone formation |
| Phosphorous | Milk<br>Meat<br>Poultry<br>Whole grains | Bone formation<br>Acid–base balance<br>Component of coenzymes |
| Magnesium | Whole grains<br>Green leafy vegetables | Protein synthesis<br>Coenzyme<br>Glucose metabolism |
| Sulfur | Protein | Component of protein |
| Sodium | Salt<br>Soy sauce | Regulation of body water<br>Nerve function |
| Potassium | Meats<br>Milk<br>Fruits<br>Vegetables | Regulation of body water<br>Nerve function |
| Chloride | Salt<br>Soy sauce | Acid–base balance<br>Gastric secretion formation |
| **Trace minerals** | | |
| Iron | Meats<br>Eggs<br>Whole grains<br>Green leafy vegetables | Hemoglobin formation<br>Coenzyme component<br>Myoglobin formation |
| Iodine | Fish<br>Dairy<br>Iodized salt | Thyroid hormone formation |
| Fluoride | Drinking water<br>Tea<br>Seafood | Tooth and bone structure |
| Zinc | Meats<br>Seafood<br>Whole grains<br>Vegetables | Component of enzymes involved in protein synthesis and energy metabolism |

| Vitamin or mineral | Major dietary source | Major functions |
|---|---|---|
| Selenium | Meats<br>Nuts<br>Seafood<br>Whole grains | Component of enzymes<br>Antioxidant enzyme |
| Copper | Organ meats<br>Seafood<br>Nuts<br>Legumes | Component of enzymes<br>Assists in use of iron and<br>hemoglobin in the body |
| Chromium | Seafood<br>Meat<br>Whole grains<br>Asparagus | Involved in glucose and energy<br>metabolism<br>Enhances insulin function |
| Manganese | Vegetables<br>Fruits<br>Nuts<br>Whole grains | Component of enzymes |
| Molybdenum | Legumes<br>Cereal<br>Vegetables | Component of enzymes |

Vitamins and minerals are essential to the diet of strength athletes as they have critical functions in the biochemical processes responsible for energy metabolism and protein synthesis.

# Supplements

Several nutritional supplements are marketed with claims of increasing muscular strength and size. Many of these claims lack scientific support. Investing in these ineffective supplements may be a waste of money for the strength athlete. However, some supplements—such as creatine, branched-chain amino acids, and L-carnitine—have supporting evidence for their use and may be beneficial to the strength athlete when used correctly. In a survey of Division I athletes, 89 percent had used or were currently using nutritional supplements, including sports drinks and bars. Additionally, about 47 percent consumed a multivitamin, and 37 percent used a creatine supplement.

## Creatine

Creatine is an amino acid derivative (from arginine, glycine, and methionine) that is available in meats and fish and is synthesized in the liver, pancreas, and kidneys. Because creatine plays a critical role in ATP metabolism, creatine supplementation theoretically increases the bioavailability of phosphocreatine (PCr) in skeletal muscle cells, enhancing muscle performance. Having more available PCr facilitates the resynthesis of ATP to provide energy for brief, high-intensity exercise (such as resistance training). This results in a better match between ATP supply and demand. PCr may also increase the force of muscular contraction and delay fatigue during anaerobic exercise by buffering the intracellular hydrogen ions formed with lactate production.

The amount of creatine in human skeletal muscle normally ranges between 90 and 160 mmole/kg (millimoles per kilogram of muscle) in dry muscle. The effectiveness of creatine supplementation appears to vary with these baseline levels, with the greatest advantage observed in those with the lowest baseline levels. Although anecdotal evidence suggests increased muscle cramping with creatine supplementation, no serious side effects have been scientifically verified.

Over two dozen studies have reported that creatine supplementation enhances the development of lean body mass and muscle strength in response to resistance training. This increased muscle strength and mass could be because of several mechanisms, including an effect on protein metabolism, synthesis, and transcriptional expression at the genetic level.

Research supports this theory; five-day oral dosages of 20 grams per day have been shown to increase muscle creatine availability by 20 percent and significantly accelerate PCr regeneration after intense muscle contraction. Significant performance enhancement has been observed in male athletes—in both brief, high-intensity work and total time to exhaustion—using creatine supplementation of 20 to 30 grams per day.

Long-term creatine supplementation has been shown to enhance the progress of muscle strength during resistance training for sedentary females. Twelve weeks of creatine supplementation enhances fat-free mass, physical performance, and muscle morphology in healthy men in response to heavy resistance training. This is likely attributable to higher-quality training sessions.

Short-term creatine loading results in enhancement of both maximal strength and weightlifting performance; therefore, part of the ergogenic (performance-enhancing) effect of creatine shown in studies is likely because of this acute effect, and part is likely because of the ability to train with higher workloads (although the relative contributions of these mechanisms remain unclear).

## Branched-Chain Amino Acids

Branched-chain amino acids include three essential amino acids (leucine, isoleucine, and valine) that are needed to maintain muscle and preserve glycogen. Branched-chain amino acids are found naturally in foods such as dairy products, meat, whey, and eggs. Because of their role in muscle metabolism, branched-chain amino acids are sometimes isolated and consumed as a dietary supplement. In a study of branched-chain amino acid supplementation during four weeks of resistance training overreaching (defined earlier), initial reductions in strength and power were attenuated.

© SportsChrome/Monte Isom

## L-Carnitine

Carnitine is synthesized in the human liver and kidneys and is found in meats and dairy products. L-carnitine (the supplement form of carnitine) is thought to benefit exercise performance because it spares muscle glycogen by increasing free fatty acid transport across mitochondrial membranes, thus increasing fatty acid oxidation and use for energy. L-carnitine also appears to delay fatigue by reducing muscle lactate accumulation associated with exercise.

Some studies have shown a decreased respiratory exchange ratio (RER)—the ratio of carbon dioxide expired to oxygen consumed at the level of the lungs—with L-carnitine supplementation (2 to 6 grams per day) during exercise, suggesting that fatty acids rather than carbohydrates were used for energy. However, another study directly measuring muscle glycogen and lactate levels (through biopsy and serum analysis) failed to demonstrate any glycogen-sparing effect or reductions in lactate levels while supplementing with 6 grams per day of L-carnitine. L-carnitine L-tartrate supplementation (a source of L-carnitine when split into L-carnitine and L-tartaric acid in the body) in healthy men for three weeks has been shown to reduce the amount of exercise-induced muscle tissue damage, leave a greater number of receptors intact for hormonal interactions, reduce the level of muscle soreness, and result in less of a rise in markers of muscle damage and free radicals (atoms or compounds with unpaired electrons, which are thought to cause cellular damage).

□■■■

To maximize the acute anabolic response, several important factors must be considered. These factors include the stimulus of resistance training combined with the availability of amino acids, the timing of supplement or macronutrient ingestion immediately before and after training, and the presence of insulin. To create a hormonal environment that enhances recovery from training, an athlete should ingest both protein and carbohydrate immediately before and after training.

Although more research is needed on the chronic adaptations to resistance training and nutrition, existing evidence suggests that protein and carbohydrate supplementation enhances the development of lean body mass in response to training. Several supplements are marketed with claims of increasing muscular strength and size; however, the only supplement with convincing scientific evidence to support its benefits to the strength athlete is creatine, which has been shown to improve the quality of the workout stimulus.

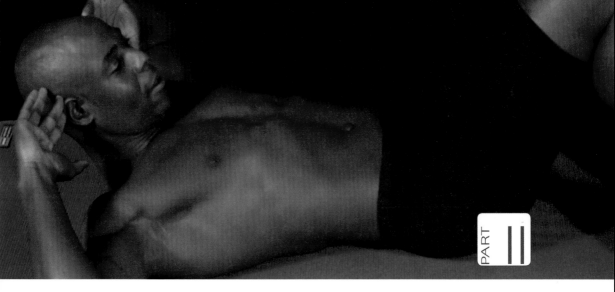

# PART II

# Resistance Training Guidelines

In this part of the book you will discover the proper methods for strength training and how to develop a program that will result in the greatest gains. You'll learn how to follow appropriate testing procedures to assess your strength; from there you will discover how to make the correct choice of training method to maximize output while minimizing risks.

Chapter 5, "Strength Assessment," lays the foundation for strength and power testing to help you define your strength training goals. These test results are interpreted so you can understand your strengths and weaknesses and then use this information to determine what areas to spend the most time on to improve your strength performance.

Chapter 6, "Types of Strength and Power Exercises," delineates the ways you can train in and out of the gym. There are a myriad of choices in the real world for training muscle, and this chapter helps you choose the one that suits your needs and time limitations.

Chapter 7, "Workout Schedule and Rest," organizes your workout into specific sections and details the purpose of each. Your workout should be a function of your goals and provide steps to accomplishing everything you want for strength and power. This chapter will allow you to adjust your variables in such a way to achieve maximum results.

Finally, chapter 8, "Safety, Soreness, and Injury," provides information on strength training in a manner that allows you to realize your goals without incurring injury. It also discusses muscle soreness, which is inevitable in some forms of resistance training, but you can minimize and control it by following proper guidelines. Finally, you can easily identify any injuries before they become serious, and proper form and methods of training can eliminate them altogether.

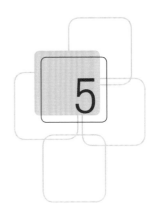

# Strength Assessment

Daniel P. Murray, Sagir G. Bera, Lee E. Brown, and Brian W. Findley

Before beginning any exercise program you must have a proper understanding of your current level of fitness. Your level of fitness has many different aspects, such as strength, power, and cardiovascular endurance. In turn, these aspects are affected by a multitude of factors, including age, body mass index, and prior training experience (training age).

This chapter discusses the ways you can assess certain aspects of your fitness level. In particular, we talk about how to test muscular strength and power. Proper assessment is a critical step in developing effective resistance training programs, because it allows you to see your particular areas of strength and weakness. You can then use this information, coupled with your personal goals, to develop an appropriate program. Furthermore, repeated assessments allow you to track your progress. Keep in mind that, regardless of your current level of fitness, resistance training can be a fun and effective way of improving your overall health and well-being.

Strength and power can be measured in many ways using reliable assessment tests, not to mention an individual self-assessment. In this chapter, we detail how to perform the most commonly used strength assessment tests to help you measure your individual strength and power.

# Setting Goals

When a person begins any exercise program, he or she usually has a personal set of goals to achieve. These can include losing weight, simply improving overall fitness, increasing muscle strength, and gaining a particular edge in his or her sport. Collecting some baseline data on where you are can help you determine the type of exercises that will assist you the most in achieving your goals. This is especially true for strength and power training exercises. Given the wide variety of resistance training methods available (discussed in further detail in chapter 6), it is important to decide which training methods to focus on and which are best suited for you.

Your resistance training goals should be specific to the things you want to accomplish through training. Before setting your goals, ask yourself, "Why am I doing this?" If you want to improve general strength, then your goals should focus on improving the amount of weight you can lift. If, on the other hand, you want to achieve something more specific, such as being a better basketball player, your goals should focus on improving your performance in the components of that specific sport.

© Fotosearch

Goals should also be realistic and attainable. This is not meant to discourage you from having lofty goals. On the contrary, setting the bar high for yourself can help keep you focused and motivated. Remember, though, the loftier the goal, the longer and harder you will likely have to work to achieve it. In other words, it is not realistic to want to be able to bench press 200 pounds (90.7 kg) after six weeks of training if your current maximum is 100 pounds (45.4 kg). The goal itself (lifting 200 pounds) will be difficult to achieve but not impossible. The short time frame, however, makes such a goal unrealistic.

Avoid setting unrealistic goals because they can lead to frustration and discouragement. Appropriate and realistic goals, on the other hand, can create satisfaction and a feeling of achievement. Once these initial goals are accomplished, you can change them to reflect the progress that you've made. Creating a sense of accomplishment through goal setting is vital because it gives you positive reinforcement for resistance training and can help you stick with the activity for the long haul.

# Assessing Strength

The choice of strength assessments may be determined by your goals. If your goal is to improve overall physical fitness then a self-assessment may be the best choice. However, if your goal is to improve a specific aspect of your performance, then more sophisticated tests such as the 1RM or computer-based assessments may be more beneficial. In addition, anthropometric measurements, such as height and weight, can be utilized by all individuals. Overall, the more assessments you take of your strength and conditioning level, the greater your understanding of your baseline fitness will be.

Note that some of the assessments noted in the following pages require more experience on the part of both the exerciser and the tester than others. For example, 1RM tests require that the exerciser have a moderate level of strength and experience lifting in the gym. Computer-based tests may require expensive equipment as well as well-trained testers, while anthropometry and self-assessments may be done with little or minimal expense and experience.

## Self-Assessment

Perhaps the easiest and most convenient way to evaluate your strength is to do a simple self-assessment. Even though many test protocols have been designed to assess strength and power, a simple self-assessment remains one of the most effective ways to understand your personal strength capabilities. This is because only you can feel your muscles at work. Thus, a quick measurement of your overall strength and power may be very valuable to eventually achieving your exercise goals.

The beauty of doing a self-assessment is that there is no single right way to complete one. Basically, all you have to do is compare the level of strength that

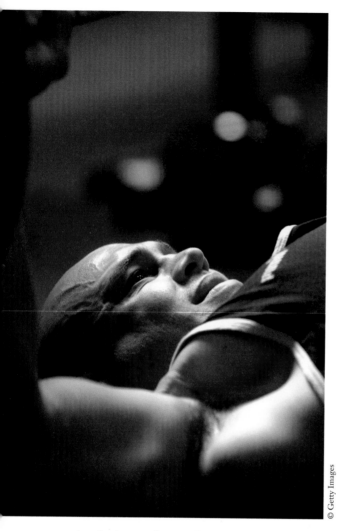

© Getty Images

you are at currently with the level you were at before; this enables you to assess whether or not you need to make changes to your strength training program. Or if you are beginning an exercise program, you simply have to determine if you are at an appropriate strength and power level for achieving the types of gains you wish to achieve.

The first step is to determine why you need or want additional strength (or power). Some of the questions you might want to ask yourself may include "Am I consistently having trouble doing the everyday tasks that I used to do?" and "Do I find it increasingly difficult to pick up items that were previously easy to pick up?" Perhaps you feel that you are not getting as much as you would like out of your body during physical activities. Or, maybe you just want to be able to run faster and jump higher when competing in athletics. For any of these situations, you want to determine how much strength you feel you are lacking or would like to gain. These deficiencies can simply be designated as "a lot," "a little," or "an average amount." You will find that a simple subjective self-evaluation can be a useful supplement to a comprehensive strength and power testing protocol. If after performing your self-assessment you still have questions regarding your strength level, you should consult a qualified strength and conditioning professional for further evaluation.

## One Repetition Maximum (1RM) Protocol

One of the most universally accepted and used methods for testing strength and power is the one repetition maximum (1RM) protocol. Essentially, a person's 1RM for a specific exercise is the maximum amount of weight that he or she can lift for no more than one complete repetition of that exercise.

Many researchers have found that 1RM protocols can be great indicators of strength and power. The 1RM test is an important tool because it allows you to establish a baseline that can be used to determine subsequent exercise intensities and loads for your workouts. In fact, the majority of the time, when people talk about doing a strength and power assessment, they are referring to doing a 1RM test. Usually, only the major muscle groups of the body are tested. Maximal upper body strength is measured using a bench press (page 176), while lower body strength is measured using the back squat (page 214). Maximum muscular power can be measured by using a power clean movement (page 259).

Determining a 1RM for any exercise is a comprehensive process. Many sets of the exercise are performed, ultimately leading up to the actual 1RM determination. This process is detailed in the following procedures.

Performing the 1RM test properly means taking appropriate safety precautions. Before performing any of these procedures, you must have an understanding of

## 1RM Test–Bench Press

Refer to pages 176 and 177 for detailed instructions for the bench press.

1. Begin with a warm-up set in which the resistance is low enough to allow you to complete 5 to 10 repetitions easily.
2. Rest for one minute.
3. Perform another warm-up set with a resistance that will allow you to complete 3 to 5 repetitions. This usually means increasing the weight about 10 to 20 pounds (4.5 to 9.0 kg) or 5 to 10 percent of the previous set.
4. Rest for two minutes.
5. Estimate another increase (10 to 20 pounds or 5 to 10 percent) that will enable you to completely perform 2 or 3 repetitions. Perform those repetitions.
6. Rest for two to four minutes.
7. Estimate another load increase of 10 to 20 pounds (5 to 10 percent) that will allow only 1 repetition of the exercise to be performed with correct form. If you were able to complete the rep, go to the next step; if you were not able to lift the weight, go to step 9.
8. Rest for two to four minutes and then estimate another moderate increase in weight (10 to 20 pounds or 5 to 10 percent), and repeat the trial.
9. If you are unable to lift the weight, rest for two to four minutes, decrease the weight by 5 to 10 pounds (2.3 to 4.5 kg), and repeat. Continue increasing or decreasing the weight as needed until you determine your actual 1RM. Try to complete the process within five sets following the warm-up sets.

Procedures for the 1RM back squat (page 214) and 1RM power clean (page 259) are very similar to those for the 1RM bench press. The same procedures are followed for the number of warm-up sets and repetitions, the difference being that you should increase the weight in 30- to 40-pound (13.6 to 18.1 kg; 10 to 20 percent) increments instead of the 10- to 20-pound (5 to 10 percent) increments. During the actual 1RM determination, the same increases in weight and rest periods apply. However, for a failed 1RM attempt, the weight is decreased in increments of 15 to 20 pounds (6.8 to 9.0 kg; 5 to 10 percent) for the back squat and power clean. ■

the proper form and technique for safely completing the exercise you choose to use (refer to part III for detailed exercise instructions). Sturdy equipment must be used to ensure that the participant and the weights are properly secured and supported. Use benches or squat racks with spotting bars, and enlist the help of a spotter to ensure proper form and technique, as well as safety, during testing. Finally, be sure to use adequate rest periods to allow for recovery and to promote proper form.

As you can see from the instructions on page 101, 1RM testing protocols take a lot of time and effort to complete. This is one of the drawbacks of the test. Fortunately, the results of the 1RM test are well worth obtaining. You will often see competitive sport teams using these tests to measure an athlete's ability, or more

Table 5.1    **Estimating 1RM Training Loads**

| Max reps (RM) | 1 | 2 | 3 | 4 | 5 | 6 | 7 | 8 | 9 | 10 | 12 | 15 |
|---|---|---|---|---|---|---|---|---|---|---|---|---|
| % RM | 100 | 95 | 93 | 90 | 87 | 85 | 83 | 80 | 77 | 75 | 67 | 65 |
| Load (lb or kg) | 10 | 10 | 9 | 9 | 9 | 9 | 8 | 8 | 8 | 8 | 7 | 7 |
| | 20 | 19 | 19 | 18 | 17 | 17 | 17 | 16 | 15 | 15 | 13 | 13 |
| | 30 | 29 | 28 | 27 | 26 | 26 | 25 | 24 | 23 | 23 | 20 | 20 |
| | 40 | 38 | 37 | 36 | 35 | 34 | 33 | 32 | 31 | 30 | 27 | 26 |
| | 50 | 48 | 47 | 45 | 44 | 43 | 42 | 40 | 39 | 38 | 34 | 33 |
| | 60 | 57 | 56 | 54 | 52 | 51 | 50 | 48 | 46 | 45 | 40 | 39 |
| | 70 | 67 | 65 | 63 | 61 | 60 | 58 | 56 | 54 | 53 | 47 | 46 |
| | 80 | 76 | 74 | 72 | 70 | 68 | 66 | 64 | 62 | 60 | 54 | 52 |
| | 90 | 86 | 84 | 81 | 78 | 77 | 75 | 72 | 69 | 68 | 60 | 59 |
| | 100 | 95 | 93 | 90 | 87 | 85 | 83 | 80 | 77 | 75 | 67 | 65 |
| | 110 | 105 | 102 | 99 | 96 | 94 | 91 | 88 | 85 | 83 | 74 | 72 |
| | 120 | 114 | 112 | 108 | 104 | 102 | 100 | 96 | 92 | 90 | 80 | 78 |
| | 130 | 124 | 121 | 117 | 113 | 111 | 108 | 104 | 100 | 98 | 87 | 85 |
| | 140 | 133 | 139 | 126 | 122 | 119 | 116 | 112 | 108 | 105 | 94 | 91 |
| | 150 | 143 | 140 | 135 | 131 | 128 | 125 | 120 | 116 | 113 | 101 | 98 |
| | 160 | 152 | 149 | 144 | 139 | 136 | 133 | 128 | 123 | 120 | 107 | 104 |
| | 170 | 162 | 158 | 153 | 148 | 145 | 141 | 136 | 131 | 128 | 114 | 111 |
| | 180 | 171 | 167 | 162 | 157 | 153 | 149 | 144 | 139 | 135 | 121 | 117 |
| | 190 | 181 | 177 | 171 | 165 | 162 | 158 | 152 | 146 | 143 | 127 | 124 |
| | 200 | 190 | 196 | 180 | 174 | 170 | 166 | 160 | 154 | 150 | 134 | 130 |
| | 210 | 200 | 195 | 189 | 183 | 179 | 174 | 168 | 162 | 158 | 141 | 137 |
| | 220 | 209 | 205 | 198 | 191 | 187 | 183 | 176 | 169 | 165 | 147 | 143 |
| | 230 | 219 | 214 | 207 | 200 | 196 | 191 | 184 | 177 | 173 | 154 | 150 |
| | 240 | 228 | 223 | 216 | 209 | 204 | 199 | 192 | 185 | 180 | 161 | 156 |
| | 250 | 238 | 233 | 225 | 218 | 213 | 208 | 200 | 193 | 188 | 168 | 163 |
| | 260 | 247 | 242 | 234 | 226 | 221 | 206 | 208 | 200 | 195 | 174 | 169 |
| | 270 | 257 | 251 | 243 | 235 | 239 | 224 | 216 | 208 | 203 | 181 | 176 |
| | 280 | 266 | 260 | 252 | 244 | 238 | 232 | 224 | 216 | 210 | 188 | 182 |
| | 290 | 276 | 270 | 261 | 252 | 247 | 241 | 232 | 223 | 218 | 194 | 189 |
| | 300 | 285 | 279 | 270 | 261 | 255 | 249 | 240 | 231 | 225 | 201 | 195 |

specifically, the athlete's strength and power. If only one test could be used to determine strength or power, then the 1RM would be the test to use.

Still, some people may find the 1RM test to be more intensive than their bodies are able to handle. As an alternative to a 1RM test, you can perform a multiple RM and then convert the value into a projected 1RM value using any of a variety of prediction equations. Table 5.1 lists some of the predicted 1RM values based on weight used and repetitions completed. Although the value that prediction equations yield is not as accurate as an actual 1RM measurement, multiple RM prediction may be adequate for the average individual. And, as discussed throughout this chapter, there are a variety of other tests that can also be used, individually or collectively, to properly determine strength and power.

Table 5.1, *continued*

| Max reps (RM) | 1 | 2 | 3 | 4 | 5 | 6 | 7 | 8 | 9 | 10 | 12 | 15 |
|---|---|---|---|---|---|---|---|---|---|---|---|---|
| Load (lb or kg) | 310 | 295 | 288 | 279 | 270 | 264 | 257 | 248 | 239 | 233 | 208 | 202 |
| | 320 | 304 | 298 | 288 | 278 | 272 | 266 | 256 | 246 | 240 | 214 | 208 |
| | 330 | 314 | 307 | 297 | 287 | 281 | 274 | 264 | 254 | 248 | 221 | 215 |
| | 340 | 323 | 316 | 306 | 296 | 289 | 282 | 272 | 262 | 255 | 228 | 221 |
| | 350 | 333 | 326 | 315 | 305 | 298 | 291 | 280 | 270 | 263 | 235 | 228 |
| | 360 | 342 | 335 | 324 | 313 | 306 | 299 | 288 | 277 | 270 | 241 | 234 |
| | 370 | 352 | 344 | 333 | 322 | 315 | 307 | 296 | 285 | 278 | 248 | 241 |
| | 380 | 361 | 353 | 342 | 331 | 323 | 315 | 304 | 293 | 285 | 255 | 247 |
| | 390 | 371 | 363 | 351 | 339 | 332 | 324 | 312 | 300 | 293 | 261 | 254 |
| | 400 | 380 | 372 | 360 | 348 | 340 | 332 | 320 | 308 | 300 | 268 | 260 |
| | 410 | 390 | 381 | 369 | 357 | 349 | 340 | 328 | 316 | 308 | 274 | 267 |
| | 420 | 399 | 391 | 378 | 365 | 357 | 349 | 336 | 323 | 315 | 281 | 273 |
| | 430 | 409 | 400 | 387 | 374 | 366 | 357 | 344 | 331 | 323 | 288 | 280 |
| | 440 | 418 | 409 | 396 | 383 | 374 | 365 | 352 | 339 | 330 | 295 | 286 |
| | 450 | 428 | 419 | 405 | 392 | 383 | 374 | 360 | 347 | 338 | 302 | 293 |
| | 460 | 437 | 428 | 414 | 400 | 391 | 382 | 368 | 354 | 345 | 308 | 299 |
| | 470 | 447 | 437 | 423 | 409 | 400 | 390 | 376 | 362 | 353 | 315 | 306 |
| | 480 | 456 | 446 | 432 | 418 | 408 | 398 | 384 | 370 | 360 | 322 | 312 |
| | 490 | 466 | 456 | 441 | 426 | 417 | 407 | 392 | 377 | 368 | 328 | 319 |
| | 500 | 475 | 465 | 450 | 435 | 425 | 415 | 400 | 385 | 375 | 335 | 325 |
| | 510 | 485 | 474 | 459 | 444 | 434 | 423 | 408 | 393 | 383 | 342 | 332 |
| | 520 | 494 | 484 | 468 | 452 | 442 | 432 | 416 | 400 | 390 | 348 | 338 |
| | 530 | 504 | 493 | 477 | 461 | 451 | 440 | 424 | 408 | 398 | 355 | 345 |
| | 540 | 513 | 502 | 486 | 470 | 459 | 448 | 432 | 416 | 405 | 362 | 351 |
| | 550 | 523 | 512 | 495 | 479 | 468 | 457 | 440 | 424 | 413 | 369 | 358 |
| | 560 | 532 | 521 | 504 | 487 | 476 | 465 | 448 | 431 | 420 | 375 | 364 |
| | 570 | 542 | 530 | 513 | 496 | 485 | 473 | 456 | 439 | 428 | 382 | 371 |
| | 580 | 551 | 539 | 522 | 505 | 493 | 481 | 464 | 447 | 435 | 389 | 377 |
| | 590 | 561 | 549 | 531 | 513 | 502 | 490 | 472 | 454 | 443 | 395 | 384 |
| | 600 | 570 | 558 | 540 | 522 | 510 | 498 | 480 | 462 | 450 | 402 | 390 |

Reprinted, by permission, from National Strength Coaches Association, 2000, *Essentials of strength training and conditioning*, 2nd ed. (Champaign, IL: Human Kinetics), 410-411.

## Anthropometric Measurements

Anthropometric measurement is another simple way to measure strength. *Anthropometry* can be defined as the scientific measurement of the body. The only instrument you need to make these measurements is a simple, flexible tape measure, not unlike the one that you would see your tailor using.

Every few weeks, use the tape measure to measure the circumference of a variety of big muscle groups, such as those of the thighs, upper arms, chest, and calves (figure 5.1). By taking the measurements every few weeks, you can chart the progress of gain (or loss) in muscle size. As you learned in chapter 2, generally speaking, the larger the circumference of the muscle, the stronger it is.

Although anthropometric measurements may seem primitive, they can be a great way to identify changes in strength. However, we recommend that anthropometric measurements be used only as a supplement to other strength and power assessment tools.

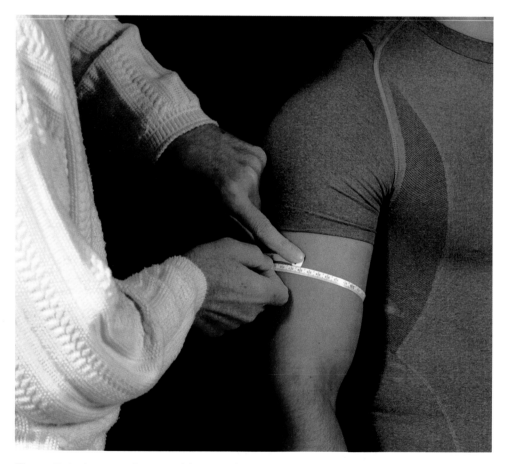

**Figure 5.1**    Increases in a muscle's circumference tend to indicate an increase in that muscle's strength.

# Computerized Measurements

On one end of the strength assessment spectrum is the simple, low-tech self-assessment. On the other end of the spectrum are the variety of available computerized measurement tools. Computers have the ability to quantify a person's actual strength and power, which can't be done with a normal self-assessment. With computers, you have the option of performing a large number of tests and getting very accurate results. In addition, computers can precisely measure muscle strength and power in all sorts of positions and movements. The two most frequently used tools are electromyography equipment and isokinetic dynamometers.

Electromyography (EMG) measures electrical signals in the body to determine general levels of strength. As you learned in chapter 1, each muscle in your body is innervated or connected by a set of nerves, or motor neurons. These motor neurons are ultimately controlled by your central nervous system, including your brain. Muscular strength is partially determined by the neuromuscular control that you have over those muscles. In fact, the initial adaptations to resistance training exercise are mostly neuromuscular adaptations (refer to page 32). (That's one of the reasons why you do not see huge gains in muscle mass until after the first few weeks of regular training.) Strength training forces your nerves to "learn" how to best and most efficiently send a signal to the muscles. As a person's muscles get stronger, the electrical activity of the muscles increases. Through EMG pads, which are connected to an EMG machine or computer, placed on various locations surrounding a muscle, the electrical activity of that muscle can be measured as it contracts. When this process is repeated after a few weeks of resistance training, it can be used to determine increases in neuromuscular activity and thus gains in muscle strength.

An isokinetic dynamometer is another piece of equipment that you can use to measure strength and power (figure 5.2). Dynamometers look like beefed-up exercise machines that are connected to a computer. This machine measures the force that is produced when someone pushes or pulls on the dynamometer attachment; a computer program then analyzes the data and provides a measure of the torque (strength) and power that the participant produced. The collected information gives you some of the most precise, accurate, and quantifiable assessment data available on strength and power.

With a few slight adjustments to the dynamometer, almost every major muscle in the body can be tested. These machines can measure muscle strength through the muscle's entire range of motion, otherwise known as the *dynamic strength* of the muscle. Isokinetic training is discussed in more detail in chapter 6.

Isokinetic dynamometers can also measure isometric or static strength at specific angles of a joint. This can be especially useful as a clinical tool in identifying areas of strength deficiency or imbalance. For instance, an athlete recovering from knee surgery can be tested to determine if the quadriceps of the leg that was operated on is as strong as the opposing side. The results of the test can be used to help determine whether this athlete is ready to return to the field of play or needs more time rehabbing.

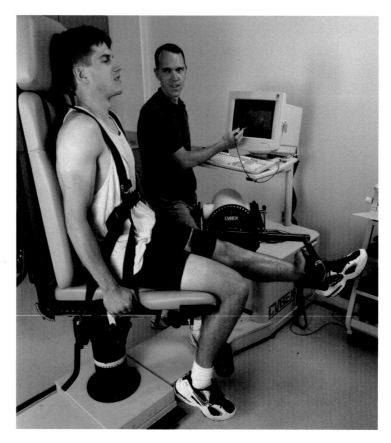

**Figure 5.2**   An isokinetic dynamometer being used for strength assessment.

For a precise measurement of strength and power, isokinetic dynamometers or EMG machines are the way to go. Unfortunately, that accuracy comes at a price—literally. Both of these machines are very expensive and are usually only found in a clinical or laboratory setting. Prior background knowledge is required to operate such machines. Also, a medical referral may be required. Much of the time, the strength and power measurements from an isokinetic dynamometer or EMG are more elaborate than what is needed by the individual. Thus, for most people, we recommend simpler and more routine assessment tests.

# Assessing Power

As with the strength assessments mentioned previously in this chapter, the test you choose to assess your power will depend on your specific goals. The 1RM and vertical jump protocols described in the next section require only simple equipment. Be aware that measures of strength relate to the maximum weight you can lift, and measures of power relate to your explosiveness (see chapter 12).

# 1RM Protocol

The 1RM protocols regarding strength assessments (see pages 100 to 103) can also be applied to power exercises. The techniques and procedures for performing the test are exactly the same as when assessing strength. The only difference is the way that the exercise is performed. Power exercises are performed ballistically, with an attempt to move the weight as fast as possible. The repetitions done during strength assessments are done more slowly, with good control of the weight throughout the entire range of motion of the exercise. Typical power exercises that are assessed with 1RM protocols are the Olympic lifts (discussed in chapter 12).

# Vertical Jump Test

More than likely, you have probably heard many sportscasters talk about a basketball player with a "48-inch vertical" or a football player with a "36-inch vertical." They are referring to these players' vertical jump test scores. Like the 1RM tests, the vertical jump test is a routinely used test to measure lower body power, especially in an athletic setting. A vertical jump test should not be used to obtain exact power measurements for individual muscles. Instead, the test is used to compare power (or vertical jump height) to that of others taking the same test. As implied above, many professional and collegiate sports teams use the vertical jump tests to determine the power level of their athletes. More specifically, the data are used to determine if an athlete needs to improve lower body power for his or her specific sport.

Like many power assessment tests, the vertical jump is a simple test that almost anyone can perform. The vertical jump height of an individual can be measured in two ways. The first way is to use a commercially available vertical jump test device, such as the Vertec (figure 5.3a). Alternatively, the test can be performed using a wall and some chalk to put on the jumper's fingertips (figure 5.3b). A commercial device will usually give slightly more accurate results, because testing conditions will always remain uniform for each trial. Nonetheless, a wall and some chalk are fairly precise and accurate in their own right.

Quite simply, the vertical jump test consists of a person jumping as high as he or she possibly can. The test begins with the participant standing directly underneath the device or six inches (15.2 cm) to the side of a wall. An initial measurement is taken with the participant reaching as high as possible with his or her feet flat on the ground. If using a wall, a mark is made at this point with the chalk. If using a commercial device, the device is adjusted so that the participant can just reach the lowest vane. For either test setting, the participant bends down, swings both of his or her arms down and back, quickly swings both arms forward and up, and jumps as high as possible. At the highest point, a chalk mark should be left on the wall, or a vane should be tapped on the vertical jump device. Vertical jump height is defined as the distance between the initial standing mark and the top of the jump. Perform three trials, recording the highest jump. A brief recovery period is allowed between each trial.

**Figure 5.3**   A vertical jump test can be performed using *(a)* a device to measure the jump or *(b)* by performing the jump beside a wall on which you can mark the height.

Vertical jump tests can help you determine your level of lower body power by comparing your score to some descriptive data for the test (see table 5.2). For most athletes or athletes-to-be, maximum vertical jump height is a very important variable that applies directly to the performance of many sports. Unfortunately, vertical jump height cannot readily be compared to quantitative power measurements from tests such as the 1RM power clean. Thus, vertical jump tests should primarily be used to measure and compare vertical jump height. As with many strength and power measurements, vertical jump tests should be used as just one portion of an overall testing protocol.

## Margaria-Kalamen Stair Sprint Test

Margaria-Kalamen may sound like a fancy cocktail, but it is actually a very useful test to calculate an individual's lower body power. The test is easy to administer and requires very little equipment—just steps and a timer.

## Table 5.2    Vertical Jump Test Descriptive Data

| Sport or group | Position | Mean or median score (in) | (cm) |
|---|---|---|---|
| NCAA Division I college football | Split ends, strong safety, and offensive and defensive linemen | 31.5 | 80 |
| | Wide receivers and outside linebackers | 31 | 79 |
| | Linebackers, tight ends, and safety | 29.5 | 75 |
| | Quarterbacks | 28.5 | 72 |
| | Defensive tackles | 28 | 71 |
| | Offensive guards | 27 | 69 |
| | Offensive tackles | 25-26 | 64-66 |
| High school football | Backs and receivers | 24 | 61 |
| | Linebackers and tight ends | 22 | 56 |
| | Linemen | 20 | 51 |
| College basketball (men) | All | 27-29 | 69-74 |
| College basketball (women) | All | 21 | 53 |
| NCAA Division II college basketball (women) | Guards | 19 | 48 |
| | Forwards | 18 | 46 |
| | Centers | 17.5 | 44 |
| College baseball | All | 23 | 58 |
| College tennis (men) | | 23 | 58 |
| College tennis (women) | | 15 | 38 |
| Competitive college athletes (men) | | 25-25.5 | 64-65 |
| Competitive college athletes (women) | | 16-18.5 | 41-47 |
| Recreational college athletes (men) | | 24 | 61 |
| Recreational college athletes (women) | | 15-15.5 | 38-39 |
| Sedentary college students (men) | | 16-20.5 | 41-52 |
| Sedentary college students (women) | | 8-14 | 20-36 |
| 17-year old boys | | 20 | 51 |
| 17-year old girls | | 13 | 33 |
| 18- to 34-year old men | | 16 | 41 |
| 18- to 34-year old women | | 8 | 20 |

The values list are either means or 50th percentiles (medians). There was considerable variation in sample size among the groups tested. Thus the data should be regarding as only descriptive, not normative.

Reprinted, by permission, from National Strength Coaches Association, 2000, *Essentials of strength training and conditioning*, 2nd ed. (Champaign, IL: Human Kinetics), 310.

You can perform a Margaria-Kalamen test on any staircase that has at least nine steps and at least 20 feet (6 m) of flat area leading up to the staircase (figure 5.4). Each step should be about 7 inches (17.8 cm) tall. Perform the test using the following instructions:

1. An electronic start timer is placed on the third step, and a stop timer is placed on the ninth step. (A simple timer will suffice if no electronic timer is available, though the results may not be as accurate. In such a case, it is better to have a second person around to get the time measurement.)

2. The participant takes three warm-up runs up the stairs.

3. The participant then stands exactly 20 feet (6 m) from the base of the staircase, facing the staircase. He or she begins to sprint from a standstill.

4. On reaching the staircase, the participant steps on the third, sixth, and ninth steps only. Timing begins immediately after stepping on the third step and ends after reaching the ninth step.

5. The time is recorded to the nearest hundredth of a second.

6. The following formula is then used to calculate power for this individual in kilogram-meters per second (kg-m/s):
$$P = (W \times H)/t$$

   a. Measure the weight (W) in kilograms of the participant.

   b. Measure the height (H) in meters of the six steps between the third and ninth steps.

   c. Plug in the time (t) to move from the third to the ninth step.

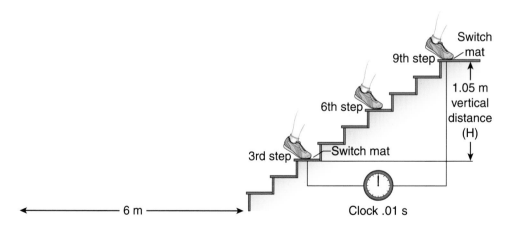

**Figure 5.4** The Margaria-Kalamen stair sprint test is a simple method for assessing your level of power relative to others in your age group.

Adapted from M. Foss and S.J. Keteyian, 1997, *Fox's physiological basis for exercise and sport*, 6th ed. (New York: McGraw-Hill Companies). By permission of the authors.

7. The calculated power for the participant can be compared to the information in table 5.3, a standardized chart used to determine the level of power.

8. Generally, power is measured using the standard unit of watts. To convert the power value from the Margaria-Kalamen test to the standard units of power, multiply the value by 9.807. This will allow you to better compare the calculated power value to that from another test, such as an isokinetic dynamometer test.

For people who do not have the facilities or resources to do other power assessment tests, the Margaria-Kalamen stair sprint test offers a simple but universally accepted power testing protocol. Since little equipment is required to perform this test and to make the power calculations, most people can perform this test correctly without prior training. Although the Margaria-Kalamen test can be used to estimate power, it is best suited for classifying the level of power into different categories, including "poor," "average," or "excellent." If you are just looking to compare your level of power to others in your age group (rather than to determine an exact numerical power measurement), then the Margaria-Kalamen stair sprint test is the solution for you.

### Table 5.3   Margaria-Kalamen Stair Sprint Test Guidelines

| | Men Age groups (yr) | | | | |
|---|---|---|---|---|---|
| Classification | 15-20 | 21-30 | 31-40 | 41-50 | Over 50 |
| Poor | < 113 | <106 | <85 | <65 | <50 |
| Fair | 113-149 | 106-139 | 85-111 | 65-84 | 50-65 |
| Average | 150-187 | 140-175 | 112-140 | 85-105 | 66-92 |
| Good | 188-224 | 176-210 | 141-168 | 106-125 | 83-98 |
| Excellent | >224 | >210 | >168 | >125 | >98 |
| | Women Age groups (yr) | | | | |
| Classification | 15-20 | 21-30 | 31-40 | 41-50 | Over 50 |
| Poor | <92 | <85 | <65 | <50 | <38 |
| Fair | 92-120 | 85-111 | 65-84 | 50-65 | 38-48 |
| Average | 121-151 | 112-140 | 85-105 | 66-82 | 49-61 |
| Good | 152-182 | 141-168 | 106-125 | 83-98 | 62-75 |
| Excellent | >182 | >168 | >125 | >98 | >75 |

Units are kg-m/s. To calculate watts (Newton-meters per second, or NM/s, a more standard unit of power), multiply the above values by 9.807.

Adapted from M. Foss and S.J. Keteyian, 1997, *Fox's physiological basis for exercise and sport*, 6th ed. (New York: McGraw-Hill Companies). By permission of the authors.

# Interpreting the Results

Regardless of which specific assessments you choose to perform, the reason for completing them is the same. Primarily, these tests give you a personal baseline from which to start building a program. They allow you to compare your strength and power levels to established norms, and they give you the means to create goals to work toward. The goals keep you focused on your reason for resistance training and help you construct an appropriate program.

The answers you get from your assessments, coupled with your goals, tell you which types of exercises to include in your program. For instance, a high school football player who scores well on a 1RM bench press test but achieves a mediocre score on a vertical jump would want to slant his program more toward improving his lower body power, even if the rest of his team is working more on upper body strength. A middle-aged woman who is just starting to resistance train for the first time might score poorly on a 10RM test on the bench press but do well on a similar squat test. If her goal is to develop more overall strength, these results may lead her to include more upper body than lower body training in her program.

We have described a broad selection of strength and power assessment protocols. Some tests are relatively simple, such as the self-evaluation, vertical jump, or Margaria-Kalamen tests, while some tests are a little more complicated, such as the 1RM or computer-controlled tests. There is really no wrong or right test to choose. Rather, the test should be determined based on the needs of the participant. For example, if you want to compare your level of power to that of others, you may choose the Margaria-Kalamen stair sprint tests. Or if you are looking for accuracy, an isokinetic dynamometer test may be appropriate. Vertical jump strength, 1RM, and power tests are staples of the competitive sports industry. No matter what test you choose, you must always look out for your health and safety by using proper form and precisely following procedure. Above all else, the results from your assessment should help you plan and determine what resistance training exercises will aid you in ultimately reaching your goals.

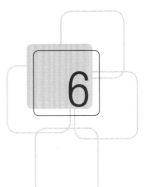

# Types of Strength and Power Exercises

Sagir G. Bera, Daniel P. Murray, Lee E. Brown, and Brian W. Findley

Almost everyone has had the experience of walking into a gym or fitness center for the first time and seeing enormous men and toned women flexing their muscles and checking themselves out in the massive wall of mirrors. On the floor itself, you see hundreds of different pieces of equipment. You hear fellow exercisers talking about running on a treadmill or elliptical trainer, or working out on the fitness machines or with free weights, or using medicine balls or exercise rubber bands. The gym can be an intimidating place for a person who does not know what types of exercises to perform and what equipment to use.

This chapter helps explain some of the different types of exercises often used for strength or power training—including isotonic, isometric, and isokinetic exercises; plyometric and medicine ball exercises; and exercises that use resistance bands and cords. As you recall, strength is the maximum force that your muscles can generate at a particular speed, while power is the force that is produced over a range of velocities. Thus, you would expect to have quick, explosive movements incorporated into power exercises—such as the power clean (page 252)—as opposed to the steady movements in strength exercises—such as the leg extension (page 224) or seated leg curl (page 223). We discuss some of the advantages and disadvantages of each of the main categories of exercises. In addition, we give our recommendations on how to use these exercises within an overall training program. You may find it helpful to refer back to the previous chapter to properly assess your level of strength as you choose the types of training that are right for you.

# Isometric Training

Exercises intended to improve muscle strength and power come in many different forms. In the past, isometric exercise was the most common form of exercise used to improve strength. However, people trying to strengthen their muscles have gradually shifted their focus to other types of exercise that are more functional in nature. Nonetheless, isometric exercise is still an effective training method for gaining strength.

Isometric exercises are those in which the exercising muscle or limb does not move. In other words, there is contraction of the involved muscle with no apparent movement of the joint. The force of the muscle contraction causes tension in the muscle without a noticeable change in its length. Isometric exercises are usually performed by mimicking a "pushing" or "pulling" action in the various joint positions. An example of an isometric exercise is pushing a fixed object, such as a wall or a bar or weight machine attached to the floor (figure 6.1a). Another example of an isometric exercise is holding a weighted object in a stationary position with muscles contracted, such as holding a dumbbell in place with your arm slightly bent (figure 6.1b).

**Figure 6.1**    An isometric exercise can be done by (a) pushing against an immovable object or (b) holding a weight in a position with the muscles contracted.

Research has shown that isometric exercise can significantly increase the tension of the muscle. Thus, a person can achieve maximum muscular contractions by performing isometric exercises, in contrast to regular isotonic weight training (which we will get to soon). In addition to gains in muscle strength, isometric exercise can also lead to an increase in muscle mass and improvements in bone strength. It also provides all the benefits associated with muscle strength including elevated muscle metabolism (energy use by the body), which is important when trying to burn fat.

You don't need to have free weights or a weight machine to do isometric exercises; therefore, it is an easy and convenient form of strength training that you can perform anywhere, such as a hotel room or bedroom. All you need is some fixed or stationary object that you can push or pull against. Typically, you perform this type of exercise by holding a muscle or joint in a set position for six to eight seconds. However, each exercise needs to be repeated between 5 and 10 times per session and over a period of six to eight weeks to really produce any noticeable improvements in strength.

Although isometric exercise can be a very effective strength training method, it has many drawbacks. Since isometric exercises are performed in a set-limb position, the involved or contracting muscle will primarily achieve gains in strength in that position. This type of gain in muscle strength is a good example of exercise specificity. *Exercise specificity* basically means that in performing an exercise, you mainly improve at the strength level and within the motion that you are training. It follows, for example, that if you wanted to become better at cycling, you would not spend the majority of your time running. Rather, you would spend most of your time cycling, since that is the specific activity that you are training for. With isometric exercise, you are strengthening your muscles in a static position, so you would expect improvements in strength in that particular position only. As a result, you would have to perform isometric exercises through the whole range of motion of the limb to get equal improvements in muscle strength across this range. Furthermore, given that isometric exercises are performed in a static position, a person may experience a reduction in speed and athletic performance. This can be contrasted with the dynamic movements performed in isotonic training, which are discussed later in this chapter.

Another drawback of isometric exercise is that it can dramatically increase blood pressure. This rise in blood pressure can be attributed to the large increase in muscle tension that may be achieved with isometric exercise. Unfortunately, the dangerous rise in blood pressure can lead to damaged or ruptured blood vessels, in addition to an irregular heartbeat. Thus, it is recommended that individuals with high blood pressure and heart problems refrain from performing isometric exercise. Additionally, since blood is not constantly pumped through the muscle (as it is in isotonic exercise), muscular endurance can decrease.

These negative side effects (decrease in athletic performance and muscle endurance) make isometric training a less appealing form of strength training exercise than some other forms. Isometric contractions are primarily used in a rehabilitative or physical therapy setting. Because of their shortcomings, isometric exercises should be treated as only one part of a larger overall program, rather than the sole workout type in a strength training program.

# Isotonic Training

Usually, when you hear people talking about strength and power exercises, they are referring to isotonic training, or simply weight training (whether with free weights or machine weights). Unlike isometric exercises, isotonic training involves an exercise movement using a constant load. In other words, the weight that you are training with always remains the same, no matter what movement or speed you are using during the exercise. This is in contrast to what you typically see with other types of resistance training. Nevertheless, like every other type of exercise, regular isotonic training has many physical and physiological benefits, as well as some disadvantages.

Compared to other resistance training methods, isotonic training may be the most beneficial to overall health. Obviously, routine weight training can lead to the development of muscle strength, muscle tone, and muscle endurance. But these are not the only benefits to isotonic training. Routine isotonic exercise has also been shown to improve tendon and ligament strength. A person can improve joint stability and posture by combining stronger tendons and ligaments with overall muscle strength. This important quality can help you reduce the risk of injury during normal physical activities. In addition, you can also decrease the chances of experiencing the effects of such mainstream problems as arthritis and lower back pain.

Some additional benefits of isotonic training include improvements in bone strength, energy, and fat loss. Continuously loading the body or placing a force on the body is necessary to build bone density (figure 6.2). Lifting a weight forces the bones in the body to support a load that they are not used to supporting, causing more minerals to be deposited on the bones, thereby increasing their strength. Increased muscle mass from weight training has also been shown to improve fat loss. Some believe that the added muscle mass improves body metabolism, though this is still a highly contested topic. In addition, a person may feel that he or she has more energy to carry out normal acts of daily living. These health benefits are supplementary to the primary purpose of weight training, which is to improve the characteristics of the muscles.

Muscles grow in response to stresses being placed on them. Resistance training overloads the muscles, or forces them to work at an intensity that they are not used to working at. As you'll remember from chapter 3 (page 54), the overload phenomenon is pretty much the basis of all types of training. Overload from resistance training can cause microscopic tears in the muscles of the body; these tears are part of the normal muscle-building process. As these tears form, the natural muscle-rebuilding process of the body is stimulated. Protein molecules are laid down to generate more muscle fibers. Accordingly, the size and makeup of muscles will adapt to the exercise and grow. (See chapter 1, pages 6 to 8, for a discussion of the types of muscle fibers.) Essentially, working at a level that it is not used to forces the body to adapt to the extra stresses, resulting in an improvement in that specific activity (as expected with exercise specificity). In the case of weight training, the specific adaptation to an overload is for your body's muscles to increase in size, strength, muscular endurance, and power (figure 6.2).

## Adjusting the Load to the Goal

Whether you are a seasoned athlete, someone recovering from a recent injury, or a chronic couch potato, we recommend that you partake in some form of resistance training. Isotonic exercises are perfect for almost any population because they can be personalized to fit specific needs. Altering the intensity, the number of sets, and the number of repetitions of an exercise is enough to influence how the muscles will adapt and grow in response to that exercise. But, with any exercise, it's also important to become familiar with what to do, how to do it, and why you are doing it. This will ensure that you know the risks and benefits of what you are doing and can correctly plan how to achieve your exercise goals. (Exercise goals and how to determine them are discussed in chapter 5.)

The main benefits of isotonic exercise include improvements in muscular strength, power, hypertrophy, and endurance. Although you may see improvements in each of these categories for any given exercise, it is best to focus specifically on improving strength, power, hypertrophy, or endurance.

**Figure 6.2**    Isotonic exercises such as this barbell overhead press can condition your body to more easily perform everyday activities.

You can accomplish this by adjusting the level of intensity or the number of sets and repetitions performed for each exercise, also known as the *training load*, to suit the desired area of improvement. The intensity of isotonic training is commonly defined as a percentage of an individual's 1RM weight lifted for a particular weightlifting exercise. Note that your 1RM can vary dramatically between exercises, and even between muscles.

As discussed in chapter 3, to improve muscle strength, you should attempt to perform between two and six sets of approximately 6 repetitions at an intensity of at least 85 percent of your 1RM for that specific exercise. For individuals trying to improve muscle power, the ideal is to perform two to five sets of 6 repetitions at 75 to 90 percent of 1RM. The proper rest period between each set for both strength and power exercises is between two and five minutes.

Improving muscular endurance or muscle tone requires approximately two or three sets of 12 or more repetitions. Muscular endurance exercises are performed at intensity levels below 65 percent of 1RM, with short rest periods lasting no longer than 30 seconds between each set. Finally, those looking to improve muscle mass (hypertrophy) should do three to six sets of 6 to 12 repetitions at 65 to 85 percent of 1RM, with rest periods between 30 and 90 seconds. Table 6.1 provides a summary of these numbers.

Table 6.1 **Adjusting Training Load to Training Goals**

| | Frequency (times per week) | Intensity (%1RM) | Volume | Rest |
|---|---|---|---|---|
| Power | 1-2 | 85-95 | 1-4 reps 1-2 sets | 4-6 min. |
| Strength | 3-4 | 75-85 | 4-8 reps 3-4 sets | 2-3 min. |
| Hypertrophy | 4-6 | 60-80 | 8-12 reps 4-6 sets | 30-90 sec. |
| Endurance | 5-7 | <60 | 12-15 reps 5-7 sets | <30 sec. |

# Choosing the Equipment

Training load is only one of the many variables in isotonic training. Another variable is the style of exercise equipment that is used during training. Generally, the two most accepted types are free weights and weight training machines. Both types of equipment are readily available in any public gym. In addition, a variety of inexpensive exercise equipment can be found at many retail stores.

Although both free weights and weight machines can be used effectively to improve muscle attributes, each has certain advantages over the other. Weight training machines are much more expensive to own than free weights. Moreover, because of their fixed nature of movement, several machines are necessary in order to target every major muscle in the body. Conversely, free weight equipment (such as dumbbells, barbells, and weight benches) is relatively inexpensive to purchase. Usually, all the weights and benches are interchangeable and stackable so that a variety of muscles can be worked at many different positions and intensities. If you do not have access to a gym or if you are looking for a convenient isotonic workout at home, a free weight system is the way to go.

Free weights and weight training machines also physically work the muscles in slightly different ways, making each ideal for different groups of people. For example, since weight training machines are fixed in the way that they can move, they are highly recommended for people who are new to weight training, recovering from an injury, or lacking in adequate muscle strength. Weight training machines encourage proper form by limiting the range of motion that is needed for the exercise (figure 6.3). The risk of injury is further reduced by built-in safety mechanisms. Weight machines can be used to work almost every major muscle group through exercises such as dumbbell biceps curls (page 204), abdominal crunches (page 235), shoulder presses (page 170), leg curls (page 223), and leg presses (page 216). Additionally, machines can be used to train isolated muscles.

Conversely, free weight systems, as the name implies, involve freestanding exercises in which the lifter can move the weights in any plane of movement. For that reason, free weights are better suited for people with adequate strength and proper

**Figure 6.3**   Exercising on a weight training machine helps ensure safety for the beginning lifter. In this exercise, the risk of injury is reduced because the machine keeps the back stationary.

training experience. The added benefit of lifting with a free moving system is that it not only forces the primary muscles to work, but it also recruits the adjoining muscles that aid in supporting the movement (figure 6.4). For instance, the bench press (page 176) is primarily used to strengthen the chest, but it can also strengthen the triceps because they aid in the movement of the exercise. This characteristic can vastly improve overall strength and joint stability, but the benefits can come at a price: If you use incorrect form and mechanics during a free weight exercise, you may put yourself at increased risk of injury. Again, a wide array of muscles can be trained using free weight exercises as you'll see in part III.

**Figure 6.4**   Having a spotter for free weight exercises helps ensure safety and proper form.

When training for muscle strength, hypertrophy, or endurance, either free weights or weight machines can be used effectively. However, training for muscle power should be performed almost exclusively with free weight systems. Power exercises—such as squats (pages 212, 214), hang cleans (page 262), and snatches —are difficult to perform and should only be done with proper training and supervision. These movements often require large loads and strenuous body movements. Power training is primarily used in competitive athletic environments in order to improve physical performance.

Isotonic training is important if you are trying to improve the attributes of your muscles, as well as your overall health. In general, isotonic exercises are the type of resistance exercises best suited for most people. After the age of 25, muscle mass gradually starts to shrink (atrophy) with inactivity. Thus, people should participate in isotonic and resistance training not only to maintain muscle strength, but to maintain the strength needed for everyday functional ability and complete independence. Nevertheless, you must set goals for your training—whether you are training for hypertrophy, strength, or other reasons—and then choose the types of exercises necessary to reach those goals. The majority of any strength and power training program should consist of isotonic exercises, with other types of training scattered in to work on specific deficiencies. Within weeks of regular training, you will start noticing and feeling the benefits of isotonic training.

# Isokinetic Training

The third main category of strength training is isokinetic exercise. This is probably the type of strength training least known to the general public, and it is rarely seen in a community fitness setting. As with isometric and isotonic exercises, isokinetic exercises hold one variable constant. In this case, it is the speed of movement that is held constant throughout the entire exercise movement (as opposed to the constant length and constant load experienced with isometric and isotonic exercises, respectively).

Specialized machines known as *isokinetic dynamometers* (see chapter 5) are generally required to perform these types of movement (figure 6.5). Dynamometers are bulky and expensive pieces of equipment that require some background knowledge in order to operate. As a result, isokinetic dynamometers are typically found in a health care or rehabilitation setting and typically not found in a regular fitness gym. However, if you are fortunate enough to work out on a dynamometer, you can take advantage of quite a few strength training benefits not offered by isotonic or isometric exercises alone.

Isokinetic exercises combine some of the best features of the other types of strength training exercises. The high-tension contractions of isometric exercise are combined with the range of motion of isotonic exercises to form isokinetic exercises. This is accomplished by the dynamometer electronically controlling the speed at which it moves, regardless of how hard or how little someone pushes.

This is known as *accommodating resistance* and means the muscle experiences over-load (refer back to figure 5.2*b*). Using the computer or control panel of the machine, you set the desired exercise speed, which typically ranges from 30 to 500 degrees per second. The slower speeds are more intense than the faster speeds. Range of motion can also be limited to a preset range, which can be useful in limiting the movement of an injured person. Also, dynamometers come with interchangeable attachments so they can be used to isolate and exercise almost every muscle group in your body. By combining these features, isokinetic dynamometers are able to provide maximum strength training resistance throughout the entire range of motion of a limb.

Strength training on an isokinetic machine is perhaps the most efficient method of exercise for gaining strength. You can gain maximum strength throughout the entire movement range, along with some of the added benefits of isotonic and isometric exercise. In addition, a lot of research is being done on whether isokinetic training can improve how fast a person can move a limb through a range of motion, which has applications for such things as improving running or throwing speed. Also, isokinetic dynamometers are very safe because of built-in safety features such as safety stops. The ability of isokinetic dynamometers to completely control the various parameters (range of motion, speed, and so forth) makes this form of exercise desirable in a physical therapy and rehabilitation setting.

Unfortunately, isokinetic exercise has many disadvantages as well. First, since isokinetic dynamometers are so expensive, they are rarely found in a public fit-ness gym. Additionally, most isokinetic machines isolate movements during exercise, thereby eliminating most of the supplementary strength gains found with free weights. Moreover, a good deal of background knowledge is required to properly use the complex computer program and the various attachments of the dynamometer.

Isokinetic exercise can be a good way to gain strength, but its many limita-tions may make it less desirable for the average person than some other methods. Isometric and isotonic exercises are much easier and much more convenient to perform. People can achieve maximal strength gains using isokinetic machines, but doing so requires a lot of time, money, and effort. Unless you have an isokinetic machine readily available, we recommend that you stick with forms of strength training that are more convenient and cost effective.

# Plyometric Training

Have you ever wanted to dunk like LeBron James? Or throw a punch like Mike Tyson? Or even run as fast as Asafa Powell, the world-record holder for the 100-meter sprint? If you answered yes to any of these questions, then you'll want to make plyometric exercise an important component of your overall training and conditioning program. Most elite athletes use some form of plyometric exercise to improve the agility, speed, and power necessary for explosive movements.

Plyometric exercise is a training protocol used to get your muscles to create the greatest force in as little time as possible. The foundation that plyometric exercise is based on is the stretch–shortening cycle (SSC) of the muscles (also discussed in chapter 3). Because of the SSC, you can generate more force by prestretching a muscle immediately before a concentric muscle contraction than when performing a concentric muscle contraction alone. To better understand the physiology of the stretch–shortening cycle, think of your muscle as a rubber band. When you stretch out a rubber band, you create an elastic force in the band. Because of the rubber band's elasticity, the strain created by the stretch causes the rubber band to return, if possible, to its original shape. Your muscles have an elastic component to them and, similar to a rubber band, will attempt to return to their original state in response to any sort of stretch (figure 6.5). Fundamentally, this is how the stretch-shortening cycle works in the body.

Plyometric exercise tries to combine the natural physiological SSC characteristics in the muscles with strength and power to create a truly explosive movement. To better describe how a plyometric activity works, consider the example of a two-legged standing long jump, focusing primarily on the quadriceps muscle group on top of the thighs. (Note that other muscles are used in this movement, but for purposes of simplification, we will not discuss them.) Before the initial takeoff, the long jumper dips down a bit, forcing the quadriceps to eccentrically contract and stretch the muscle. Soon after, the quadriceps will concentrically contract, causing the leg to straighten out and spring off of the ground (see page 24 for a review of eccentric and concentric contraction). Plyometric exercise focuses on training the period of time *between* the eccentric and concentric phases.

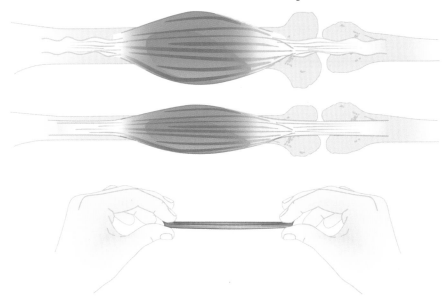

**Figure 6.5**   Similar to a stretched rubber band, a stretched muscle will attempt to return to its natural state. This phenomenon is known as the stretch–shortening cycle and provides the basis for plyometric training.

The transition period between the eccentric and concentric phases is known as the *amortization phase*. Quickly transitioning through the amortization phase enables the body to generate a powerful contraction using the SSC. But the body can only produce this additional power when the amortization period is relatively short, typically in the hundredths of a second. This short time frame allows the elastic component and the stretch reflex to add power to the relative strength of the muscle. Plyometric exercises focus on training the muscles to quickly move through this amortization phase and thereby produce more powerful movements. By minimizing the amortization phase and improving the SSC, you can learn to run faster, jump higher, and perform better than you have before.

Plyometric exercises are rarely done in a public fitness setting; rather, they are usually performed in an athletic strength and conditioning setting. Fortunately, a variety of plyometric exercises can be performed with various pieces of equipment that are easy to find, such as sturdy wooden boxes or crates and weighted balls. One of the most popular plyometric exercises is the depth jump. For this exercise, you begin by standing on a box. You then step off the box, and upon landing on the ground, you push up and jump as high as you can with both feet (figure 6.6, *a* through *c*). Depth jumps are frequently used to train basketball or volleyball players to jump higher.

A variety of plyometric exercises can also be performed with the upper body. Upper body plyometric exercises commonly involve medicine balls. (We discuss more about medicine balls in the next section.) The chest pass is one example of a medicine ball exercise; it can either be performed with two people passing the ball (figure 6.7, *a* and *b*) or with one person throwing against a wall. Basically, you use a chest pass to throw the ball to another person (or the wall), and when the ball is returned to you, you immediately throw another chest pass. This plyometric drill focuses on training the upper body to produce powerful throwing or pushing movements, such as those used when passing a basketball or when blocking in football.

As with any other type of resistance training, there are many benefits to performing plyometric exercises. You get many of the same benefits of other types of strength and power training, such as increases in muscle and bone strength. Additionally, because of the nature of plyometric exercise, you improve functional power. In other words, since the movements of plyometric drills mimic those that are used during athletic activities, they produce improvements in power and performance that transfer to those activities. This is one of the main reasons plyometric exercises are primarily done in athletic strength and conditioning settings. With proper plyometric training, athletes can learn to use the maximum power their body generates on the court, track, or playing field.

Like many other types of exercise, plyometric exercise has its drawbacks and limitations. First, most public fitness settings do not have the appropriate space and equipment for plyometric exercise (though as we previously mentioned, with a little imagination, you can create your own equipment from items such as sturdy wooden boxes). And because of the highly intensive nature of plyometric exercise, it should not be performed without a proper strength foundation. Build

**Figure 6.6** The depth jump is an ideal plyometric exercise for athletes who wish to improve their vertical jumping power.

**Figure 6.7**   A properly performed chest pass requires that the athlete pass the medicine ball back to his partner immediately upon catching it.

up a routine training program and develop a minimum base of strength before adding plyometric activities. Then, learn the proper techniques for performing these exercises from a trained professional or another reliable resource. In addition, these activities should be performed no more than two or three times per week so that your muscles have time to rest and recover from the activity.

As you can see, plyometric exercise can be very beneficial to people trying to maximize the power that their muscles can generate. These exercises can help you improve your athletic performance while giving you an active, high-intensity workout. Realistically, plyometrics need only be performed if you are taking part in competitive sports and you want to exploit every last bit of power your muscles can generate.

# Medicine Ball Training

Medicine balls are not spherical containers of prescription drugs as the name may imply. Rather, they are weighted balls that come in a variety of weights (ranging from .5 to 30 pounds [.2 to 13.6 kg]), colors, and sizes (ranging in diameter from 3.5 to 10.6 inches [8.9 to 26.9 cm]). Medicine balls come in many different forms (figure 6.8a), with the two most distinct forms resembling a dodgeball from your childhood years and an extremely old leather basketball. Most public fitness gyms are beginning to carry medicine balls and make them readily available to members.

**Figure 6.8**   *(a)* Medicine balls of varying style, weight, and size. *(b)* Some medicine balls are designed with handles that allow them to be used as dumbbells.

Medicine balls can be used in a variety of ways for strength and power training. Since medicine balls are available in specified weights, they can be used with ordinary isotonic or isometric strength training exercises, similar to the way dumbbells, barbells, or weight plates are used. In fact, some medicine balls actually come with handles to allow you to easily mimic many of the exercises you could perform with dumbbells (figure 6.8*b*). Although medicine balls can be useful as a tool for gaining strength, they are most often used to train for power.

The texture and composition of most medicine balls allow them to be easily handled and used for a variety of exercises. For example, they can be thrown up in the air or against the wall and caught with relative ease, as shown in the chest pass example (pages 124 and 126). Many basketball players and boxers use this type of exercise to develop the ability to quickly pass the ball or throw a punch. Additionally, medicine balls can be used to build core strength and stability. The core muscles (abs, lower back, and muscles of the trunk) are often neglected, but they play an essential role in any power training program. Although strengthening the muscles surrounding the abs will not directly lead to gains in power, core training with a medicine ball will help you better transfer the power of the movement from your body into whatever action you are performing. For example, stronger abs can help a baseball pitcher transfer power from the legs to the abs and ultimately to the arms to throw the ball. This is the kind of strength that allows pitchers such as Roger Clemens and Randy Johnson to throw a baseball upward of a hundred miles per hour.

Be aware that there are some disadvantages to using medicine balls in your training program. First, many gyms do not have enough space in their facilities to allow people to safely throw medicine balls against the wall or in the air, which limits the number and type of exercises that can be performed there. This is one of the reasons power training with medicine balls is rarely seen in a public setting (and is seen more often in a collegiate or professional athletic setting).

Second, medicine balls raise safety concerns similar to those that isotonic or isometric weights do, though the material medicine balls are made of decreases the amount of damage that people or surroundings may suffer if the ball is accidentally mishandled. People using medicine balls to train for power must ensure that they have adequate strength to be taking part in power exercises—and that they use correct form and technique when performing the exercises—to minimize the risk of injury.

Training with medicine balls can greatly improve and diversify any strength and power training program. Medicine balls are relatively inexpensive and can be a convenient type of training exercise to perform at home. As with other types of exercise, medicine balls should not be the sole means of exercise. They should always be used in conjunction with other types of training to achieve your ultimate training goals. Again, safety must always be your primary concern when performing this type of exercise. If you have appropriate facilities in which to use medicine balls in your workout, this type of training can add variety and enjoyment to your normal exercise regimen.

# Resistance Band Training

The use of resistance (exercise) bands and cords as a form of exercise is becoming increasingly popular. These are not regular rubber bands from your local office supply store. Exercise bands and cords usually come in a variety of bright colors (such as red, blue, green, and yellow) and in either flat sheets (resistance bands) that are approximately 4 inches wide by 6 feet long (10 cm × 2 meters) or longer cables (resistance cords). Each color corresponds to a particular degree of tension: extra thin, heavy, super heavy, and maximum resistance. As with normal rubber bands or bungee cords, the tension in resistance bands and cords increases as they are stretched. This provides the resistance that is necessary for strength training and exercise. You can combine different levels of resistance to create a customized workout.

Resistance bands and cords are an effective complement or alternative to any strength and power training workout. Like other strength training exercises, these bands and cords can provide strength gains in both muscle and bones by providing resistance. But resistance bands and cords also have the characteristic "recoil" or "pulling back" effect found in normal rubber bands. This produces the added benefit of exercising agonist muscles while stretching out antagonist muscles (see chapter 1 for a full discussion of agonist and antagonist muscles). For example, when performing a biceps curl, the agonist muscles would be your biceps and any other muscle aiding in the movement, while the triceps would be the antagonist (or opposing) muscle. This tendency for the band or cord to return back to its original shape leads not only to improvements in overall strength but also to improvements in joint stability.

It is not uncommon to see resistance bands and cords used in a rehabilitation setting. The light resistance that they can provide make them a perfect way for beginning exercisers as well as people who have limited muscle strength or who are recovering from injuries to gain strength. However, resistance bands are also a good way to increase power for specific movements. A great example of this is a boxer wrapping a resistance band around his back with the ends of the band gripped in each of his hands and then throwing a variety of punches (figure 6.9). This is a great way to build punching power and strength in a manner that isn't possible with other equipment.

Most resistance bands and cords are relatively inexpensive to buy. Like medicine balls, resistance bands and cords offer a convenient and inexpensive form of exercise. Connect one end to a stable or stationary object and you are ready to perform a variety of different exercises. Also, the compact size of these pieces of equipment makes them easy to travel with so you can get a strength training workout almost anywhere. Since these cords and bands provide constant resistance, they make it possible to strengthen the corresponding muscle throughout the entire range of motion of the exercise.

Regrettably, resistance bands and cords do not come without some limitations. It can be difficult to find resistance bands or cords in many public gyms. Moreover,

**Figure 6.9**  Resistance bands can help you build strength by enabling you to simulate movements from your sport while offering added resistance.

very few sporting goods stores carry these items for retail purposes. However, a simple Internet search for a fitness, training, or rehabilitation equipment store can help you get your hands on a set of resistance bands or cords. Another drawback of the bands and cords is that since the resistance gets greater the farther you stretch them out, you only get minimal resistance at the beginning of the movement, resulting in minimal gains in strength and power at these early angles. As a result, users may experience uneven gains in muscle strength and power. Fortunately, though, resistance bands and cords are very safe and require no specific training to use.

Resistance bands and cords can be great additions to your overall exercise plan. Nonetheless, they should not be used as your sole means of gaining strength and power. Rather, they should be used to supplement the existing exercises that you already do.

Some sort of resistance training is necessary to maintain muscle strength and health, but such training is also beneficial to the strength of bones, tendons, and ligaments. Resistance training has been shown to increase the overall feeling of energy as well. Having the proper strength and power to perform functional everyday activities is essential to a person's well-being and independence—not to mention that they can also be very useful when competing in athletic events, either recreationally or professionally. Fortunately, a wide selection of resistance training exercises is available to fit almost anyone's needs.

All it takes to begin any strength and power training program is the understanding of what your exercise goals are and what types of exercises you can do to achieve those goals. For instance, if you are rehabilitating a previously injured area, you may choose to perform isometric exercises. You may look to isokinetic training if you want to improve limb movement speed, or to plyometric exercises if you want to train for powerful, explosive movements. Or if you just want to improve general strength and muscle health, you can perform isotonic exercises. Whatever your goals or intentions may be, there is some type of resistance training exercise that can be useful and convenient to your lifestyle.

# Workout Schedule and Rest

Lee E. Brown, Brian W. Findley, Daniel P. Murray, and Sagir G. Bera

Now that you have learned how to assess your baseline strength (chapter 5), as well as what types of strength and power exercises are best for different goals (chapter 6), you need to understand the components that go into creating a successful resistance training program. This chapter will familiarize you with the different variables involved in creating a workout schedule. It also introduces some of the lingo that strength training professionals use in developing and modifying strength programs. In part IV of this book, you will learn how to take the information presented here and manipulate it to develop a goal-specific strength training program.

The benefits you can get from resistance training are highly dependent on the time and effort you are able to devote to your program. But busy schedules and hectic workdays should not discourage you from working out. Remember that any time or effort that you devote to resistance training, especially when it is a new form of exercise for you, is beneficial. As you grow accustomed to resistance training, however, you will need to devote more energy to each workout in order to continue to achieve strength gains.

This chapter covers the specific variables you must consider to construct an effective resistance training program. Through the manipulation of these variables, you can alter the outcome of your training—that is, you can further develop things such as your muscles' strength or power or endurance. While some of this material may appear to overlap that of previous chapters, the information presented here is designed to help you create a goal-centered resistance training program.

© Jumpfoto

# Adjusting Training Variables to Goals

The best way to begin planning your workout schedule is to determine why you want to start a resistance training program. This is where performing a needs analysis comes in (see chapter 5). As you learned in chapter 5, strength training has many different potential benefits. Adaptations to resistance training are not limited to increased muscle size and strength. You can also train to improve muscular endurance, muscular power, and athletic performance. The personal goals you establish will greatly affect how you design your program. These goals will influence the workout variables you will use in your program.

You'll recall from chapter 3 that there are several acute training variables that can be adjusted to help you meet your goals:

**Load.** This is simply the amount of weight that is lifted during each repetition. The load is often given as a percentage of 1RM, which is the maximal amount of weight that can be lifted in just one repetition.

**Repetitions (reps).** The number of repetitions is the number of times a given movement is performed continuously without resting.

**Sets.** Repetitions are grouped together to create sets. Each set is separated by a rest interval.

**Rest interval.** This is the amount of time spent recovering between each set.

**Intensity.** In strength training, intensity refers to the load being lifted in comparison to the maximum load. The closer a load is to maximum, the higher the exercise intensity.

**Volume.** This is determined by multiplying sets, reps, and load. Volume is expressed as a weight and can be used to describe a single exercise or a complete workout session.

The following are some common goals of resistance training and how they might affect your workout planning.

## Hypertrophy

One of the most common reasons that people get started in resistance training is to achieve increased muscle size, also called *hypertrophy*. If you are new to training, it may take as long as six weeks before you notice differences in muscle size and improvements in strength (Moritani and deVries 1979). Keep this in mind so that you don't get frustrated with the lack of results in the initial stages of training.

Even in individuals who have previously participated in resistance training, hypertrophy is not maximized unless the program is designed correctly. In general, hypertrophy training is most effective when you use moderate loads (between 6 and 12RM) and large training volumes (four or five sets; Kraemer and Ratamess 2004).

Hypertrophy protocols require rest periods between 30 and 90 seconds. This allows sufficient time for some recovery between sets, but it also ensures that the muscle is completely fatigued by the completion of the last set.

## Increasing Maximal Strength

Another common goal of resistance training is to increase maximal strength. As discussed in chapter 3, the greater the muscular overload during resistance training, the greater the adaptations that occur. In keeping with this principle, resistance training carried out with the goal of improving maximal strength is most successful when you use heavy loads or high intensities—loads lifted near the 1RM and few repetitions (two to four). A moderate to high number of sets (four to six) is recommended for maximal strength gains.

© Jumpfoto

The exact load that best produces improvements in maximal strength has been widely debated. It is generally agreed that loads between 85 and 95 percent of 1RM create the muscular overload needed for maximal strength improvements. A recent analysis of existing research suggests that the lower end of this range (85 percent of 1RM) may be the best load for producing maximal gains in muscular strength (Peterson, Rhea, and Alvar 2004).

Maximal strength protocols require the longest rest intervals. When intensity is at its highest, as it is when training for maximal strength, you should take at least three minutes between sets. Many professionals have recommended that up to five minutes of rest should be taken between high-intensity sets, but recent research has revealed that performance is similar on subsequent sets when rest periods are three or five minutes (Kraemer and Ratamess 2004).

Beginner and novice lifters will experience changes in maximal strength with a wide range of training loads. Therefore, it is usually better for beginners to start out with lower-intensity and higher-volume programs. They can then advance to higher-intensity programs when their progression of strength improvements reaches a sticking point or plateau.

## Improving Muscular Power

In physics terms, *power* is the amount of force applied to move an object divided by the time it takes to move the object. In other words, the quicker an object is moved, or the greater the force applied to move the object, the greater the power. The same holds true for muscular power. Because power is a combination of both strength and speed, it is often an important variable for those seeking improvements in athletic performance.

The goal of power exercises is to move the given load as quickly as possible. This is intended to improve explosive strength and the speed with which a given load can be moved. Power training has traditionally been performed with heavy loads, similar to those prescribed for maximal strength training. Heavy loads were believed to be necessary to produce significant muscular overload. Since the goal of training is to lift the heavy load *explosively*, it was thought that doing so in training would create maximal improvements in power.

More recently, it has become apparent that moving lighter loads (30 to 40 percent of 1RM) with low volumes (few sets and few repetitions) as quickly as possible can be more effective in producing greater power gains (Jones et al. 2001; McBride et al. 2002; Wilson et al. 1993). This load is light enough to move quickly but heavy enough to require some force for it to be moved. Thus, the combination of force production and speed of movement yields peak power.

Although lighter loads allow the lifter to achieve greater movement speeds during training—and thus train the speed component of power—heavier loads train the strength component of power. Either strategy can be effective in improving muscular power, but it appears that training with lighter loads (which allow greater movement speeds) may accomplish this goal more effectively.

The problem with lighter-load power training, however, is that there is no consensus on the amount of sets and repetitions that should be performed; the research done in this area has been concerned strictly with the comparison of heavy and light loads, and not with training volume. Studies of power training with light loads have used volumes anywhere from two to five sets of 5 to 15 repetitions.

You should allow for three to five minutes of rest between sets of power exercises, similar to the rest periods used for maximal strength training.

## Increasing Muscular Endurance

Another goal of resistance training is to improve local muscular endurance. Training for endurance is quite different than training for maximal strength, because muscular endurance training aims to improve the ability to perform more contractions and sustain them for longer periods of time. As a result, this type of training calls for light loads (generally between 50 and 60 percent of 1RM) and high volume (three to five sets of 15 to 20 repetitions).

Muscular endurance protocols require very little rest time between sets, usually 30 seconds or less. In fact, the purpose of muscular endurance training is to produce greater duration of muscular work and resistance to fatigue. The short duration of rest time promotes longer durations of muscle activity and helps stave off neuromuscular fatigue.

Muscular endurance training protocols can be very effective for beginners and special populations, as well as for athletes training for endurance sports such as mountain climbing and orienteering. People who are unaccustomed to resistance training may be opposed to the amount of work required to lift higher percentages of their 1RM. Since new resistance trainers will see benefits with nearly any combination of training volume, a muscular endurance protocol is often a good way to introduce them to the activity.

For intermediate and advanced resistance training, muscular endurance protocols provide variety and balance to a program. Although a desire to increase muscular endurance usually isn't the main reason people start resistance training, the benefits of doing so are widespread and can make it easier to perform the activities of daily living, such as gardening or carrying things. As you will see in later chapters, providing balance and variety in a workout program is essential to maximizing progress.

## Improving Athletic Performance

For decades, athletes of all sports have used resistance training as an essential preparatory tool. It is well established that improvements in strength and power enhance athletic performance. To be effective in creating these enhancements, workout programs need to be designed with the specific characteristics of the sport in mind. For example, the exercises and training goals included in the program must fit with the muscle groups and movement patterns used in the sport. A close

examination of the sport's requirements will reveal not only what muscle groups to train, but also whether strength, power, or muscular endurance should be the main focus. For example, a sport such as basketball requires explosive leg power for jumping as well as muscular strength to shoot and pass the ball. So explosive power exercises for the lower body and exercises for overall muscular strength would be important to include for most basketball players.

# Organizing Workouts

Several factors must be considered as you schedule and organize your training workouts. First, determine how much time you have available for each session—for example, can you spend 30 minutes per session or do you have a full 2 hours to spend at one time? You also need to determine how many times you can work out each week (frequency). We discuss more issues relative to exercise frequency and how to be efficient in your workouts in the next section.

Next, you must determine what exercise equipment you have at your disposal. Do you have a facility with free weights and machine weights? Do you have access to things such as plyometric boxes and medicine balls? Or do you need to rely on more standard equipment when you work out? Answers to these questions will factor into what exercises you choose to include in your workout. We discuss more about choosing exercises and the order in which to do them later in this chapter.

Finally, you need to consider your training background. Are you prepared physically and do you have enough strength training experience to begin an advanced, complex, or difficult workout? Or do you need to follow a program for beginners? Part IV of this book provides some samples of beginner, intermediate, and advanced strength training programs—as well as guidelines on how to determine which program is right for you.

## Workout Frequency

The first thing to decide when developing a workout schedule is the frequency with which you will train. Workout frequency is generally considered the number of workouts a person completes each week. Typically, an effective workout frequency is from two to five times a week.

Obviously, frequency has a direct relationship to how much time you have available and are willing to devote to resistance training. You will experience greater results when you are able to "hit the gym" more often in a given week, but this greater frequency also needs to be balanced with proper rest periods to maximize the gains. Although a greater frequency will result in greater overall gains, you should not be discouraged if you only have one or two days on which you can train. You can still achieve positive results with as few as two days per week. Any time spent resistance training is beneficial and helps contribute to a healthy lifestyle.

© SportsChrome/Monte Isom

Of course, the total amount of time you spend in the gym is determined by your busy schedule, but you should realize that greater benefits will result from more consistent and regular training. Also, remember that the load you lift and the frequency of the workout should be inversely related. In other words, if you lift relatively heavy or near maximal loads, then you will need more rest between workouts; therefore, your workouts will be less frequent than those of someone who is lifting relatively lighter loads. (We discuss more about rest periods between workouts later in this chapter.)

To continue making strength gains, you should increase your workout frequency as you become more experienced in the gym. Again, beginners are able to advance and see strength gains when they undertake any sort of resistance training. Having a lower workout frequency when you are starting out allows your muscles to experience the appropriate rest and recovery between sessions. As you establish consistency with your workouts, gains become more difficult to achieve. Adding more days to your program allows you to achieve greater results.

Several methods can be used to optimize your strength training so that you are working efficiently and achieving the greatest gains possible while allowing enough rest between sessions. These methods include using a split routine (alternating workouts according to body part or region, muscle group, or type of movement), alternating heavy and light days, and using circuit training, pyramid training, or super or compound sets.

## *Split Routine*

A good way to add days to your workout frequency is to use a split routine in which you complete different sets of exercises on different days of the week. This common approach allows you to work some body parts and rest others on a given day. It also permits you to train on consecutive days; since different muscle groups are being trained on different days, you don't have to worry about training fatigued muscles from the day before.

Trying to fit everything you want to accomplish into one workout can become tedious and overwhelming. You may want to have a comprehensive program that encompasses all major muscle groups of the body; however, you might not have a block of time large enough to accomplish all that in one workout. Splitting your routine maximizes your time and effort by allowing you to exercise a broad range of muscle groups without spending hours in the gym for each workout.

Split routines also help give your workouts variety. Performing the same set of exercises every time you work out can get boring and stale. Changing things up from day to day and focusing on two or three body parts per session, rather than the entire body, allows you to have more diversity in your program and helps limit tediousness.

You can split your routine in a variety of ways. One method is to design body part or muscle group workouts, such as working the upper and lower body on different days. Another method is to group muscles that produce similar body movements together, such as putting all pushing or pulling movements in one workout.

**Body Part or Muscle Group Workouts**   Probably the most common ways that people split their workouts is by body part or muscle group. This type of split allows you to either create a well-balanced generalized program or focus your workout on a single body part that needs attention.

One way to organize your training is by alternating upper body and lower body workouts. This provides balance between training the upper and lower body muscles and ensures that appropriate recovery takes place between workouts. This method is a good way to introduce beginners to resistance training, because each workout can be designed to include one exercise for each major muscle group of either the upper or lower body.

Because each training session is intended to be general in nature (either upper or lower body), you are able to pick from a wide variety of available exercises. This variety is another reason that beginners favor this kind of workout. Performing the same routine over and over again can turn resistance training into a boring, monotonous activity.

For more experienced participants in resistance training, body part routines can be used to target specific focus areas. As you become more familiar with working out, you may become aware of certain muscle groups that you would like to focus more heavily on or that you simply enjoy training. Specific body part routines can also center your workouts on muscle groups that are not progressing as well as others. For instance, suppose your bench press workouts have hit a standstill

© Eyewire/Photodisc/Getty Images

because you are unable to finish the movement on the last few repetitions without help from your spotter. Since the triceps are heavily involved in the elbow extension at the end of the bench press motion, you decide to focus your next few upper body workouts on your triceps. In a few weeks, you see your bench press load increase again because you now have the strength to finish off the movement.

**Push-Pull Workouts**  You can also split your workout by separating lifts into pushes and pulls and doing each on separate days. Pushes consist of movements where a load starts close to the body and is moved away. Conversely, pulls involve the load starting farther away and ending up closer to you.

Pushes and pulls often use opposing muscle groups to perform the given action. Pushes tend to be dominated by muscles of the chest, shoulders, and posterior arm (triceps)—as in the bench press (page 176) and other overhead lifting movements. Pulls tend to be dominated by muscles of the back and anterior arm (biceps)—as in the lat pulldown (page 191) and in rowing movements. Lower extremity muscle groups are difficult to place in either push or pull categories, because most tend to be involved in both categories of movement.

The push-pull concept can also be used within a single workout. Beginners may sometimes want to alternate push and pull exercises within a workout when they are working their upper bodies. This technique allows for appropriate rest of muscle groups between exercises and ensures balanced training between the major muscle groups of the upper body.

## Alternating Heavy and Light Days

Varying the volume and the main goal (hypertrophy, maximum strength, and so forth) of your training is a great way to maximize gains and avoid plateaus during training. A scheduled cycle of changes in training variables is known as *periodization* of training and is discussed relative to muscle training in chapter 3; applications of this kind of training are shown in part IV. Switching the volume scheme of your workout (for a few training sessions) can enable you to make breakthroughs during times when progress might otherwise have slowed.

Let's illustrate this point with an example. Say you have been training for eight weeks using a hypertrophy program for your upper body. For the last two weeks of those eight weeks, you have been unable to increase the load while trying to maintain the appropriate amount of repetitions (8 to 10). This could be because your maximum strength has not improved to the same extent that your 8 to 10RM has. In this instance, performing the next few workouts with a maximum strength protocol (increasing load and decreasing reps) may help get you through your plateau.

On the other hand, if your trouble with progression relates to an inability to recover between sets, you may be lacking in muscular endurance. In this case, you may want to perform the next few workouts with lighter loads and increased repetitions. This could improve your muscular endurance enough to recover better between sets when you return to your hypertrophy protocol.

## Circuit Training

Circuit training is a unique resistance training method in which single sets of several different exercises (usually 10 to 12) are completed in succession, with little or no rest between exercises. Typically, one to three circuits of these exercises are performed during a training session. Loads are kept very light (generally 40 to 60 percent of 1RM), and exercises are either performed with a high number of repetitions (12 to 15), or more often, are performed for a set time (e.g., 30 seconds) using very short or no rest time between exercises. The purported benefit of this form of training is that it produces improvements in strength, muscular endurance, and aerobic conditioning in one workout.

The routine is usually "full body" (for example, leg press, bench press, sit-ups, leg extension, standing military press, seated leg curl, biceps curl, standing calf raise, lat pulldown, machine back extension, seated cable row; see chapters 9 through 11); all the major muscle groups around each joint are trained every workout. To provide rest for the body, most circuits are sequenced to alternate exercises from leg to arm to leg to arm, and so on. Heart rates during circuit training are typically higher than during most other weight training programs because of the short rest periods.

Because circuit training places high cardiovascular demands on the body, people often use this type of training to try to improve cardiovascular fitness. Like strength, cardiovascular fitness can improve quickly and with little training in those who are very unfit. Although it is likely that circuit training can improve cardiovascular conditioning in people with lower base levels of fitness, the aerobic effects are much less pronounced when it comes to those who are more fit (Gotshalk, Berger, and Kraemer 2004). Even if this type of training does affect cardiovascular fitness to some degree, larger gains will be achieved with actual aerobic endurance training.

Similarly, improvements in basic strength following circuit training are also more potent in previously untrained people. The protocols for developing maximal strength and hypertrophy by using heavier loads are much more likely to improve strength to a greater degree. Circuit training may be a good introductory form of training because it is fast moving and usually shorter in duration than a more traditional resistance training session.

In fact, one of the most compelling reasons to engage in circuit training is that a workout can be accomplished in a short period of time. Performing three circuits of 10 exercises for 30 seconds each with 30 seconds between exercises could take as little as half an hour. Circuit training is a great option for those people who otherwise would not resistance train because they don't have the time.

Undoubtedly, the greatest effect that circuit training has is to improve local muscular endurance. The combination of light loads, high repetitions, and short rest intervals is perfect for those seeking such gains.

## Pyramid Training

Pyramid training refers to a change in the intensity of an exercise from set to set. Pyramids can be ascending, descending, or triangular (Drought 1992). Ascending pyramids begin with lighter loads, and each subsequent set is performed with a heavier load. Descending pyramids begin with a heavy load, and each subsequent set is performed using a lighter load. Triangular pyramids ascend and descend with the heaviest load being lifted in the middle sets. Repetitions vary during pyramid training in order to accommodate the changing loads. An example of this would be performing a 10RM, 8RM, 6RM, 4RM, 2RM, 4RM, 6RM, 8RM, and 10RM with the resistance set to allow only the listed number of repetitions. As mentioned in chapter 3, this type of training is very time intensive so is often reserved for only a few exercises in a given workout.

Pyramid training combines several aspects of both maximal strength and hypertrophy protocols. Volume is relatively high because many sets are performed and some sets contain a high number of repetitions. This characteristic of hypertrophy training is coupled with the inclusion of at least one set in which a heavy load is lifted. This high-intensity set is indicative of maximal strength protocols.

Although this method does allow for a variety of muscle stimuli within a single workout, the volume may not be appropriate for individuals with a specific goal in mind. For example, if your goal is maximal strength, this type of routine may lead to an undue amount of muscular fatigue by the time you perform the high-resistance, low-repetition sets (e.g., the 2 to 4RM sets in the previous example) that would help you meet that goal. This fatigue may prevent the neuromuscular adaptations necessary for building maximal strength. However, like circuit training, pyramid training may be used occasionally to break up the monotony that comes with repeating the same workout over and over.

## Super Sets and Compound Sets

Using compound sets and super sets is a good way to increase the time efficiency during your workouts. These terms are often used interchangeably, but they refer to two distinct techniques. For the purpose of this discussion, *super sets* are multiple sets of exercise in which a set that uses the antagonist muscle group is

© BananaStock

immediately followed by an exercise that uses the agonist muscle group (e.g., biceps curls followed by triceps pushdowns). *Compound sets*, on the other hand, are sets in which the first set of the second exercise uses the same muscle group as the first exercise and is immediately followed by a third set of the first exercise (e.g., the triceps pushdown exercise would be followed by triceps extensions and then another round of the triceps pushdown exercise).

Super sets are useful when you are lifting for maximal strength and don't need long rest periods between sets. Ordering the exercises so that agonists and antagonists are trained back-to-back can allow you to move from exercise to exercise with less time spent resting.

Furthermore, experts previously thought that performing super sets allowed the antagonist, which is trained second, to produce greater force, because the agonist is fatigued and cannot resist the movement of the antagonist. However, recent evidence shows that the opposite is actually true (Maynard and Ebben 2003). Since the antagonist is somewhat involved during the contraction of the agonist, the antagonist is slightly fatigued itself during the previous set. This fatigue causes a slight decrease in its ability to produce force.

This effect is better understood using an example. You may expect the quadriceps to perform better immediately following a set of leg curls, because the hamstrings are fatigued and less likely to be able to resist (eccentrically) the action of the quadriceps. Instead, the quadriceps performance will be slightly hindered because they were somewhat active (providing a stabilizing cocontraction) during the previous hamstring exercise.

Compound sets are done with the purpose of exercising a muscle in a fatigued state. The idea is to completely exhaust the muscle being worked and produce a greater amount of overload.

## Types of Exercises and Exercise Order

Now that you understand some of the methods you can use to enhance the frequency of your workouts, it's time to discover what types of exercises are out there to help you accomplish your goals.

Exercises can be grouped into three categories based on how they relate to your goals—power, core, and assistance exercises.

© Human Kinetics

**Power exercises** are explosive movements in which the lifter attempts to move the weight as quickly as possible. Some classic power exercises include the power clean (page 252) and the push jerk (page 270). Power exercises use many muscle groups and require the movement of several joints (as do core exercises; see page 147). When performing power exercises, the lifter should be at his or her freshest in order to minimize fatigue. Therefore, if you will be performing power movements, you should place them first in the workout program, before the core lifts. Power exercises are important to include in a well-balanced resistance training program, especially for those seeking to improve athletic performance. Use caution with these exercises, though, because proper form is vital to their performance. Instruction and supervision from a qualified exercise professional are always recommended when performing power lifts.

**Core exercises** use large muscle groups located close to the center of the body. They generally incorporate several muscle groups across the movement of multiple joints. These exercises primarily work the muscles of the chest, shoulders, back, and hips; they include such exercises as the front squat (page 212), the lunge (page 217), and the bench press (page 176). Since core exercises work multiple muscle groups, you should perform them before assistance exercises.

**Assistance exercises** work smaller muscle groups in the arms and legs and are usually limited to the movement of one joint. They are used to work specific muscle groups in isolation, and they include such exercises as the dumbbell biceps curl (page 204), triceps extension (page 203), and exercises that focus on the calf muscles. Assistance exercises are generally performed after core exercises so that the individual muscle groups don't get fatigued before they are called upon to execute multijoint movements.

## Rest Between Workouts

You've already learned that the rest you take between sets of a given exercise during a training session is directly related to the intensity with which you are performing the training. In other words, as intensity increases, the body requires more time to recuperate in preparation for the next set (see chapter 3). We discussed earlier in this chapter how this factor affects your training in various ways depending on your goals (see pages 134 to 139).

The time taken between workouts can be referred to as the *inter-training-session rest period* (Weiss 1991). Specific recommendations are not often given for inter-training-session rest periods; rather, these rest periods are usually the by-product of the chosen frequency of training sessions per week. It is widely believed that at least 48 hours of rest is necessary for a muscle to sufficiently recover following a training session. The problem is that little is known about the optimal time frame between training sessions.

Research scientists have had difficulty establishing a gold standard for inter-training-session rest periods because of the inability to design experiments to test different options. For instance, let's say that two experimental training groups are to perform bench presses using equal intensity, volume, and rest. The only difference in the training groups is the frequency of training (or inter-training-session rest). Within the 12-week experiment, the group that trains with higher frequency will improve more simply because their overall training volume is higher.

Regardless of whether we are able to determine the optimal inter-training-session rest time to promote the greatest gains, this variable needs to be guided by your training experience. When you are new to training, you need to keep your frequency at two or three sessions per week. In fact, some research has shown that beginners can improve with as little as one session per week. As your experience mounts, improvements in recovery will allow you to increase your training frequency.

© BananaStock

Similarly, when progress is slowing or lacking, training frequency or rest should be one of the variables that you examine. When frequency is too low, the muscles are not receiving enough of an overload to incur change. When training frequency is too high, there is insufficient inter-training-session rest, and the muscles are unable to recover well enough to perform at their best during the next training session. Tinkering with training frequency can be another good way to manage your training plateaus.

Remember that your training goal will dictate in some way how you manipulate your training variables. In other words, plan to train the correct way for the desired outcome and adjust your plan as needed, instead of just doing the same thing each workout.

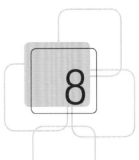

# Safety, Soreness, and Injury

Brian W. Findley, Lee E. Brown, Daniel P. Murray, and Sagir G. Bera

This chapter discusses one of the most important topics in the field of resistance training. Although no one is interested in reading long-winded explanations about proper form and technique or the importance of following safe training guidelines, learning how to avoid an injury is much better than trying to figure out how to fix one. Practicing preventative techniques goes a long way toward reducing the occurrence and severity of injuries that can cause pain, dysfunction, and a costly loss of training time.

We must emphasize that resistance training prevents and aids in the recovery of far more injuries than it causes. People who avoid working with weights because of the fear of developing or exacerbating an injury are misguided in their thinking. In fact, with qualified instruction and strict adherence to proper technique, the incidence of injuries actually created by resistance training is extremely small. In other words, the positives of resistance training far outweigh the potential negatives.

Throughout this chapter, we discuss the importance of safely engaging in resistance training. We also address the soreness associated with unaccustomed exercise and how this soreness passes in a short time. Finally, we give some information to help you identify and manage injuries that may occur from lifting incorrectly.

# Lifting Safely

Lifting safely is of paramount importance when exercising because it greatly reduces the chance of injury. In the weight room, injuries most often occur when individuals do not follow directions or do not use proper form. In addition to properly warming up for and cooling down from your strength training workout, you should always wear appropriate clothing and shoes, and you must learn the proper techniques for each lift.

## Warming Up and Cooling Down

Like aerobic exercise, resistance training demands a proper warm-up. Beginners should start a strength training session by performing 5 to 10 minutes of light aerobic exercise, jogging, or cycling on a cycle ergometer. From there, performing one or two warm-up sets—using a light load (around 50 percent of 1RM)—for each new exercise improves blood flow to the muscles that will be exercised. Warm-up sets also improve a muscle's ability to produce force during subsequent training sets. Performing these sets before each exercise takes only a short amount of time, and the first training set can be performed almost immediately following the last warm-up. Warm-up sets should not be counted in your total number of sets for the day. Proper warm-up sets are especially important before high-intensity workouts. It is a dangerous practice to exercise a muscle at or near its maximum intensity without first preparing it physiologically.

Cool-down periods following workouts help the body bounce back. The by-products of muscular contraction (e.g., lactic acid) tend to sit in the muscle following training unless they are cleared back into the blood for processing and waste removal. Cooling down is one way to facilitate this clearance and help the muscle recover more quickly between workouts. Cool-down periods don't have to be excessive in duration. Spending 5 to 10 minutes on a bike or treadmill (at a low to moderate intensity) following lower body workouts is sufficient. Similarly, performing 5 to 10 minutes of upper body aerobic training (e.g., on an upper body bike) will help clear waste products following an arm workout.

## Stretching

Stretching is another beneficial activity to include in your resistance training program. Muscular flexibility and good range of motion of the joints improve your ability to perform exercises using the appropriate form. Improved flexibility, especially of the lower extremities, also seems to help limit lower back injuries.

Many experts advocate stretching as part of the warm-up process before resistance training. Recent evidence indicates that this practice may not be as helpful as was once thought. Some studies have shown that stretching a muscle just before training may in fact decrease its ability to produce force (Cramer et al. 2004).

Instead, stretching programs seem most worthwhile when performed following the active cool-down period. The increase in blood flow from training warms the muscle, which allows it to stretch farther and better maintain gains in flexibility.

There are several different methods of stretching, including static, ballistic, and proprioceptive neuromuscular facilitation (PNF) stretching. We will focus on static stretching, which is as effective as any other form and is the easiest to understand.

Static stretching technique involves slowly stretching a muscle to its end range (i.e., as far as you can stretch it) and holding that stretch for a prescribed duration of time. Intensity of the stretch should be moderate in order to achieve good results without overstretching and causing pain (figure 8.1). The best duration for static stretching seems to be 30 seconds with a brief pause between repetitions. Performing two or three repetitions of the stretch is common practice, although better results are often described if repetitions and stretching sessions per day are increased (Malliaropoulos et al. 2004). After any strength training workout, you should be sure to stretch the entire body, emphasizing the major joints.

**Figure 8.1**    After the cool-down period following your workout, it is beneficial to perform some moderate static stretches on the muscles that were the focus of your exercise.

# Dressing for Lifting

Wearing proper attire while resistance training helps to regulate the temperature of the body and facilitate lifting movements. Wearing long pants and long sleeves made out of heavy, restrictive material may inhibit movement during exercise and may trap heat that the body needs to release. If the body is unable to release enough heat, or if the sweat it produces cannot evaporate, the core temperature of the body may rise, leading to dehydration. Wearing comfortable, breathable materials during training sessions helps to prevent overheating. Clothing that allows for optimal mobility is best.

Footwear is also an important consideration in the gym. Open-toed shoes or sandals are not appropriate for resistance training. Comfortable athletic shoes help protect the feet and toes from being stubbed or scraped against heavy equipment, and they also offer good support for the feet when lifting heavy weights. Athletic shoes won't likely save you from injury if you drop a 45-pound plate on your foot, but they can help cushion your feet and avoid minor traumas.

# Performing Exercises Correctly

Although injuries directly attributable to resistance training are rare, they do occur from time to time. The vast majority of these injuries stem from the lifter not using the proper form for an exercise. One of the biggest misconceptions about resistance training is that it will lead to injury of the lower back or neck. It is true that these areas are vulnerable to injury when lifting heavy weights, but by paying attention to proper positioning and avoiding poor technique, you can eliminate the causes of these injuries.

Watch out for the following pitfalls as you strive to execute proper form:

- ☐ Resist the temptation to load up the bar with as much weight as you possibly can and turn an individualized resistance training program into a competition among peers. Overloading the bar is never a good idea. It leads to using momentum to perform lifts, which does not optimally isolate the targeted muscle.

- ☐ Don't lurch or twist body parts during a lift. This is obviously poor form. Equipment that enables you to lift while sitting and provides a high back support, such as an adjustable bench, can help keep you from overcompensating with accessory muscles or using momentum.

- ☐ Avoid performing a partial range of motion during an exercise. This can also be a sign that the load is too great. The length–tension relationship of a muscle tells us that the most difficult segments of muscle actions are at the beginning and end of a given range of motion. Some people tend to perform only the easiest (i.e., the middle) portion of the range using a heavier load than is necessary. You should avoid this practice because a muscle needs to be exercised through its entire range of motion.

☐ Don't deviate from proper positioning of the neck during resistance training exercises performed in the seated and standing positions. Maintaining good form can be a challenge. A common mistake is to bring the head forward when performing lifts; this places undue stress on the musculature of the back of the neck, and it places strain on the delicate structures of the posterior aspect of the cervical spine. During seated and standing resistance exercises, the head is in the correct position when the ears are in line with (or slightly in front of) the shoulders (figure 8.2). Proper positioning can be monitored by a spotter or by performing the exercise in front of a mirror.

**Figure 8.2** Aligning your ears evenly with (or slightly in front of) your shoulders while performing a standing (or seated) lift will help ensure that your head is properly positioned, thereby keeping your neck and cervical spine free from undue stress and strain.

☐ Don't compromise proper positioning of the lower back. This can be a challenge during all lifts, but especially during core exercises. Overarching of the back is a common compensatory technique when loads are heavier than they need to be. You need to identify and eliminate this flawed technique in order to provide safe lifting for the lower back. Underarching of the lower back is often seen when lifts are performed from the floor, such as in the deadlift. This rounding of the back places the lumbar muscles at a mechanical disadvantage and makes them vulnerable to strain while performing the lift. Appropriate position entails the lifter holding his or her abdominal muscles tight while maintaining a slight arch in the lower back. This ensures that the lumbar spine is held in what is known as the *neutral spine* position, and that undue stress is not placed on either the anterior or posterior aspects.

As an exerciser gains experience and consistently achieves good form, he or she should progress from doing more machine weight exercises, to more free weight exercises.

The rampant use of bad form that you can observe in almost any gym in the country has led some exercise professionals to discourage people from performing some potentially dangerous exercises altogether. The lat pulldown in which the bar is pulled behind the head, and squats in which the lifter goes below 90 degrees of knee flexion, are two of the exercises that some call "bad" or "illegal" exercises. However, there is no such thing as a bad exercise, but there are exercises performed with improper form and exercises that are contraindicated for certain individuals.

Take the lat pulldown, for example. Some argue that performing this exercise behind the head puts the shoulder in a position where it is vulnerable to injury and causes the lifter to bring the head too far forward. This is true for those individuals who lack the appropriate external rotation range of motion of the shoulder to perform the exercise correctly. If the appropriate range of motion exists, and if the lifter takes care to pull the bar around and behind the neck (instead of pushing the head forward to avoid the bar), then this exercise can be safe and effective. Moreover, the lat pulldown behind the neck may be important to include in training programs for certain athletes, such as overhand throwers, who are required to place their shoulder in this position when they participate in their sport.

Part III of this book details the correct form for many strength training exercises. Refer to those descriptions and use a spotter when necessary to ensure that you are using proper form.

## Using Straps, Wraps, and Belts

Lifting straps, wraps, and belts are commonly used by bodybuilding and powerlifting professionals who often engage in high-intensity training.

Straps are used to help a lifter improve his or her grip on the bar by taking up some of the stress that would otherwise be felt by the hand and forearm. One strap is used for each hand. One end of the strap is wrapped around the wrist several

**Figure 8.3** The closed grip is shown here using lifting straps. Notice that the thumb wraps around the bar to prevent slippage.

times, while the other end is wrapped around the bar or dumbbell to be lifted (figure 8.3). Straps are often used with power lifts such as the clean and jerk or heavy lifts such as the deadlift.

Wraps are used around the knees when performing high-intensity exercises for the lower body, such as the squat or leg press. Some people feel that the wraps help support the knees during these heavy lifts and prevent them from incurring undue stress. The wraps should be applied directly around the joint doing the lifting in order to provide greater support for the joint.

Weight belts are also commonly used for high-intensity and power lifts. These belts are designed to increase support for the lower back and trunk by increasing interabdominal pressure during these lifts. They may also help cue the lifter to maintain proper lower back positioning during heavy lifting.

The negative aspect of using these pieces of equipment is that the lifter may become dependent on them, which can promote detraining of stabilizer muscles that are also supposed to be working during these lifts. For example, when performing a squat, keeping the back in a slightly arched position and holding the abdominal muscles tight are important parts of correct form. Using a weight belt creates the same stabilizing pressure that the abdominal contraction is supposed to create. When the belt is used, the abdominal muscles and the stabilizer muscles in the lower back can relax during the lift. This may contribute to their weakness and may therefore be detrimental rather than beneficial. As a result, you should not use a belt when lifting less than maximal loads.

## Using Spotters

Exercising with a workout partner or spotter is integral to safe resistance training. This obviously becomes even more important when you are performing high-intensity training or when you are attempting to exercise the muscle to exhaustion. Having a spotter is not a sign of weakness or inexperience. Rather, it is an intelligent decision that shows both a commitment to working your muscles to their limits and a regard for the practice and promotion of proper safety.

A spotter's most obvious contribution to safe weightlifting is being there to help you complete a lift in case you are unable to do so on your own. Not only does this allow you to eliminate any fears of being trapped under a bar, but it lets you work the muscle to fatigue. You are able to get the most out of each set because you are lifting the load until you no longer can.

© Eyewire/Photodisc/Getty Images

The spotter is also useful for encouragement and motivation. Lifting with a friend or workout partner can make the training session more enjoyable and provide you with motivation to work harder. The encouragement and feedback your spotter gives you can also help you press through days when your usual motivation and desire are lacking.

A good workout partner can also coach you to avoid improper form. He or she may notice that you are not completing full-range repetitions or that you are arching your back too much with each lift. A well-trained spotter can be key in helping you avoid injuries that might otherwise develop because of bad form. Instructions for spotting on particular exercises are included in part III of this book.

When you are the one acting as a spotter, you must use good spotting form. Getting as close to the weight as possible without disturbing the lift helps to ensure proper form. Also, be prepared to offer as much help as needed. In other words, don't underestimate how much you may need to help the person you're spotting. If he or she only needs a little help, it is easy to decrease your contribution to the lift. This is a safer and more effective practice than underestimating the weight at first and then trying to contribute more.

Occasionally, when very heavy loads are being used, two spotters are necessary. This usually takes place with bar lifts, and the appropriate technique is for the spotters to position themselves on both ends of the bar. If the lifter needs help, the spotters must communicate so that even contributions can be made from both ends.

## Dealing With Muscle Soreness

Unfortunately, muscular soreness is something that often comes with the territory when you begin resistance training. This soreness is the result of the muscle undergoing unaccustomed stress. Although the actual physiological processes involved in producing this soreness are not well understood, the most likely theory is that unaccustomed exercise actually leads to microscopic tears in the muscle cells. These tears produce swelling and inflammation in the muscle, which creates the associated pain and stiffness.

The soreness can begin as soon as a few hours following a resistance training session, but often it will not peak until 48 to 72 hours after the session. For this reason, the soreness associated with any type of resistance exercise is referred to as *delayed-onset muscle soreness*, or DOMS.

The lack of understanding of the actual process involved in DOMS provides us with little ability to treat or prevent it. Everything from heat compresses, to stretching, to ibuprofen has been used to treat DOMS. Unfortunately, none of these remedies has been met with universal success.

The only thing we truly know about DOMS is that it occurs to a lesser and lesser degree as resistance training is repeated. This is known as the *repeated bout effect.* Although you may experience significant discomfort after your first few training sessions, this phenomenon is drastically reduced the more you continue to train.

© Jumpfoto

DOMS occurs to a greater degree when exercise is intense, and it is especially evident following intense eccentric training. Therefore, it is recommended that beginners work out with less intensity than intermediate and advanced lifters. There is no reason for beginners to start their training with high-intensity workouts when they can accomplish significant gains with lower intensities, and in doing so, reduce the degree of DOMS.

It is generally recommended that you wait for the soreness of a prior workout session to fade before lifting again. This is because DOMS significantly lowers your strength. Once the soreness has worked itself out, you will be able to return to training without decrements in strength.

# Identifying and Treating Injuries

As stated earlier, if proper guidelines are followed, the actual incidence of resistance training injuries is very low. Regardless, it is important to be able to distinguish the difference between muscular soreness and injury. And once an injury is identified, you need to know what steps to take to ensure its proper treatment.

You can distinguish muscular soreness from injury in that soreness is diffuse and broad based, while injuries tend to be local, or specific, in nature. Pain that is felt in a localized area—for instance, on one side of the body or in only one muscle or joint—is indicative of injury rather than soreness. Since similar loads are lifted with both sides of the body, soreness tends to present itself evenly on each side.

Injuries also last much longer than typical muscular soreness does. If pain does not fade following the 72-hour peak that is often seen with muscular soreness, an injury may be present. If injuries are mismanaged in this early time frame, they can become prolonged and disruptive.

Of course, the best recommendation when dealing with an injury is to see a qualified health care professional as soon as possible. Take this step right away so that the injury can be taken care of early and appropriately. In the meantime, follow the PRICE principle for treating an injury in its early stages. PRICE is an acronym that stands for protect, rest, ice, compression, and elevation. Practicing these techniques is an effective means of dealing with an acute injury until you can see an appropriate practitioner.

The most important aspect of any resistance training program is your personal safety, which can be ensured by following the guidelines in this chapter. Be mindful of the distinction between soreness and injury. Soreness is an expected outcome of almost any new resistance training program. However, injury can result from bad form and technique and is usually associated with unusual or unexpected pain. Injury should always be referred to a qualified physician.

# Exercise Technique

This part of the book discusses general technique for strength training exercises. The exercises are grouped into those that target the upper body, lower body, and torso. I also cover explosive lifts.

Before you get started strength training, you should review several safety issues. Although weight training is one of the safest activities, at no time should you compromise safety. Chapter 8 details several precautions you can take to reduce the potential for injury. Please review those precautions (pages 150 to 157) before attempting any strength exercise. In addition to those precautions, keep in mind the following safety issues:

- **Medical clearance.** Obtaining medical clearance from a qualified physician before participating in a strength training program is advised. The physician will look for any condition that may compromise your health and safety—things such as coronary risk factors, medications, orthopedic concerns, recent operations, and lifestyle management. This is extremely important information to take into account before you begin training. If any condition exists that has not yet manifested itself, the doctor may detect it during this examination.

- **Grip.** To reduce the likelihood of having a barbell, a dumbbell, or the handle of another piece of equipment slip out of the hands, wrap the thumbs around the bar or handles. This is called a *closed grip* (refer back to figure 8.3). It is often tempting to use an open grip in which the thumb is not wrapped around the bar or handle; however, this hand position increases the likelihood that the handle will slip from the hands.

- **Physical space.** Physical space around a lifter can ensure safety as well. The immediate area around a lifter will vary slightly with the exercise, but generally there should be three feet (91.4 cm) of space in any direction around a lifter who is performing a lift. Space is often limited in high-traffic areas and during high-usage times. Be sure to stay away from areas in which the physical space is compromised.

- **Breathing.** Continue to breathe throughout the lift. Generally, you should breathe in during the lowering, or eccentric, phase and breathe out during the lifting, or concentric, phase. The most important thing to remember is that you should never hold your breath while performing resistance training exercises.

- **Lifting technique.** As discussed in chapter 8, lifting technique must never be compromised in an effort to lift more weight or perform more repetitions. Using improper technique results in slower strength gains and can lead to injury. Although everyone uses slightly different technique because of differences in body size and shape, the acceptable range of variance in technique is limited (as you will see in the exercise descriptions in this part of the book). Common lifting errors that compromise technique include swinging the weight to initiate a repetition, moving from the recommended foot position, raising the hips off the bench, not completing the full range of motion, and leaning forward or backward to assist with the movement. Lifting in a controlled manner in both directions is ideal.

- **Proper progression.** Gradually add volume and intensity as the body adapts to training. What may be the ideal training program for one person could be counterproductive for someone else. Therefore, it is best to start with a basic program and add more work over time as the body allows. (The progressive overload principle is discussed in further detail in chapter 3.)

- **Neutral spine.** The spine has three natural curves—cervical, thoracic, and lumbar. The neutral spine position is the position in which the alignment of the vertebrae allows equal distribution of force in all directions. This is the position of the spine typically seen when a healthy person stands erect. A neutral spine position is desirable because it allows for the greatest application of force while also limiting the risk of injury. Injury to the spine can occur if its range of motion is exceeded.

- **Spotting.** The spotter is responsible for the lifter's safety, and by spotting correctly, he or she can further reduce the likelihood of injury. A detailed description of the correct spotting technique is included in the exercise descriptions where appropriate, with specific instructions for lifts such as those in which the weight is supported overhead (pressing movements) or on the trunk (squats). Clear communication between the spotter and lifter is critical. Before any lifting attempts, the spotter should know exactly how the lifter wants to be assisted as well as the number of reps planned; he or she should also be familiar with the lifter's strength levels. The spotter is also accountable for using collars on the weights and ensuring that the bar is loaded evenly on both sides.

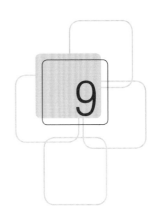

# Upper Body Exercises

Michael Barnes and Keith E. Cinea

There are an infinite number of exercises that you can perform to strengthen the upper body. In this chapter, we focus on the fundamental exercises that strengthen the muscles of the chest, shoulders, upper back, and arms (figure 9.1, *a* through *c*) as well as some more advanced movements. The exercises in this chapter serve several purposes. They can help you achieve good general health and fitness, improve athletic performance, condition your body for bodybuilding, and prevent injuries.

As you perform each of these exercises, pay particular attention to your exercise technique. Properly executing movements will ensure you will maximize your strength gains and minimize your chances of injury. Use a spotter when performing movements in which you support the bar over the head or face.

To achieve balance in your lifting regimen, follow each pressing exercise with a pulling exercise. For example, if you perform three sets of the bench press exercise, complement your program with three sets of a seated row. This creates a balance in both the strength and appearance of the muscle groups and ensures joint stability. Most people enjoy training the upper body muscles because the results are easy to see in the mirror and are easy to quantify on the barbell or machine.

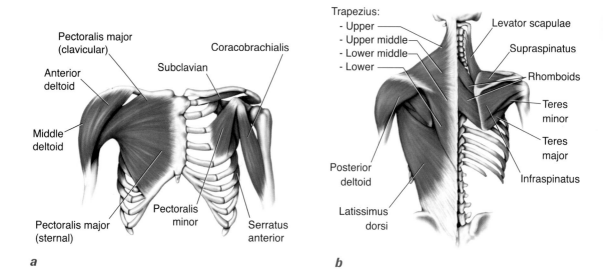

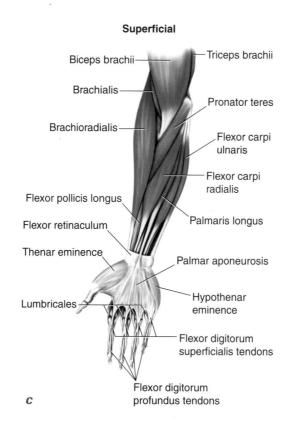

**Figure 9.1**  Major muscles of the *(a)* chest and anterior shoulders, *(b)* upper back and posterior shoulders, and *(c)* upper arm.

Reprinted, by permission, from W.S. Behnke, 2006, *Kinetic Anatomy*, 2nd ed (Champaign, IL: Human Kinetics), 47, 47, and 81.

# Barbell Shrug

upper trapezius

**◄ Starting Position**

1. Position the barbell about mid thigh, slightly below arm length.

2. With a flat back and neutral spine, hold the bar against the thighs and stand with the feet hip-width apart.

3. Position the shoulders back and chest up.

**▼ Action**

4. Elevate the shoulders directly upward as high as possible, ideally three to four inches from the starting point.

5. Return along the same path used for the upward movement.

Maintain a flat back and neutral spine; avoid rounding the upper back.

Prevent the shoulders from rolling either forward or backward at the midpoint.

Avoid initiating the movement with the legs.

# Standing Military Press

medial deltoids, triceps brachii

### ▲ Starting Position

1. Begin with the bar on the front of the shoulders and the feet hip-width apart.
2. Take a shoulder-width grip on the bar with the palms facing forward.
3. Stand up straight and pull the shoulders back, elevating the chest.

Prevent the shoulders from slumping forward; allowing them to slump could injure the lower back.

Keep the muscles of the torso tight and active.

Avoid leaning backward with the bar overhead.

## ▲ Action

4. Press the weight off the shoulders in an arc so that the bar moves around the head and ends up overhead (and slightly behind the head). The arms should be fully extended and in line with the hips. You may have to pull the head back to avoid contacting the bar with the chin and face.

5. Keep the back flat, the chest up, and the feet flat on the floor, a hip-width apart.

6. Return to the starting position, following the same arc used in the upward movement.

# Seated Barbell Overhead Press

anterior and medial deltoids, trapezius, triceps brachii

## ▲ Starting Position

1. Adjust the rack so that you can remove the bar at shoulder height.

2. As you sit on the bench, be sure that your body makes contact with the floor and the bench at five points: both of the feet, the hips, the upper back, and the head.

3. Use an overhand shoulder-width grip to hold the bar.

Maintain the five points of contact throughout the movement.

Perform the full range of motion.

Keep the muscles of the torso tight to stabilize the movement.

You can also perform this lift using dumbbells.

## ▲ Action

4. After removing the bar, initiate the movement by pressing the bar in front of the head.

5. Move the bar overhead, supporting it directly over the shoulders with the elbows fully extended.

6. Return to the starting position, following the same path used for the upward movement.

# Machine Shoulder Press

medial deltoids, anterior deltoids, triceps brachii

### ➤ Machine Setup

1. Adjust the seat height so that the handles are aligned with or above shoulder height.

2. Select the appropriate resistance on the weight stack.

3. Grip either set of handles (with the palms facing forward or toward each other).

4. Position the body with the chest up and the shoulders and head back against the back pad.

### ◄ Action

5. Extend the handles in a slow, controlled motion until the arms are fully extended.

6. Return the handles to the starting position without letting the resistance rest on the weight stack between reps.

# Dumbbell Upright Row

medial deltoids, upper trapezius

### ◄ Starting Position

1. Stand with the feet shoulder-width apart, keeping the back flat and the chest up.
2. Face the palms toward the thighs with the elbows pointed outward.

### ▼ Action

3. Initiate the movement by bending at the elbows to raise the hands to shoulder level.
4. Keep the dumbbells close to the body and the elbows pointed outward.
5. Once the hands reach shoulder level, elevate or shrug the shoulders.
6. Lower the shoulders while simultaneously extending at the elbows to return to the starting position before beginning the next repetition.

Keep the muscles of the torso tight to stabilize the movement.

Perform the full range of motion, and avoid swinging the weight upward to initiate the movement.

You can also use a barbell to perform this movement.

# Dumbbell Side Raise

medial deltoids, trapezius

### ◄ Starting Position

1. Stand with the feet shoulder-width apart, slightly bending the knees and keeping the back flat in a neutral spine position.
2. Hold the dumbbells at the sides of the body with the palms facing in and a slight bend in the elbows.

### ▼ Action

3. While maintaining a neutral spine position and a slight bend in the elbows, raise both arms simultaneously to the sides in a smooth, controlled fashion until they are horizontal.
4. Lower the dumbbells, following the same path used for the upward movement, keeping the spine in a neutral position and the elbows slightly bent.

Maintain the elbow angle at all times, making sure that you lift the arms to a horizontal position.

Avoid flexing and extending at the hips to complete the repetitions.

You can also use cables to perform this movement.

# Machine Lateral Raise

anterior deltoids, medial deltoids

➤ **Machine Setup**

1. Adjust the seat height so that the shoulder joints are aligned with the machine's axis of rotation.
2. Select the appropriate resistance on the weight stack.
3. Place the elbows at the sides or slightly in front of the body.
4. Position the body with the chest up.

▼ **Action**

5. Lift the elbows to the sides in a slow, controlled motion until they reach the level of the shoulders.
6. Slowly return to the starting position without letting the resistance rest on the weight stack between reps.

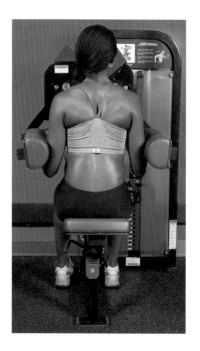

# Dumbbell Front Raise

anterior deltoids, trapezius

◄ **Starting Position**

1. Stand with the feet shoulder-width apart, the knees slightly bent, and the back flat in a neutral spine position.
2. Hold the dumbbells in front of the body with the palms facing the thighs (or facing in).

▼ **Action**

3. While maintaining a neutral spine position, raise one arm to the front in a smooth, controlled fashion until the dumbbell is at shoulder level.
4. Lower the dumbbell, following the same path used for the upward movement, keeping the spine in a neutral position and the elbows slightly bent.

Maintain the elbow angle at all times and lift the arms to shoulder height.

Avoid flexing and extending at the hips to complete the repetitions.

You can also use cables to perform this movement.

# Dumbbell Rear Raise

posterior deltoids, trapezius

➤ **Starting Position**

1. Stand with the feet shoulder-width apart and the knees slightly bent.
2. Bend at the waist until the torso is near horizontal, maintaining a flat back in a neutral spine position.
3. Hold the dumbbells below the shoulders with the palms facing each other.

▼ **Action**

4. While maintaining a neutral spine position raise both arms simultaneously to the sides in a smooth, controlled fashion until the dumbbells are at shoulder level.
5. Lower the dumbbells, following the same path used for the upward movement, keeping the spine in a neutral position.

Maintain the elbow angle at all times and lift the arms to shoulder height.

Avoid lifting the torso up to assist with the movement.

You can also perform this movement in a seated position.

# Bench Press

pectoralis, anterior deltoids, triceps brachii

◄ **Starting Position**

1. As you lie on the bench, be sure that your body makes contact with the floor and the bench at five points: both of the feet, the hips, the upper back, and the head.

2. Hold the bar with a grip slightly outside of shoulder width, wrapping the thumbs around the bar.

3. Have the spotter assist with removing the bar from the rack; support the bar over the shoulders.

**Spotter**

☐ Load the bar evenly and use collars.

☐ Ask the lifter how many repetitions he or she will be attempting to complete.

☐ Stand behind the bar at the head of the lifter and assist with lifting the bar off the rack, using one overhand and one underhand grip.

☐ Slowly transfer the weight to the lifter when he or she is in the starting position.

☐ Stand with the knees slightly bent and the hands in a ready position close to the bar; most lifters need assistance in the upward movement phase of the bench press.

☐ Smoothly transfer the barbell back to the rack once the set is completed or the lifter needs assistance.

Use the same movement path for every repetition and avoid bouncing the bar off the chest.

Maintain the five points of contact.

## ▲ Action

4. While maintaining the five points of contact, lower the bar in a controlled motion, arcing the movement of the bar until it lightly touches the lower portion of the chest.

5. Maintain an upper arm angle of approximately 45 degrees from the torso.

6. Press the barbell up to the starting position, using the same path and body position as used for the downward movement.

# Dumbbell Bench Press

pectoralis, anterior deltoids, triceps brachii

## ▲ Starting Position

1. As you lie on the bench, be sure that your body makes contact with the floor and the bench at five points: both of the feet, the hips, the upper back, and the head.

2. Hold the dumbbells in each hand with the thumb wrapped around the handle.

3. Place the dumbbells slightly to the side of the chest in the down position.

---

**Spotter**

☐ Clear the area of any equipment in case the lifter has to drop the weight for any reason.

☐ Ask the lifter how many repetitions he or she will be attempting to complete.

☐ Stand at the head of the bench, prepared to assist the lifter when he or she lies back on the bench.

☐ Keep the hands in a ready position throughout the lift, under the lifter's forearms.

☐ Assist the lifter in sitting up after the set is complete.

---

Use the same movement path for every repetition, and perform the full range of motion.

Maintain the five points of contact.

## ▲ Action

4. Maintaining the five points of contact, press the dumbbells upward in a controlled and smooth fashion until the arms are extended over the shoulders.

5. Lower the dumbbells using the same path and body position as for the upward movement.

6. The set is complete when the dumbbells are over the shoulders.

7. Once the set is complete, the lifter lowers the weight, places the face of the dumbbells on each thigh, and sits up with the help of the spotter.

# Incline Bench Press

pectoralis, anterior deltoids, triceps brachii

## ▲ Starting Position

1. As you lie on the incline bench, be sure that your body makes contact with the floor and the bench at five points: both of the feet, the hips, the upper back, and the head.

2. Hold the bar with a grip slightly outside of shoulder width, and wrap the thumbs around the bar.

3. Have the spotter assist with removing the bar from the rack.

---

**Spotter**

☐ Load the bar evenly and use collars.

☐ Ask the lifter how many repetitions he or she will be attempting to complete.

☐ Stand behind the bar at the head of the lifter and assist with lifting the bar off the rack, using one overhand and one underhand grip.

☐ Slowly transfer the weight to the lifter when he or she is in the starting position.

☐ Stand with the knees slightly bent and the hands in a ready position close to the bar; most lifters need assistance in the upward movement phase.

☐ Smoothly transfer the barbell back to the rack once the set is completed or the lifter needs assistance.

---

Avoid bouncing the bar off the chest.

Maintain the five points of contact.

## ▲ Action

4. While maintaining the five points of contact, lower the bar in a controlled and smooth fashion until it lightly touches the upper portion of the chest.

5. Make sure that the path of the bar is fairly linear from the shoulders to the upper portion of the chest.

6. Keep the upper arm angle at approximately 45 degrees from the torso.

7. Press the barbell up to the start position, following the same path used for the downward movement.

# Incline Dumbbell Bench Press

pectoralis, anterior deltoids, triceps brachii

## ▲ Starting Position

1. As you lie on the incline bench, be sure that your body makes contact with the floor and the bench at five points: both of the feet, the hips, the upper back, and the head.
2. Hold the dumbbells in each hand with the thumb wrapped around the handle.
3. Place the dumbbells slightly to the side of the chest in the down position.

### Spotter

☐ Clear the area of any equipment in case the lifter has to drop the weight for any reason.

☐ Ask the lifter how many repetitions he or she will be attempting to complete.

☐ Stand at the head of the incline bench, prepared to assist the lifter when he or she lies back on the bench.

☐ Place the hands in a ready position under the lifter's forearms.

☐ Assist the lifter in sitting up after the set is complete.

Maintain the five points of contact.

Perform the full range of motion.

## ▲ Action

4. While maintaining the five points of contact, press the dumbbells in a controlled and smooth fashion until the arms are extended over the shoulders.

5. Make sure that the path of the dumbbells is fairly linear from above the sides of the chest to above the shoulders.

6. Keep the upper arm angle at approximately 45 degrees from the torso.

7. Lower the dumbbells, following the same path used for the upward movement. The set is complete when the dumbbells are in the down position after the last rep.

8. Once the set is complete, the lifter lowers the weight, places the face of the dumbbells on each thigh, and sits up with the help of the spotter.

# Machine Chest Press

pectoralis major, anterior deltoids, triceps brachii

**◄ Machine Setup**

1. Adjust the seat height so that the handles are aligned with the mid chest.
2. Adjust the start location for the handles so that they are just in front of the chest.
3. Select the appropriate resistance on the weight stack.
4. Grip the handles with an overhand grip, and position the elbows slightly below the shoulders.
5. Position the body with the chest up and with the shoulders and head against the back pad.

**▼ Action**

6. While maintaining a flat back, extend the handles outward in a slow, controlled motion until the arms are fully extended.
7. Slowly return to the starting position without letting the resistance rest on the weight stack between reps.

Focus on drawing the elbows toward each other as opposed to pressing on the arms.

# Machine Chest Fly

pectoralis, anterior deltoids

### ➤ Machine Setup

1. Adjust the seat height so that the elbows are slightly below the shoulders when holding the vertical handles.
2. Select the appropriate resistance on the weight stack.
3. Keep the elbows slightly bent and grip the vertical handles.
4. Position the body with the chest up and the shoulders back.

### ▼ Action

5. Bring the arms together in a slow, controlled motion until they touch in front of the body.
6. Slowly return to the starting position without letting the resistance rest on the weight stack between reps.

Bring the arms together instead of bringing the handles together.

Maintain elbow angle (determined by the machine) throughout the movement.

# Dumbbell Fly

pectoralis, anterior deltoids

## ▲ Starting Position

1. As you lie on the bench, be sure that your body makes contact with the floor and the bench at five points: both of the feet, the hips, the upper back, and the head.

2. Hold the dumbbells in each hand with the thumb wrapped around the handle.

3. Position the hands directly above the shoulders with the palms facing in and the elbows slightly bent.

**Spotter**

☐ Clear the area of any equipment in case the lifter has to drop the weight for any reason.

☐ Ask the lifter how many repetitions he or she will be attempting to complete.

☐ Stand at the head of the bench, prepared to assist the lifter when he or she lies back on the bench.

☐ With the lifter lying on the bench, place the hands in a ready position under the lifter's forearms.

☐ Assist the lifter in sitting up after the set is complete.

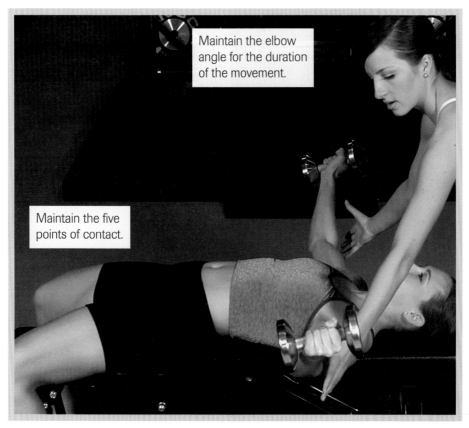

Maintain the elbow angle for the duration of the movement.

Maintain the five points of contact.

You can also perform this movement on an incline bench or stability ball (refer to page 241).

## ▲ Action

4. While maintaining the five points of contact, lower the dumbbells in a controlled and smooth fashion to the sides until they form a horizontal line with the shoulders.

5. Make sure that the path of the dumbbells forms an arc from the starting position to the horizontal position.

6. Keep the upper arm angle at approximately 90 degrees from the torso.

7. Raise the dumbbells, following the same path used for the downward movement, performing the full range of motion.

8. Once the set is complete, the lifter lowers the weight, places the face of the dumbbells on each thigh, and sits up with the help of the spotter.

# Pull-Up

latissimus dorsi, rhomboids, biceps brachii

◄ **Starting Position**

1. Using an overhand grip with the hands shoulder-width apart, hang from a pull-up bar with the arms straight.

2. Align the body vertically.

➤ **Action**

3. Pull the body upward by bending at the elbows and shoulders until the chin is over the bar.

4. Lower the body along the same path used for the upward movement, performing the full range of motion.

Maintain the vertically aligned body position and use the same movement path throughout the movement.

Avoid bending at the knees and hips to initiate repetitions.

# Assisted Chin-Up

biceps brachii, latissimus dorsi

➤ **Machine Setup**

1. Select the appropriate resistance on the weight stack.
2. Rotate the lower bar handles outward.
3. Lower the knee pad and lock it into place if assistance is desired.
4. Stand on the foot plates and choose a set of upper handles to perform the chin-up.
5. Place the knees on the pad while stepping off the foot plates.

◄ **Action**

6. Bend at the elbows and shoulders to pull upward until the chin is above the level of the hands.
7. Lower the body along the same path used for the upward movement.
8. When finished, remove one knee from the pad while it is in the down position and step onto the foot plate. Remove the second knee when the pad gets near the top position.

The weight you select is subtracted from body weight when you perform the exercise. Therefore, the more weight you select, the easier the exercise.

# Lat Pulldown

latissimus dorsi, biceps brachii

➤ **Machine Setup**

1. Sit down and adjust the thigh pads to a secure leg position.
2. Select the appropriate resistance on the weight stack.
3. Stand up and grip the bar slightly wider than shoulder width.
4. Sit down with the thighs under the pads, pulling the bar down to an overhead position.
5. Lean back slightly from the hips, with the chest up and the arms extended overhead.

▼ **Action**

6. Draw the bar down to the front of the chest in a slow, controlled manner.
7. Pull the elbows in toward the body.
8. The midpoint is reached when the bar almost makes contact with the chest.
9. While remaining seated, slowly return the bar to the overhead position without letting the resistance rest on the weight stack between reps.

# Bent-Over Row

latissimus dorsi, rhomboids, biceps brachii

◄ **Starting Position**

1. Stand with the feet shoulder-width apart and slightly bend the knees.
2. Grip the barbell using an overhand grip with the thumbs wrapped around the bar; extend the arms.
3. Bend over at the waist so that the torso is almost horizontal to the floor and the back is flat in a neutral spine position.

▼ **Action**

4. By bending the elbows and shoulders, pull the bar upward until it touches the mid torso.
5. Extend the arms, following the same path used for the upward movement, performing the full range of motion.

Maintain the correct torso angle with relation to the floor and use the same movement path for every repetition.

Avoid initiating the movement with the legs.

# One-Arm Dumbbell Row

latissimus dorsi, rhomboids, biceps brachii

### ➤ Starting Position

1. Place one hand and one knee on a utility bench; with the torso almost horizontal, maintain a flat back in a neutral spine position.
2. Slightly bend the knee of the supporting leg.
3. With the hand that is not on the bench, grip the dumbbell using an overhand grip (with the thumb wrapped around the dumbbell) and extend the arm to the side.

### ▼ Action

4. By bending at the elbow and shoulder, pull the dumbbell upward until it reaches the torso.
5. Extend the arm, following the same path used for the upward movement, performing the full range of motion.

Avoid using the legs or rotating at the torso to initiate the movement.

Maintain the horizontal torso and flat back and use the same movement pattern throughout each repetition.

# Seated Cable Row

latissimus dorsi, rhomboids, biceps brachii

### ▲ Starting Position

1. Position yourself on a seated cable row apparatus with the knees bent and the feet flat on the supporting platform.
2. Keep the back flat in a neutral spine position with the torso approximately vertical.
3. Grip the handle using a closed grip (with the thumbs wrapped around the handle), and extend the arms forward.

### ➤ Action

4. Bend at the elbows and shoulders to pull the handle inward to the torso; keep the angle between the torso and the upper arm at approximately 15 degrees.
5. Extend the arms, following the same path used for the inward movement, performing the full range of motion.

Maintain a nearly vertical body position and use the same movement path for every repetition.

Avoid initiating the movement with the legs.

# Seated Machine Row—Rear Deltoids

latissimus dorsi, trapezius, rhomboids, posterior deltoids, biceps brachii

◄ **Machine Setup**

1. Adjust the seat height to align the mid chest with the top of the chest pad.
2. Adjust the chest pad to allow for full arm extension.
3. Select the appropriate resistance on the weight stack.
4. Grip the desired handles with the palms facing each other (row) or the palms down (rear deltoid).
5. Sit with the head and chest up.

➤ **Action**

6. Pull the shoulders backward in a slow, controlled manner.
7. Slowly return to the starting position without letting the resistance rest on the weight stack between reps.

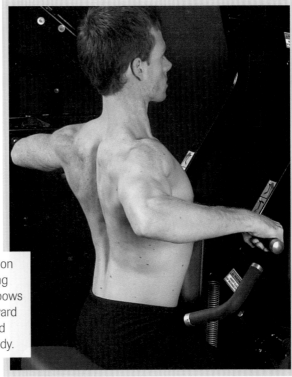

Focus on drawing the elbows backward beyond the body.

# Dip

pectoralis, anterior deltoids, triceps brachii

### ➤ Starting Position

1. Use the dip equipment to either step up or jump to the starting position, extending the elbows to support the body weight.
2. Keep the torso nearly vertical. The knees may have a slight bend in them.

### ▼ Action

3. Maintaining a slightly forward body lean, lower the body in a controlled and smooth fashion by bending at the elbows and shoulders until the upper arm is horizontal.
4. Keep the upper arm angle at approximately 45 degrees from the torso.
5. Rise upward along the same path used for the downward movement, performing the full range of motion.
6. Complete the set in the down position of the movement, then step off to the floor.

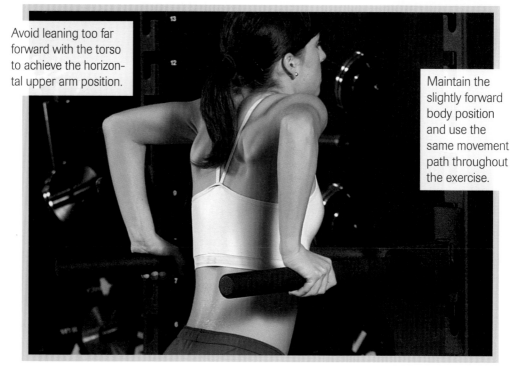

Avoid leaning too far forward with the torso to achieve the horizontal upper arm position.

Maintain the slightly forward body position and use the same movement path throughout the exercise.

# Assisted Dip

triceps brachii, anterior deltoids

### ◀ Machine Setup

1. Select the appropriate resistance on the weight stack.
2. Rotate the lower bar handles inward.
3. Lower the knee pad and lock it into place if assistance is desired.
4. Stand on the foot plates and grip the lower bar handles.
5. Place the knees on the pad while stepping off the foot plates.

### ▼ Action

6. Keeping the back straight and the head up throughout the movement, bend at the elbows and shoulders to lower the body in a controlled and smooth fashion until the upper arm is horizontal.
7. Keep the upper arm angles at approximately 45 degrees from the torso.
8. Return to the starting position, following the same path used for the downward movement.
9. When finished, remove one knee from the pad while it is in the down position and step onto the foot plate. Remove the second knee when the pad gets near the top position.

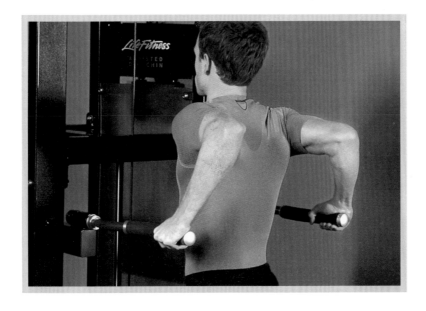

# Close-Grip Bench Press

triceps brachii

## ▲ Starting Position

1. As you lie on the bench, be sure that your body makes contact with the floor and the bench at five points: both of the feet, the hips, the upper back, and the head.

2. Grip the bar with the hands directly above the shoulders, wrapping the thumbs around the bar, and position the bar above the shoulders.

3. Have the spotter assist with removing the bar from the rack; support the bar over the shoulders.

### Spotter

☐ Load the bar evenly and use collars.

☐ Ask the lifter how many repetitions he or she will be attempting to complete.

☐ Stand behind the bar at the head of the lifter and assist with lifting the bar off the rack, using one overhand and one underhand grip.

☐ Slowly transfer the weight to the lifter in his or her starting position.

☐ Stand with the knees slightly bent and the hands in a ready position close to the bar; most lifters need assistance in the upward movement phase of the close-grip bench press.

☐ Smoothly transfer the barbell back to the rack once the set is completed or the lifter needs assistance.

Maintain the five points of contact; avoid lifting the hips off the bench in the upward movement.

Avoid bouncing the bar off the chest.

## ▲ Action

4. While maintaining the five points of contact, lower the bar in a controlled motion, arcing the path of the bar until it lightly touches the lower portion of the chest.

5. Maintain an upper arm angle of approximately 30 degrees from the torso.

6. Press the barbell up to the starting position using the same path and body position as for the downward movement.

# Lying Triceps Extension

triceps brachii

## ▲ Starting Position

1. Lie back on a utility bench, and use an EZ curl bar to perform the movement.

2. As you lie on the bench, be sure that your body makes contact with the floor and the bench at five points: both of the feet, the hips, the upper back, and the head.

3. Hold the bar with an overhand inside grip, wrapping the thumbs around the bar.

4. Have a spotter assist with placing the bar over the shoulders for the starting position.

**Spotter**

☐ Load the bar evenly and use collars.

☐ Ask the lifter how many repetitions he or she will be attempting to complete.

☐ Stand behind the bar at the head of the lifter, and transfer the weight to him or her using one overhand and one underhand grip.

☐ Stand with the knees slightly bent and the hands in a ready position close to the bar; most lifters need assistance in the upward movement phase of the lying triceps extension.

☐ When the set is completed, or if the lifter needs assistance, take the bar from the lifter.

Maintain the five points of contact throughout the movement; avoid lifting the hips off the bench in the upward movement.

Avoid letting the bar touch the forehead.

## ▲ Action

5. Maintaining the five points of contact, bend the elbows to lower the bar in an arc toward (but not touching) the forehead.

6. Keep the movement controlled, with the elbows over the shoulders for the duration of the movement.

7. Press the bar up to the starting position, following the same path used for the downward movement.

# Triceps Pushdown

## triceps brachii

◄ **Starting Position**

1. Use a selectorized cable pushdown machine for the triceps pushdown.
2. Stand in front of the machine with the elbows bent to full flexion and at the sides.
3. Keep the elbows directly beneath the shoulders, where they should remain for the course of the movement.
4. Grip the handle and wrap the thumbs around it.
5. Keep the abdominal muscles tight in order to maintain body position.

Keep the cable in front of the head and within vision.

➤ **Action**

6. Push down with the hands by extending at the elbows until they are fully extended.
7. Keep the upper arms close to the sides.
8. Return to the starting position, following the same path used for the downward movement.

Avoid bending at the knees to initiate the movement.

Maintain a vertical body position through-out the movement by keeping the abdominal muscles tight and the elbows at the sides; avoid leaning forward and over the hands.

# Machine Triceps Extension

## triceps brachii

### ➤ Machine Setup

1. Adjust the seat height so the arms rest flat on the arm pad, aligning the elbows with the machine's axis of rotation.
2. Select the appropriate resistance on the weight stack.
3. Rotate the handles backward and grip them firmly.
4. Position the back flat against the back pad.

### ▼ Action

5. Extend the handles in a slow, controlled motion until the arms are fully extended.
6. Slowly return to the starting position without letting the resistance rest on the weight stack between reps.

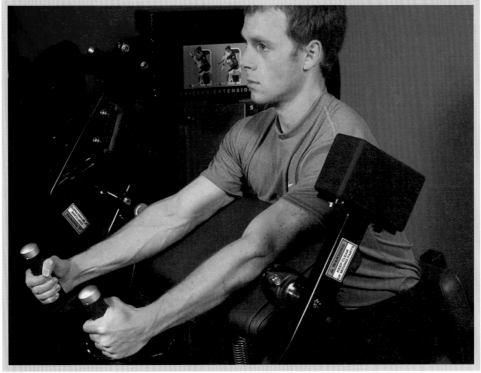

# Dumbbell Biceps Curl

biceps brachii

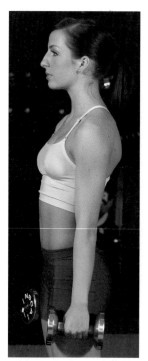

### ◄ Starting Position

1. Stand with the feet shoulder-width apart, the knees slightly bent, and the back flat and in a neutral spine position.
2. Hold the dumbbells with an underhand grip, wrapping the thumbs around the dumbbells and extending the arms fully.

### ▼ Action

3. Raise the dumbbells in a controlled and smooth fashion by bending at the elbows until they are fully flexed.
4. Lower the dumbbells, following the same path used for the upward movement.

Maintain the starting body position and use the same movement path every repetition.

Avoid flexing and extending at the knees and hips to initiate the movement.

You can also perform this lift using a barbell.

# EZ Bar Curl

biceps brachii

➤ **Starting Position**

1. Stand with the feet shoulder-width apart, the knees slightly bent, and the back in a neutral spine position.

2. Hold the bar with an underhand grip, wrapping the thumbs around the bar and extending the arms fully.

▼ **Action**

3. Raise the bar in a controlled and smooth fashion by bending at the elbows until they are fully flexed.

4. Lower the bar, following the same path used for the upward movement.

Maintain the upright body position with the knees slightly bent and the back in a neutral spine position and use the same movement path every repetition.

Avoid flexing and extending at the knees and hips to initiate the movement.

# Dumbbell Hammer Curl

biceps brachii, brachioradialis

◀ **Starting Position**

1. Stand with the feet shoulder-width apart, the knees slightly bent, and the back flat and in a neutral spine position.
2. Hold the dumbbells with the palms facing inward, wrapping the thumbs around the dumbbells.
3. Extend the arms fully.

▼ **Action**

4. Raise the dumbbells in a controlled and smooth fashion by bending at the elbows until they are fully flexed. The palms should remain facing toward the torso.
5. Lower the dumbbells, following the same path used for the upward movement.

Maintain the starting body position and use the same movement path every repetition.

Avoid flexing and extending at the knees and hips to initiate the movement.

# Machine Biceps Curl

biceps brachii

## ▲ Machine Setup

1. Adjust the seat height so that the backs of the upper arms rest flat on the arm pad.
2. Align the elbows with the machine's axis of rotation.
3. Select the appropriate resistance on the weight stack.
4. Rotate the handles forward and grip them firmly.
5. Position the body with the chest up and the shoulders back, leaning forward slightly if necessary to increase stability.

## ◄ Action

6. Flex the arms in a slow, controlled manner, curling the handles up to the shoulders until the arms are fully flexed.

7. Slowly return the handles to the starting position without letting the resistance rest on the weight stack between reps.

# Lower Body Exercises

Michael Barnes and Keith E. Cinea

Most people who start a strength training program initially focus on performing the upper body exercises described in chapter 9. However, it is important not to neglect the muscles of the lower body (figures 10.1, *a* through *d*) and the movements they perform on a daily basis. This chapter covers a variety of exercises that will be useful to everyone from beginning exercisers to professional athletes.

To lift a bag of groceries or run full speed for a touchdown, you need to activate the lower body. The muscles of the hips, thighs, and lower legs all are coordinated in a specific manner that allows these movements to occur. Additionally, ground-based movements like the squat (pages 212, 214), lunge (pages 217, 218, 219), and step-up (page 220) are particularly effective for knee stability and health.

If you are just beginning strength training for the lower body, start with one or two lower body exercises twice a week. If you are consistent with the exercises and perform each movement correctly, you will soon find the lower body exercises as enjoyable as any other exercises.

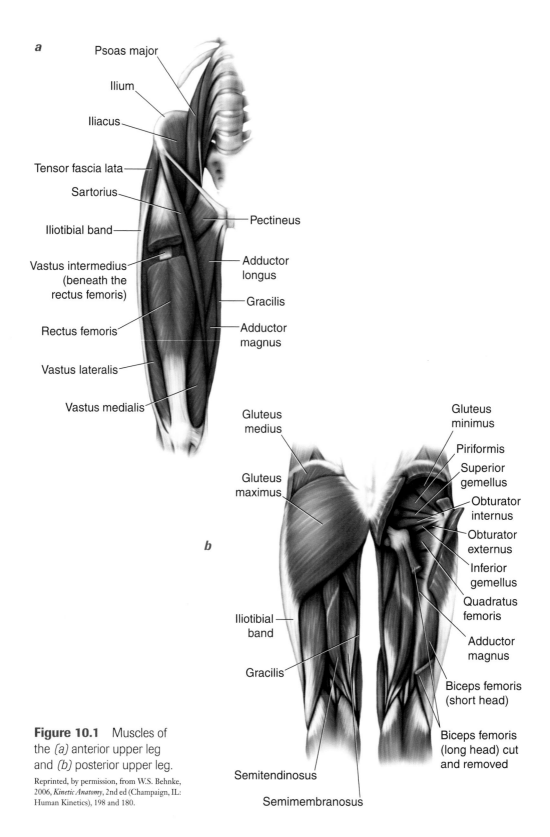

**Figure 10.1** Muscles of the *(a)* anterior upper leg and *(b)* posterior upper leg.

Reprinted, by permission, from W.S. Behnke, 2006, *Kinetic Anatomy*, 2nd ed (Champaign, IL: Human Kinetics), 198 and 180.

*c*

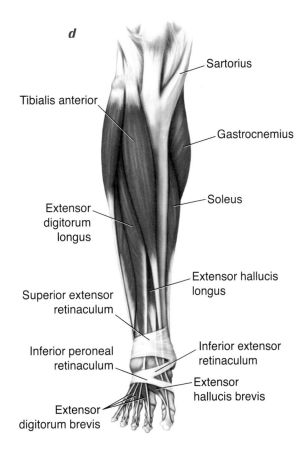

Plantaris

Gastrocnemius
(medial head)

Gastrocnemius
(lateral head)

*d*

Sartorius

Tibialis anterior

Gastrocnemius

Soleus

Extensor
digitorum
longus

Extensor hallucis
longus

Superior extensor
retinaculum

Inferior extensor
retinaculum

Inferior peroneal
retinaculum

Extensor
hallucis brevis

Extensor
digitorum brevis

**Figure 10.1**   Muscles of
the *(c)* posterior lower leg
and *(d)* anterior lower leg.

Reprinted, by permission, from W.S. Behnke,
2006, *Kinetic Anatomy*, 2nd ed (Champaign,
IL: Human Kinetics), 202 and 216.

# Front Squat

quadriceps, gluteals, hamstrings

➤ **Starting Position**

1. Using a squat rack, adjust the height of the rack to a level where you can remove and replace the bar without rising up on the toes.

2. Hold the bar with a grip slightly wider than shoulder width, and let the shoulders come forward to make a "shelf" to support the bar in front of the body.

3. Lift the bar off the rack, with the feet directly below the bar, then take one step back, and place the feet about shoulder-width apart, with the toes pointed slightly outward. Use the elbows to support the bar.

**Spotter**

☐ Before the lift, ask the lifter how he or she would prefer to be spotted—from the bar, the chest, or the arms. When spotting for female lifters, be especially sensitive to their spotting preference.

☐ Load the bar evenly and use collars.

☐ Ask the lifter how many repetitions he or she will be attempting to complete.

☐ While the bar is still in the rack, stand behind the lifter as he or she gets into position.

☐ Once the lifter steps away from the rack with the bar, move as close to the lifter as possible without touching him or her.

☐ Keep the hands in a ready position near the bar while the lifter lowers and raises the weight.

☐ Assist the lifter with returning the bar to the rack once the set is completed (or when the lifter needs assistance). This is typically done by holding the bar with the hands and guiding it back to the rack.

## ▼ Action

4.  Keeping the back neutral and the chest up throughout the movement, let the hips move backward, then immediately bend at the knees.

5.  Lower until the crease formed at the hips is horizontally aligned with the top of the knees. Keep the knees over, but not beyond, the toes.

6.  For each repetition, return to the starting position by following the same path used for the downward movement. Prevent the hips from moving backward or rising faster than the bar during the upward movement phase.

Keep the back flat and the spine in a neutral position.

Avoid bending at the knees to initiate the movement.

# Back Squat

quadriceps, gluteals, hamstrings

◀ **Starting Position**

1. Using a squat rack, adjust the height of the rack to a level where you can remove and replace the bar without rising up on the toes.

2. Hold the bar with a grip slightly wider than shoulder width, and place the bar on the upper portion of the back.

3. Lift the bar off the rack, with the feet directly below the bar, then take one step back, and place the feet about shoulder-width apart, with the toes pointed slightly outward.

**Spotter**

☐ Before the lift, ask the lifter how he or she would prefer to be spotted—from the bar, the chest, or the arms. When spotting for female lifters, be especially sensitive to their spotting preference.

☐ Load the bar evenly and use collars.

☐ Ask the lifter how many repetitions he or she will be attempting to complete.

☐ While the bar is still in the rack, stand behind the lifter while he or she gets into position.

☐ Once the lifter steps away from the rack with the bar, move as close to the lifter as possible without touching him or her.

☐ Keep the hands in a ready position near the bar while the lifter lowers and raises the weight.

☐ Assist the lifter with returning the bar to the rack once the set is completed (or when the lifter needs assistance). This is typically done by holding the bar with the hands and guiding it back to the rack.

## ▼ Action

4. Keeping the back neutral and the chest up throughout the movement, let the hips move backward then immediately bend at the knees.

5. Lower until the crease formed at the hips is horizontally aligned with the top of the knees. Keep the knees over, but not beyond, the toes.

6. For each repetition, return to the starting position by following the same path used for the downward movement. Prevent the hips from moving backward or rising faster than the bar during the upward movement phase.

Keep the back flat and the spine in a neutral position.

Avoid bending at the knees to initiate the movement.

You can also perform this lift using dumbbells.

# Leg Press

quadriceps, hamstrings, gluteals

### ▲ Machine Setup

1. Adjust the starting position so that the knees are bent to about 90 degrees.
2. Position the feet on the foot plate, about hip-width apart, with the toes slightly pointed out.
3. Select the appropriate resistance on the weight stack.
4. Position the body with the chest up, the head back, and the back flat against the back pad.

### ▼ Action

5. Pushing the foot plate, extend the knees and the hips until they have almost reached complete extension.
6. Slowly return to the starting position without letting the resistance rest on the weight stack between reps.

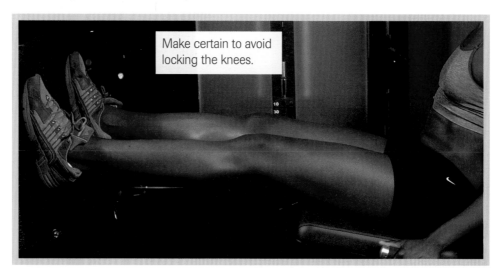

Make certain to avoid locking the knees.

# Dumbbell Front Lunge

quadriceps, gluteals, hamstrings

### ➤ Starting Position
1. Stand with the feet shoulder-width apart, and hold a dumbbell at each side.

### ▼ Action
2. Keeping the torso vertical, take a large step forward.
3. Once the front foot makes contact with the floor, move the body more downward than forward until the knee of the rear leg is just above the floor. This will ensure that the front knee does not move beyond the toes of the front foot.
4. For each repetition, return to the starting position by following the same path used for the downward movement.

Avoid swinging the dumbbells.

Keep the back flat in a neutral spine position.

# Dumbbell Reverse Lunge

quadriceps, gluteals, hamstrings

### ➤ Starting Position
1. Stand with the feet shoulder-width apart, and hold a dumbbell at each side.

### ▼ Action
2. Keeping the torso vertical, take a large step backward.
3. Once the rear foot makes contact with the ground, move downward so that the knee of the rear leg is just above the floor.
4. Ensure that the front knee does not move beyond the toes of the front foot.
5. For each repetition, return to the starting position by following the same path used for the downward movement.

Avoid swinging the dumbbells.

Keep the back flat in a neutral spine position.

# Dumbbell Side Lunge

quadriceps, gluteals, hamstrings

### ➤ Starting Position

1. Stand with the feet shoulder-width apart, and hold two dumbbells in front of the torso.

### ▼ Action

2. Keeping the torso vertical, take a large step to the side such that the stepping leg is at a 45-degree angle relative to the body.

3. Once the stepping foot makes contact with the ground, move more downward than forward. This will ensure that the knee of the stepping leg stays directly over the toes of the stepping foot.

4. The midpoint is reached when the knee of the opposite leg is just above the floor.

5. For each repetition, return to the starting position by following the same path used for the downward movement.

Keep the back flat in a neutral spine position; avoid leaning too far forward in the downward phase.

Avoid swinging the dumbbells.

# Dumbbell Step-Up

quadriceps, gluteals, hamstrings

◀ **Starting Position**

1. Choose a step or box high enough that when you step on it, you form a 90-degree angle at the knee and hip.

2. Stand with one foot on top of the box, and hold a dumbbell at each side.

Keep the back flat and in a neutral spine position; avoid leaning too far forward in the upward phase.

➤ **Action**

3. Keeping the torso upright, lean slightly forward to initiate the movement of the lead leg. Lift upward until both feet are on the box, minimizing the effort of the rear leg.

4. For each repetition, return to the starting position by following the same path used for the upward movement and gently landing the rear foot on the floor. You may repeat the exercise on the same leg to complete the set or alternate legs with each repetition.

Avoid swinging the dumbbells.

# Romanian Deadlift

## hamstrings

### ➤ Starting Position

1. Stand with the feet shoulder-width apart, the knees slightly bent, and the back flat in a neutral position.
2. Hold a bar against the thighs with a closed overhand grip.

### ▼ Action

3. "Press" the hips slightly backward, letting the bar move downward until you feel a slight stretch in the hamstrings.
4. For each repetition, return to the starting position by following the same path as used for the downward movement.

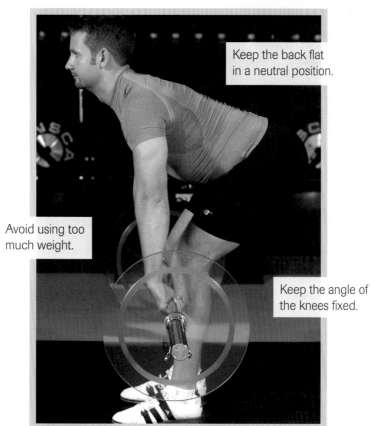

Keep the back flat in a neutral position.

Avoid using too much weight.

Keep the angle of the knees fixed.

# Deadlift

quadriceps, gluteals, hamstrings

> **Starting Position**

1. Stand with the feet shoulder-width apart, the knees slightly bent, and the back flat in a neutral position.

2. Bend at the waist so that the torso is at 45 degrees, and drop the arms forward so that they are straight and vertical.

3. Grasp the bar using one overhand and one underhand grip, with the hands slightly wider than shoulder width.

**◄ Action**

4. Using the legs, lift the bar off the floor to the knees. Keep the hips low and the chest up, maintaining the 45-degree angle.

5. Once the bar reaches the top of the knees, simply move to an upright position.

6. For each repetition, return to the starting position by following the same path used for the upward movement.

Keep the back flat.

Avoid using too much weight.

Avoid raising the hips in advance of the bar.

# Seated Leg Curl

## hamstrings

### ➤ Machine Setup

1. Sit down and adjust the back pad so that the knees line up with the machine's axis of rotation.
2. Adjust the ankle pad so that it is positioned just under the ankles.
3. Select the appropriate resistance on the weight stack.
4. Position the body with the back straight and the head up; grasp the handles.

### ▼ Action

5. Curl the pad down by flexing the knees in a slow, controlled motion until the heels are underneath the seat and past 90 degrees.
6. Slowly return to the starting position without letting the resistance rest on the weight stack between repetitions.

# Leg Extension

## quadriceps

### ➤ Machine Setup

1. Adjust the back pad so that the knee joints align with the machine's axis of rotation.
2. Adjust the leg pad to a comfortable position just above the ankles.
3. Adjust the starting position to a 90-degree bend of the knees.
4. Select the appropriate resistance on the weight stack.
5. Position the body with the back straight and the head up; grasp the handles.

### ▼ Action

6. Extend the knees in a slow, controlled motion until the knees are fully extended.
7. Slowly return to the starting position without letting the resistance rest on the weight stack between repetitions.

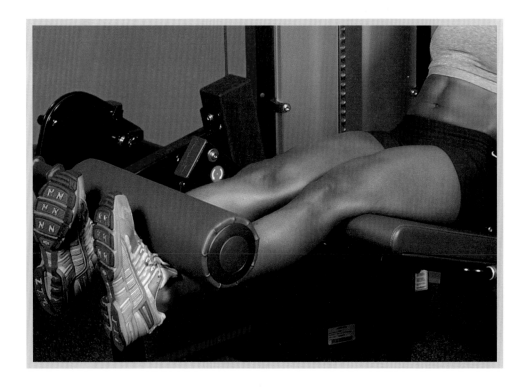

# Seated Hip Adduction

hip adductors

➤ **Machine Setup**

1. Sit down with the feet on the foot pegs so that the knees are bent at 90 degrees; you should feel a slight stretch on the inner thighs.
2. Adjust the start position if necessary.
3. Select the appropriate resistance on the weight stack.

▼ **Action**

4. Hold the handles, and with a slow, controlled motion, move the pads inward by pushing with the knees until the pads touch.
5. Slowly return to the starting position without letting the resistance rest on the weight stack between repetitions.

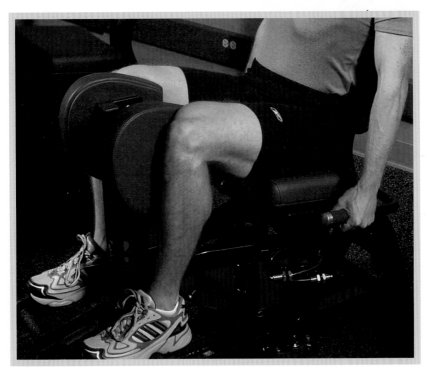

# Seated Hip Abduction

hip abductors

### ➤ Machine Setup

1. Sit down with the feet on the foot pegs so that the knees are bent at 90 degrees.

2. Adjust the start position if necessary.

3. Select the appropriate resistance on the weight stack.

### ▼ Action

4. Hold the handles, and with a slow, controlled motion, move the pads out by pushing with the knees until the legs reach the farthest outward position.

5. Slowly return to the starting position without letting the resistance rest on the weight stack between repetitions.

# Standing Calf Raise

## gastrocnemius

### ➤ Starting Position

1. Stand on one leg on a step or platform, holding a dumbbell out to the same side as the weighted leg.
2. Keep the body upright for the duration of the movement.
3. Keep the knee of the weighted leg straight throughout the movement, and keep the ankle fully flexed in the down position.

Maintain an upright body position and a straight knee.

Fully extend the ankle.

Avoid bouncing in the bottom position.

### ◄ Action

4. Rise upward by extending fully at the ankle.
5. For each repetition, return to the starting position by following the same path used for the upward movement.

You can work the soleus by performing this same exercise in a seated position with the hips and knees at a 90-degree angle and a weight plate on your thighs for resistance.

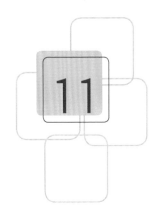

# Torso Exercises

Michael Barnes and Keith E. Cinea

The musculature of the torso (figure 11.1, *a* and *b*) serves several functions, including stabilizing the spine and assisting in transferring forces generated by the lower body to the arms. You can think of the muscles of the torso as the ones that connect the lower body muscles to the upper body muscles.

Strength and conditioning professionals and health care professionals often prescribe exercises like the ones in this chapter for rehabilitation and general strengthening. Abdominal crunches (page 232) are effective for training one specific muscle group, but you need to perform several different movements to more completely train the other muscles of the torso. This chapter offers many exercises at varying levels of difficulty. Along with performing torso exercises, following a proper diet may have you buying new clothes or even admiring your own six-pack in the mirror. Some of the exercises for the torso or core area rely on a stability ball (see pages 236 to 241). When using a stability ball, select one that is the proper size for your body. When you are seated on the ball, your hips and knees should both be at about 90-degree angles. Also be certain that the stability ball is inflated to the proper size before using it. If the ball is under- or overinflated, serious injuries could result. Table 11.1 provides a general guide for finding the right-size ball based on your height.

**Table 11.1    Stability Ball Sizing Guidelines**

| If your body height is | You need a ball this size |
| --- | --- |
| Up to 4'10" (147 cm) | Small: 45 cm (18") |
| 4'10" to 5'5" (147 to 165 cm) | Medium: 55 cm (22") |
| 5'5" to 6'0" (165 to 183 cm) | Large: 65 cm (26") |
| 6'0" to 6'5" (183 to 196 cm) | X-Large: 75 cm (30") |
| Over 6'5" (196 cm) | XX-Large: 85 cm (33") |

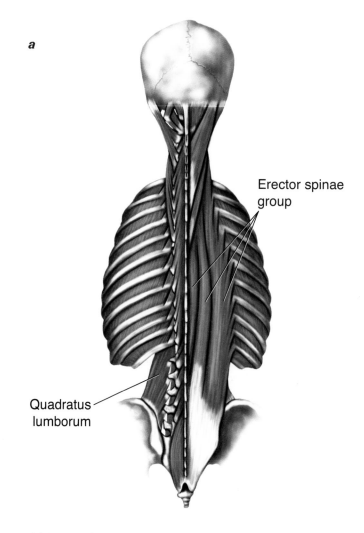

*a*

Erector spinae group

Quadratus lumborum

**Figure 11.1**    Major muscles of the torso, including *(a)* the muscles of the lower back.

Reprinted, by permission, from W.S. Behnke, 2006, *Kinetic Anatomy*, 2nd ed (Champaign, IL: Human Kinetics), 135.

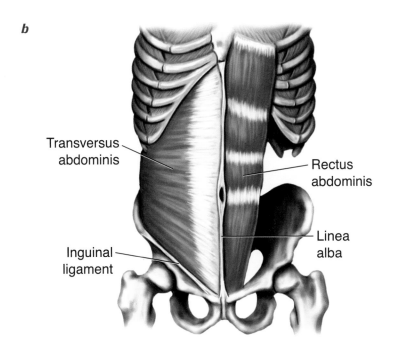

*b*

Transversus abdominis

Rectus abdominis

Linea alba

Inguinal ligament

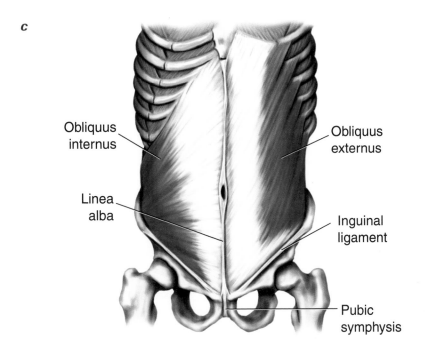

*c*

Obliquus internus

Obliquus externus

Linea alba

Inguinal ligament

Pubic symphysis

**Figure 11.1** Major muscles of the torso, including *(b* and *c)* the abdominal muscles.

Reprinted, by permission, from W.S. Behnke, 2006, *Kinetic Anatomy*, 2nd ed (Champaign, IL: Human Kinetics), 132.

# Abdominal Crunch

rectus abdominis

## ▲ Starting Position

1. Lie on the floor with the fingertips lightly touching each side of the head.
2. Bend the knees to place the feet flat on the floor, and lift the head off the floor.

## ▼ Action

3. Keeping the feet flat on the floor, curl the torso off the floor, moving the head and shoulders toward the thighs until the upper back is off the floor.
4. Return to the starting position following the same path used for the upward movement.

Curl all the way up until the upper back is off the floor.

Keep the feet flat on the floor throughout the movement.

You can turn this crunch into a sit-up by curling the torso upward as far as you can.

# 90–90 Crunch

## rectus abdominis

### ▲ Starting Position

1. Lie on your back on the floor with the feet on a bench to allow for a 90-degree bend at the knees and hips.
2. With the fingertips at each side of the head, lift the head off the floor.

### ▼ Action

3. Keeping the feet in position on the bench, curl the torso off the floor, moving the head and shoulders toward the thighs until the upper back is off the floor.
4. Return to the starting position following the same path used for the upward movement.

Curl all the way up until the upper back is off the floor.

Keep the feet on the bench throughout the movement.

# Ankle Touch

rectus abdominis

### ▲ Starting Position

1. Lie on the floor and bend the knees to place the feet flat on the floor.
2. Place the arms to the sides, and lift the head off the floor.

### ▼ Action

3. Keeping the feet flat on the floor, curl the torso off the floor, moving the hands until they touch the ankles.
4. Return to the starting position following the same path used for the upward movement.

Curl until you touch the ankles or until you cannot move any farther.

Keep the feet flat on the floor throughout the movement.

# Machine Abdominal Crunch

## rectus abdominis

### ➤ Machine Setup

1. Adjust the seat height so the chest pad is positioned at mid chest.
2. Using the adjustment knob located on the machine cam, adjust the exercise arm downward for more entry room, then sit down.
3. Position the feet behind the lower roller pads.
4. Select the appropriate resistance on the weight stack.
5. Use the adjustment knob to change the starting position for the desired range of motion.
6. Hold the handles.
7. Keep the chest up and the shoulders back.

### ▼ Action

8. Contract the abdominal muscles by bending the torso downward (about 45 degrees) in a crunch motion.
9. Return to the starting position without letting the resistance rest on the weight stack between repetitions.

Use caution if you have past or present lower back injuries.

Beginning the exercise from a slightly extended spinal position is a good way to challenge the abdominal muscles.

# Stability Ball Crunch

rectus abdominis

**◄ Starting Position**

1. Start in a seated position on the ball and roll forward until the middle of the back is supported on the ball.

2. Keep the feet flat on the floor and place the fingertips at each side of the head.

**▼ Action**

3. Keeping the feet flat on the floor, curl the torso off the ball by moving the head and shoulders upward until the upper back is off the ball.

4. Return to the starting position following the same path used for the upward movement.

Avoid rolling on the ball.

Keep the feet flat on the floor throughout the movement.

You can work the obliques by performing this same movement while lying with the side of the torso on the ball and then curling the torso upward.

# Roll-Out

rectus abdominis

▲ **Starting Position**

1. Kneel on the floor and place the forearms on the ball.
2. Position the feet slightly wider than shoulder width.

▼ **Action**

3. Reach forward and roll out on the forearms until the movement becomes too difficult for you to go any farther forward, or until the body is fully extended.
4. Return to the starting position following the same path used for the outward movement.

Maintain a neutral spine position.

Keep the abdominal muscles tight.

# Jackknife

rectus abdominis

## ▲ Starting Position

1. Start at the side of the ball and place one leg at a time on top of the ball until both upper shins are in contact with the ball.
2. Support the body with the hands on the floor, slightly wider than shoulder width.

## ▼ Action

3. Keeping the feet together, slowly pull the feet and knees in toward the torso until they are fully drawn in.
4. Slowly return to the starting position following the same path used for the inward movement.

Maintain a neutral spine position.

Keep the abdominal muscles tight.

Avoid letting the ball move to the side of the legs or letting the hips drop.

# Stability Ball Push-Up

rectus abdominis

### ▲ Starting Position

1. Start at the side of the ball and place one foot at a time on top of the ball so that both feet are in contact with the ball.
2. Support the body with the hands on the floor, slightly wider than shoulder width.

### ▼ Action

3. Bend at the elbows and shoulders, slowly lowering the torso until the head is just above the floor.
4. Slowly return in the same path used for the downward movement.

Maintain a neutral spine position.

Avoid letting the ball move to the side of the legs or letting the hips drop.

Keep the abdominal muscles tight.

Although this movement actively uses the chest and triceps, the anterior muscles of the torso are extremely involved in an effort to stabilize the body and control the movement.

# Medicine Ball Overhead Reach

rectus abdominis

## ➤ Starting Position

1. Sit on a stability ball (slightly to the front of the top of the ball), and hold a medicine ball directly in front of the torso with the arms straight.
2. Keep the torso at about a 45-degree angle.

Avoid using a medicine ball that is too heavy.

Keep the abdominal muscles tight.

## ◄ Action

3. Keeping the arms straight and the spine neutral, slowly raise the medicine ball upward until it is directly overhead or until it reaches a level just before the torso position cannot be maintained.
4. Slowly return to the starting position following the same path used for the upward movement.

Although this movement actively uses the shoulders, the muscles of the torso are extremely involved in an effort to stabilize the body and control the movement.

# Stability Ball Dumbbell Overhead Fly

## rectus abdominis

➤ **Starting Position**

1. Lie back on the stability ball (keeping the hips near the top of the ball), and hold dumbbells approximately above the chin with the arms straight.

2. Keep the torso at about a 45-degree angle and maintain a neutral spine position.

▼ **Action**

3. Keeping both arms straight, slowly lower one arm directly to the side until the hand reaches shoulder height.

4. Slowly return to the starting position following the same path used for the downward movement.

5. Alternate arms with each repetition.

Avoid using dumbbells that are too heavy.

Keep the abdominal muscles tight and avoid rotating the torso.

Although this movement actively uses the shoulders, the muscles of the torso are extremely involved in an effort to stabilize the body and control the movement.

# 90–90 Alternate Touch

rectus abdominis, internal obliques, external obliques

### ▲ Starting Position

1. Lie on your back on the floor with the feet on a bench to allow for a 90-degree bend at the knees and hips.
2. With the fingertips placed lightly behind the head, lift the head off the floor.

### ▼ Action

3. Keeping the feet on the bench, twist the torso by leading with the shoulder toward the opposite knee until the upper back is off the floor.
4. Return to the starting position following the same path used for the upward movement.
5. Alternate side to side with each repetition.

Rotate until the upper back is off the floor.

Keep the feet on the bench throughout the movement.

# Figure-Four Touch

rectus abdominis, internal obliques, external obliques

## ▲ Starting Position

1. Lie on the floor and create a figure four by crossing the legs.
2. Place the fingers of the right hand behind the head but avoid using them to pull in any way during the movement.
3. Raise the head off the floor.

## ▼ Action

4. Keeping the one foot firmly on the floor, rotate the torso by leading with the elbow toward the opposite knee. Rotate until the upper back is off the floor.
5. Return to the starting position following the same path used for the upward movement.

Avoid pulling the head with the arm.

Keep the one foot on the floor throughout the movement.

# Outside Calf Touch

rectus abdominis, internal obliques, external obliques

## ▲ Starting Position

1. Lie on the floor and bend the knees so the feet are flat on the floor.
2. Place the hands on top of one another, reaching toward the knees.
3. Lift the head off the floor.

## ▼ Action

4. Keeping the feet flat on the floor, curl and rotate the torso off the floor, moving the hands toward the outside of one calf until they touch it.
5. Return to the starting position following the same path used for the upward movement.
6. Alternate from one side to the other with each repetition.

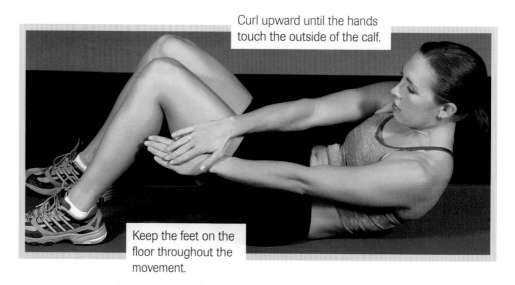

Curl upward until the hands touch the outside of the calf.

Keep the feet on the floor throughout the movement.

# Prone Plank

rectus abdominis, internal obliques, external obliques

## ▼ Position

1. Lying facedown with the feet straight behind, bend the elbows to about 90 degrees and push off the floor.
2. Keep the spine neutral and align the head with the torso.
3. Hold the position until failure or for the desired duration.

Keep the spine neutral by activating the abdominal muscles.

Focus on the lower portion of the abdominal muscles.

# Side Plank

internal obliques, external obliques

### ▼ Position

1. While lying on your side, bend one elbow to about 90 degrees and rise off the floor.
2. Keep the spine neutral and align the head with the torso.
3. Hold the position until failure or for the desired duration.

Keep the spine neutral by activating the internal and external obliques.

Focus on the lower side of the torso.

# Torso Rotation

internal obliques, external obliques

### ➤ Machine Setup

1. Adjust the seat height so that the hips and knees are at 90-degree angles.
2. Adjust the back pad so that the head is directly under the machine's axis of rotation.
3. Select the appropriate resistance on the weight stack.
4. Adjust the starting point so that the weight stack is slightly elevated from the bottom position upon starting the exercise.
5. Position the body in an upright posture with the chest up, the back flat, and the abdominal muscles tight.
6. Grasp the handles.

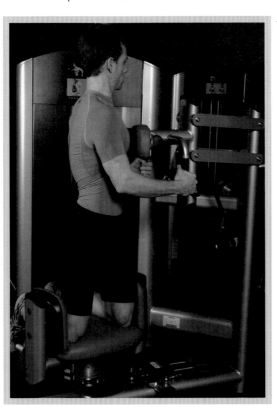

### ◄ Action

7. Rotate the hips to the side in a slow, controlled motion until they are facing the direction opposite the starting position.
8. Slowly return to the starting position without letting the resistance rest on the weight stack between repetitions.
9. Repeat the motion while maintaining proper body positioning.

# Stability Ball Shoulder Roll

erector spinae, internal obliques, external obliques

### ▲ Starting Position

1. Start in a seated position on the ball and roll forward until the upper back is supported on the ball and the knees are bent at 90 degrees.
2. Keep the feet flat on the floor, slightly wider than shoulder width.
3. Cross the arms over the chest.

### ▼ Action

4. Keeping the feet flat on the floor, rotate the torso by rolling up on the ball with one shoulder until the upper back is off the ball.
5. Return to the starting position following the same path used for the upward movement.
6. Alternate from one side to the other.

Curl all the way up until the upper back is off the ball.

Keep the feet flat on the floor throughout the movement.

# Machine Back Extension

## erector spinae

### ➤ Machine Setup

1. Adjust the foot plate so that the knees are bent.
2. Adjust the start position on the back pad to select the desired range of motion.
3. Push the hips back against the lumbar pad.
4. Select the appropriate resistance on the weight stack.

### ◄ Action

5. Grasping the handles, slowly extend the torso in a controlled motion until the lower back contacts the lumbar pad.
6. Slowly return to the starting position without letting the resistance rest on the weight stack between repetitions.

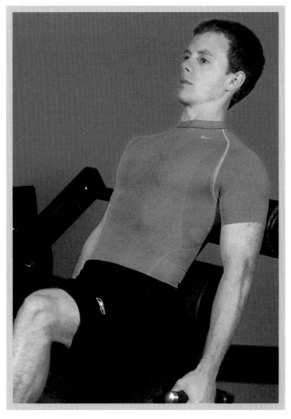

# Back Extension and Hyperextension

erector spinae, gluteals, hamstrings

### ➤ Machine Setup

1. Adjust the foot-position bar so that the upper pad rests on the hips and upper thighs.

2. Position yourself in the machine so that the legs are nearly straight and the torso is approximately 90 degrees from the legs.

3. Cross the arms over the chest.

© Jumpfoto

Avoid exaggerating the range of motion and rounding the back and shoulders during the movement.

Maintain a flat back and a neutral spine position.

© Jumpfoto

### ◄ Action

4. Extend at the hips, raising the torso in a controlled and smooth motion until it forms a straight line with the legs.

5. Return to the starting position following the same path used for the upward movement.

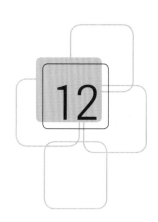

# Explosive Movements

Michael Barnes and Keith E. Cinea

Explosive weight training has many advantages for lifters at all levels. Doing explosive exercises will result in the ability to produce force more rapidly. The ability to produce force more rapidly can be especially advantageous for athletes. Sports such as basketball, volleyball, and football all involve explosive, powerful movements. That is, they require the athlete to move very quickly and forcefully in order to jump, accelerate, or defend against an opponent. By performing the exercises listed here, your explosive ability will be maximized. This increased explosive ability also has implications for the activities of everyday life in which speed of movement is beneficial, such as lifting a child, emptying a wheelbarrow, or enjoying a brisk walk.

Performing ground-based explosive movements such as the ones described in this chapter offers the distinct advantage of maximizing your ability to produce explosive power by pushing off the ground. Since almost all sports require some measure of explosive ability while the feet are in contact with the ground, it follows that performing specific activities of that nature in training will enhance sport performance. Many activities of everyday life are done when the feet are in contact with the ground while a force is transferred through the body, as is the case when closing a car door or throwing a ball. During such activities, muscles coordinate themselves and work together to perform the movement.

There are many explosive resistance movements. Some explosive movements are specialized and geared to enhance sport performance. The following five explosive movements detailed here were selected because they are the most fundamental in nature. When properly employed, explosive exercises are safe and likely to reduce the risk of injury during sports and everyday activities of life.

# Power Clean

gluteals, hamstrings, quadriceps, gastrocnemius, soleus, deltoids, trapezius

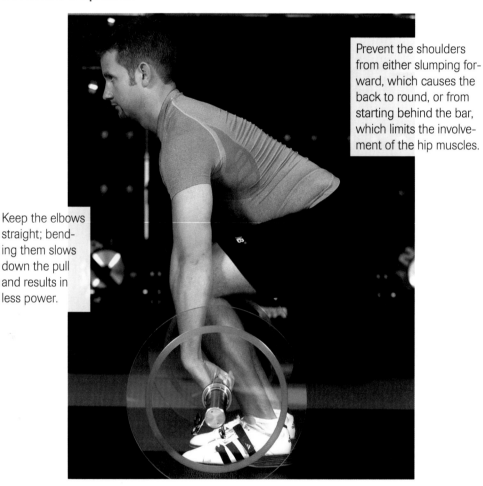

Prevent the shoulders from either slumping forward, which causes the back to round, or from starting behind the bar, which limits the involvement of the hip muscles.

Keep the elbows straight; bending them slows down the pull and results in less power.

## ▲ Starting Position

1. Approach the barbell on the floor and take an approximately shoulder-width overhand grip on the bar.
2. Keep the arms straight, the wrists slightly flexed, and the elbows locked and rotated outward.
3. Stand with the feet hip-width apart and pull the barbell against the shins.
4. Pull the shoulders, elevate the chest, and keep the eyes looking forward.
5. Squat down.
6. Keep the shoulders in front of the barbell and the weight on the forward half of the feet.

## ➤ First Pull

7. Keeping the back flat and the arms straight, extend the hips and knees to lift the barbell off the ground to the mid thigh. Avoid jerking the bar off the ground and rounding the back. Also avoid locking out the knees when moving the barbell from below knee height to mid-thigh height.

8. Look straight ahead and raise the shoulders and hips at the same speed.

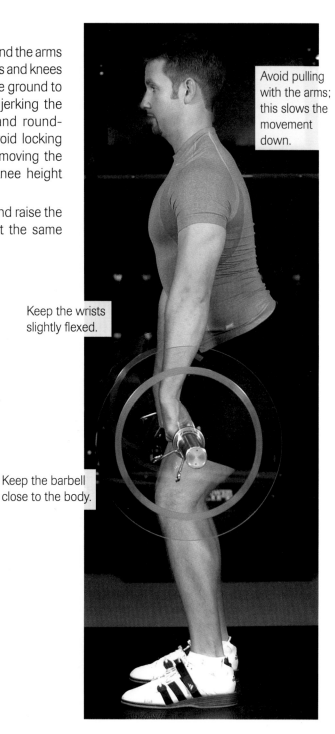

Avoid pulling with the arms; this slows the movement down.

Keep the wrists slightly flexed.

Keep the barbell close to the body.

*(continued)*

# Power Clean *(continued)*

### ➤ Second Pull

9. Keeping the arms straight and the wrists slightly flexed, violently extend the hips, rise up on the toes, and elevate the shoulders explosively.

10. Continue looking straight ahead as you pull the barbell as high as possible, to around chest level, without using the muscles in the arms.

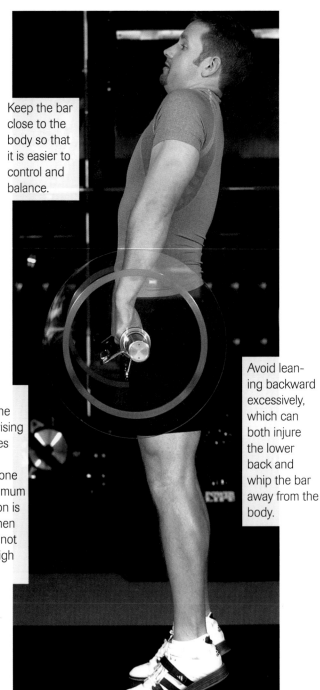

Keep the bar close to the body so that it is easier to control and balance.

Beware of executing the shrug and rising onto the toes too early. If these are done before maximum hip extension is achieved, then the bar will not be pulled high enough.

Avoid leaning backward excessively, which can both injure the lower back and whip the bar away from the body.

Keep the elbows high and pointing nearly straight forward.

Avoid moving the knees forward while entering the squat.

Avoid receiving the bar while on the toes; this will cause a loss of balance.

▲ **Receiving Position**

11. When the bar has reached its maximum height, drop under it into a quarter squat, lifting the elbows up and under the bar. If this is done properly, the bar is received on the front of the shoulders at the same time that you reach the quarter squat. The shoulders should not slump forward.

*(continued)*

255

# Power Clean *(continued)*

### ➤ Ending Position

12. Keeping the elbows high and the chest elevated, stand straight up.

Avoid allowing the shoulders to slump forward.

# High Pull

gluteals, hamstrings, quadriceps, gastrocnemius, soleus, deltoids, trapezius

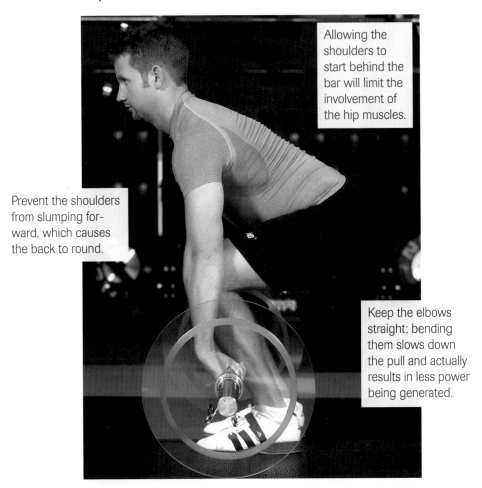

Allowing the shoulders to start behind the bar will limit the involvement of the hip muscles.

Prevent the shoulders from slumping forward, which causes the back to round.

Keep the elbows straight; bending them slows down the pull and actually results in less power being generated.

## ▲ Starting Position

1. Approach the barbell on the floor and take an approximately shoulder-width overhand grip on the bar.
2. Keep the arms straight, the wrists slightly flexed, and the elbows locked and rotated outward.
3. Stand with the feet hip-width apart and pull the barbell against the shins.
4. Pull the shoulders back, elevate the chest, and keep the eyes looking forward.
5. Squat down.
6. Keep the shoulders in front of the barbell and the weight on the forward half of the feet.

## High Pull *(continued)*

Keep the shoulders from slumping forward.

Keep the wrists slightly flexed and avoid pulling with the arms.

Keep the barbell close to the body.

▲ **First Pull**

7. Keeping the back flat and the arms straight, extend the hips and knees to lift the barbell off the ground to the mid thigh in a slow and controlled manner. Avoid jerking the bar off the ground which will cause the back to round. Avoid locking out the knees when moving the barbell from below knee height to mid-thigh height.

8. Look straight ahead and raise the shoulders and hips at the same speed.

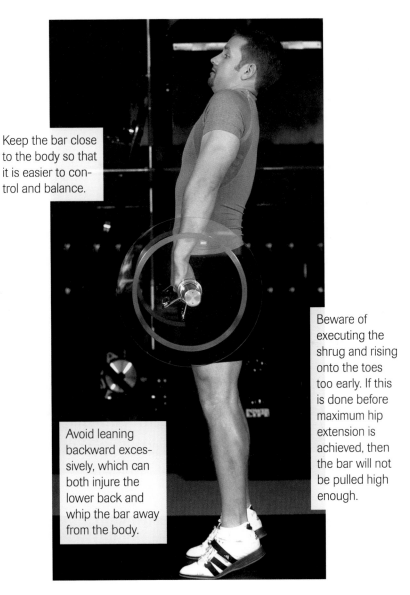

Keep the bar close to the body so that it is easier to control and balance.

Beware of executing the shrug and rising onto the toes too early. If this is done before maximum hip extension is achieved, then the bar will not be pulled high enough.

Avoid leaning backward excessively, which can both injure the lower back and whip the bar away from the body.

▲ **Second Pull**

9. Keeping the arms straight and the wrists slightly flexed with the bar at mid-thigh level, violently extend the hips, rise up on the toes, and elevate the shoulders explosively.

*(continued)*

# High Pull *(continued)*

▲ **Second Pull** *(continued)*

10. Continue looking straight ahead as you pull the barbell as high as possible, to about chest level, without using the muscles in the arms.

## ▲ Ending Position

11. When the bar has reached its maximum height, around the level of the chest, let the bar return to a resting position on the thighs.

12. Once the bar is on the thighs return it to the floor by squatting down with the back flat and the spine in neutral position.

# Hang Clean

gluteals, hamstrings, quadriceps, gastrocnemius, soleus, deltoids, trapezius

Prevent the shoulders from starting behind the bar because this limits the involvement of the hip muscles.

Avoid locking the knees; this will place more stress on the lower back.

Prevent the shoulders from slumping forward, causing the back to round.

## ▲ Starting Position

1. Approach the barbell on the floor and take an approximately shoulder-width overhand (closed) grip on the bar (see pages 161 and 252).

2. Keep the arms straight, the wrists slightly flexed, and the elbows locked and rotated outward.

3. Stand with the feet hip-width apart and lift the bar from the floor along the shins toward the knees.

4. Pull the shoulders back so that they are in front of the barbell, elevate the chest, and bear the weight on the middle of both feet.

Look straight ahead.

Avoid leaning backward excessively, which can both injure the lower back and whip the bar away from the body.

Beware of executing the shrug and rising onto the toes too early. If this is done before maximum hip extension is achieved, then the bar will not be pulled high enough.

## ▲ The Pull

5. Keeping the arms straight and the wrists slightly flexed, violently extend the hips, rise up on the toes, and elevate the shoulders explosively.

6. Pull the barbell as high as possible without using the muscles in the arms and keep the bar close to the body so that it is easier to control and balance.

*(continued)*

# Hang Clean *(continued)*

Keep the elbows high and pointing nearly straight forward.

Avoid moving the knees forward while entering the squat.

Avoid receiving the bar while on the toes; this will cause a loss of balance.

## ▲ Receiving Position

7. When the bar has reached its maximum height, around the level of the chest, drop under it into a quarter squat and lift the elbows up and under the bar. If this is done properly, the bar is received on the front of the shoulders at the same time that the quarter squat position is reached. Avoid allowing the shoulders to slump forward; this will make it more difficult to control the bar and could place more strain on the lower back.

Avoid letting the elbows drop down.

Avoid allowing the shoulders to slump forward.

Avoid allowing the hips to rise up faster than the shoulders; this will make bar control very difficult.

## ▲ Ending Position

8. From the quarter squat position, stand straight up, keeping the elbows high and elevating the chest.

# Push Press

gluteals, hamstrings, quadriceps, gastrocnemius, soleus, deltoids

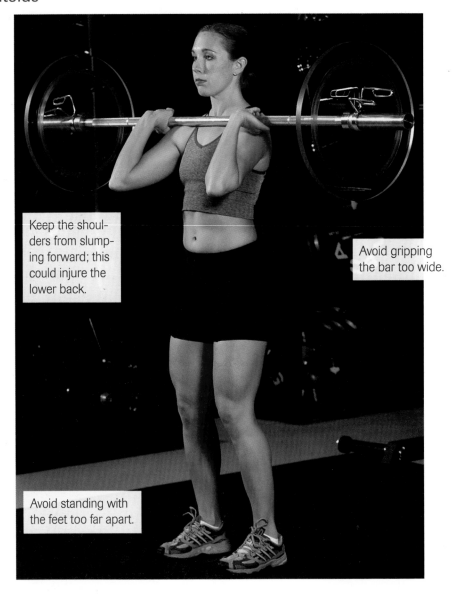

Keep the shoulders from slumping forward; this could injure the lower back.

Avoid gripping the bar too wide.

Avoid standing with the feet too far apart.

## ▲ Starting Position

1. Begin by holding the bar on the front of the shoulders with a shoulder-width grip, palms facing forward.
2. Stand with the feet hip-width apart and the eyes looking straight ahead.
3. Pull the shoulders back, elevate the chest.

Do not allow the shoulders to slump forward. This will make the bar harder to control.

Do not allow the bar to leave the shoulders while dipping. This will cause the exercise to be more difficult to perform.

Avoid initiating the squat by pushing the knees forward; sit back into the squat and avoid squatting too deeply.

### ▲ The Dip

4. Keeping the weight on the heels and the barbell on the shoulders, move into a quarter squat by pushing the hips back, flexing the knees, and keeping the chest up.

*(continued)*

## Push Press *(continued)*

Keep the chest up.

Drive straight up; moving forward or backward will throw the bar in that direction.

▲ **The Drive**

5. Without pausing at the bottom of the squat, push upward with the legs and shoulders. The act of driving upward will force the bar up off the shoulders.

Be sure to align the bar, the shoulders, and the hips vertically.

▲ **Ending Position**

6. When the bar has reached its greatest height from the drive, continue to press until the arms are extended and the barbell is in line with the hips.

# Push Jerk

gluteals, hamstrings, quadriceps, gastrocnemius, soleus, deltoids

Avoid taking too wide a grip on the bar.

Keep the shoulders from slumping forward; this could injure the lower back.

Avoid standing with the feet too far apart.

## ▲ Starting Position

1. Begin by standing straight with the feet hip-width apart and the bar on the front of the shoulders.

2. Take a shoulder-width grip on the bar, with the palms facing upward.

3. Elevate the chest, pull the shoulders back, and tuck the chin.

Keep the bar on the shoulders and keep the shoulders from slumping during the dip.

Avoid initiating the squat by pushing the knees forward; instead, sit back into the squat.

Avoid squatting too deeply.

**▲ The Dip**

4. Keeping the weight on the heels, the barbell on the shoulders, and the chest up, quickly move into a quarter squat by pushing the hips back and flexing the knees.

*(continued)*

271

## Push Jerk *(continued)*

Keep the chest up.

Make sure you drive straight up; driving forward or backward will throw the bar in that direction.

### ▲ The Drive

5. Without pausing at the bottom of the squat, explosively reverse directions, driving straight up with the legs until rising up onto the toes. The act of driving up will force the bar up off the shoulders.

Align the bar, the shoulders, and the hips vertically.

▲ **Ending Position**

6. When the bar has reached its greatest height from the drive, continue to press it until the arms are extended and the barbell is in line with the hips (slightly behind the head).

# PART IV

# Sample Programs

Regular participation in a strength training program offers numerous health and fitness rewards for most adults. Once thought of as a method of conditioning reserved for elite athletes, strength training is now recommended by professional health and fitness organizations and researchers as an effective means for adults of any age to enhance and maintain musculoskeletal health, functional ability, and quality of life. Strength training has become a popular mode of exercise that can be performed in health clubs, recreation centers, and homes. The key to safe and effective strength training is a well-designed program that involves the correct exercise technique (described in chapters 9 through 12), proper prescription of program variables (described in chapter 3), and a sensible progression to keep the workout effective and enjoyable (see chapter 7).

For a long time, coaches and trainers searched for the optimal combination of sets, repetitions, and exercises that would maximize gains in strength and muscle size. But now we know that a training program that works for one individual may not be effective for another. Thus, strength training programs need to be based on individual needs, goals, and abilities in order to maximize training outcomes, minimize the risk of injury, and increase the likelihood that strength training becomes a lifelong activity. The first step is to identify "at-risk" adults with medical ailments such as high blood pressure, heart disease, or diabetes who should obtain medical clearance before they begin a strength training program (see chapter 8). This important first step will ensure that participation in strength-building activities will be beneficial rather than harmful to those adults who are managing injuries or illnesses. Once an adult is cleared for participation by his or her health care provider, a personalized strength training program can be developed.

The second step is to identify realistic goals and a sensible starting point for each individual. Too often, adults begin strength training at a level that exceeds their current fitness level. Not only can this approach lead to excessive muscle soreness and nonadherence to the program, but it can also result in injury. Moreover, beginners often make dramatic improvements in muscle strength during the first few weeks of strength training; it doesn't make sense for beginners to participate in more advanced training programs, because strength gains will not be any greater and the likelihood of injury will increase. Since strength training programs should be both effective and realistic, the best approach is to design a training program that is consistent with a person's current fitness status and individualized goals.

In addition, when planning your training program, think about the time you have available for training, the equipment that is available to you, your strength training experience, and your health history. Consider the following questions before beginning a strength training program:

- ☐ Are there medical concerns that may limit or prevent your participation in a strength training program? Individuals with medical conditions such as heart disease, high blood pressure, diabetes, and arthritis should check with their physician or health care provider before they begin strength training.

- ☐ Do you currently participate in a strength training program? While individuals with no experience strength training should start with the beginner program, individuals who have been strength training regularly for more than two or three months may want to start at a higher level of training depending on their training experience and fitness goals.

- ☐ What type of strength training equipment is available at home or at your gym? There are advantages and disadvantages to using free weights (barbells), weight machines, and body weight exercises, but all modes of strength training can be effective provided that appropriate training guidelines are followed. The key is to choose a mode of training that is consistent with your needs, goals, and abilities.

- ☐ How much time do you have available for strength training during the week? A well-designed strength training program for a beginner can be completed in less than 30 minutes, whereas an advanced program may take longer than 60 minutes to finish. Strength training programs can be tailored to meet specific time requirements.

- ☐ What are your specific training goals? A strength training program for a beginner who wants to increase muscle strength is quite different from a program for an athlete who needs to enhance sport performance (see chapter 7). Since there is not one combination of sets and repetitions that will optimize gains for everyone, each individual must prioritize his or her training goals and then follow a program that is specifically designed to achieve those goals.

- ☐ Would individualized instruction from a qualified fitness professional be beneficial for you? It is a lot easier to develop good habits from the start than to try to break bad habits once they develop. Qualified fitness professionals can provide motivation, guidance, and instruction on safe exercise technique.

Once these questions are answered, you can design a safe, effective, and enjoyable strength training program that is consistent with personalized goals. As discussed in chapter 7, while there are many different program goals (e.g., to increase muscle strength, to reduce body fat, and to reduce stress), most beginner programs are designed to improve general fitness, strengthen connective tissue (tendons and ligaments), and build a foundation for more advanced workouts. These programs should be distinguished from more advanced training programs, which are typically designed to maximize gains in muscle strength, muscle power, and muscle size. Nevertheless, don't think of a beginner program as a simple, short-term workout. Strength training needs to be continued, progressed, and when necessary, modified in order to make continual gains in health and fitness. Otherwise, the training-induced gains from strength training begin to dissipate.

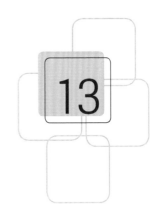

# Beginner Programs

Avery Faigenbaum and Jay Hoffman

Adults with no strength training experience and those who have not trained for several months or years should begin strength training by following a general preparation program in which the resistance is light and the focus is on learning proper exercise technique.

All too often, beginners do too much too soon. You must give your body a chance to gradually adapt to the physical stress of strength training while making fitness gains. Using the 12-week beginner program detailed in this chapter will help you to gradually increase your body's ability to tolerate the stress of strength training with minimal muscle soreness. The idea is to develop healthy habits early in the training program so that strength training becomes an enjoyable, meaningful, and lifelong fitness experience. Regardless of how much weight everybody else is lifting at the local fitness center, beginners need to proceed slowly during the first few weeks of strength training as they build a foundation for more advanced training programs in the future.

Although all strength training programs need to be based on the fundamental principles of overload, progression, and specificity (see chapter 3), beginners respond favorably to most strength training protocols provided the exercise intensity is adequate. As you become more trained, the rate of improvement tends to slow down (figure 13.1). While it is not uncommon for a beginner to increase muscular strength by about 40 percent during the first 8 to 12 weeks of strength training, an advanced lifter may only improve by about 5 to 10 percent during this same time period.

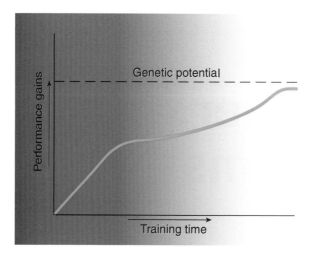

**Figure 13.1**  A theoretical training curve. Gains are made easily on the lower portion of the curve as individuals start to train and come more slowly as they approach their genetic potential.

Reprinted, by permission, from S. Fleck and W. Kraemer, 2004, *Designing resistance training programs*, 3rd ed. (Champaign, IL: Human Kinetics), 175.

As strength training experience increases, the individual gets closer to his or her genetic potential, and it becomes increasingly difficult to make strength gains. After you have completed the beginner program successfully, you will need to modify your strength training program if you want continued gains in muscular fitness. Instead of discouraging you from continuing a strength training program, this slower rate of improvement should motivate you to put additional time and effort into your program design as your training experience increases. Of course, you need to weigh the increased time that you will need in order to maximize gains in muscular fitness. Although small gains in strength may be the difference between winning and losing in some athletic events, some beginners may only want to maintain their current level of fitness. In any case, all strength training programs must be based on an individual's needs, goals, and abilities as well as an understanding of fundamental strength training principles.

## Program Design Considerations

Although men and women can benefit from strength training, the act of strength training itself does not ensure that optimal gains will be made. In other words, simply lifting light weights for a few exercises will not enhance muscular fitness. Individual effort and a systematic progression of program variables result in the most effective training outcomes. This does not mean that beginners should jump right to training with heavy weights or performing advanced exercises, but rather that the program should be structured in a way that maximizes training adaptations while minimizing the risk of muscle soreness or injury. During the early phase of

## General Strength Training Guidelines for Beginners

Make sure the exercise environment is free of clutter.

Warm up for about 5 to 10 minutes before strength training.

Take time to learn proper exercise technique.

Perform about 8 to 12 exercises that train the major muscle groups.

Perform exercises for large muscle groups before exercises for small muscle groups.

Begin with a weight you can handle for 8 to 12 repetitions.

Begin with one set and progress to two or three sets on selected exercises.

Rest about one to two minutes between sets and exercises.

Perform all exercises through the full range of motion.

Avoid jerky, uncontrolled movements while strength training.

Strength train two or three days per week on nonconsecutive days. ■

training, great variations in training repetitions and sets are not needed to enhance muscle strength. Therefore, a general program design is used during the first 8 to 12 weeks of strength training. Over time, the strength training program can become more specific in order to maximize gains in muscle strength or muscle size.

All strength trainers should warm up before every strength training workout by performing at least five minutes of low- to moderate-intensity aerobic exercise followed by several calisthenics and stretching exercises. Not only does a warm-up reduce the risk of injury, but it also enhances muscular performance by preparing the body for the demands of strength exercise. It is a good idea to exercise with an experienced training partner who can serve as a spotter on selected exercises and can provide motivation and encouragement when needed. Be sure to review the safety precautions discussed in chapter 8 as well as in the list at the top of this page.

As discussed in parts I and II of this book, several variables must be considered when setting up a strength training program, including the choice and order of exercises, the intensity, the volume, the frequency, and the progression of the training. Let's review each of these variables as they apply to a strength training program for beginners.

## Choice and Order of Exercises

Beginners should perform a total body workout that includes exercises that strengthen all the major muscle groups (one or two exercises for each major muscle group). This is an effective and time-efficient method for improving muscular fitness. Both single-joint exercises (e.g., dumbbell biceps curl, page 204, and leg extension, page 224) and multijoint exercises (e.g., bench press, page 176, and leg press, page 216) are effective for increasing muscular strength. Although it's important to include both exercise types in a strength training workout, over time you need to emphasize multijoint exercises in order to maximize gains. Multijoint exercises are more complex and involve more muscle mass, consequently more weight can be lifted. In addition, multijoint exercises more closely mimic activities of daily life and sport activities. As you learned in chapter 7, it's best to perform multijoint exercises early in a workout when the muscles are fresh and fatigue is minimal.

A beginner can include exercises using both weight machines and free weights (barbells and dumbbells) in his or her program. Many beginners enjoy strength training on weight machines because the exercises are relatively easy to learn and to perform correctly. Weight machines help stabilize the body and limit movement around specific joints. However, since weight machines are expensive and take up a lot of floor space, most people do not have these machines at home. If weight machines are not available, barbells and dumbbells can be used to strengthen all the major muscle groups. Free weight exercises require more balance and coordination than weight machines; therefore, it may take a longer period of time to learn proper exercise technique. If a variety of training equipment is available, beginners can use a combination of weight machine and free weight exercises. In any case, all beginner exercises should be performed at a controlled movement speed during the lifting and lowering phases. That means beginners should be able to stop any lifting or lowering action at will without momentum carrying the movement to completion. Uncontrolled, jerky movements are not only ineffective, but may result in injury.

## Exercise Intensity

Since heavy weights are not required to increase the muscular strength of beginners, weights corresponding to about 60 to 70 percent of 1RM are recommended for the first month of strength training (when individuals are learning the correct exercise technique). This training zone corresponds to about 8 to 12 repetitions. Although weights that can be lifted for more than 15 to 20 repetitions are effective for increasing local muscular endurance, light weights rarely result in meaningful gains in muscular strength. Since beginners do not typically perform maximal 1RM strength tests before training (see page 100), the best approach for beginners is to first establish a repetition range (e.g., 8 to 12), and then by trial and error determine the maximum load that can be handled for the prescribed training range. It may take two or three workouts to find the desired training weight on all exercises.

As a beginner progresses into the second and third months of training, he or she can use additional sets and slightly heavier loads (up to 80 percent of 1RM) to keep the training stimulus effective. Performing the same training program for a long period of time will likely result in training plateaus, boredom, or overtraining (characterized by a decrease in muscle performance). Thus, the best advice is to systematically vary the training program every month or so by changing one or more of the program variables. Not only do heavier loads and multiple sets maximize gains in muscular fitness, but other tissues (such as bone) respond more favorably to more advanced training programs than to single-set training with a light weight.

When training within a repetition range, the magnitude of individual effort determines the outcome of the strength training program. For example, training within an 8 to 12RM (estimated at 60 to 70 percent of 1RM) zone means that an individual should be able to perform no more than 12 repetitions with a given weight. Simply performing an exercise for 8, 9, 10, 11, or 12 repetitions does not necessarily mean an individual is training within the 8 to 12RM zone. Although you never want to sacrifice the proper form, the training weight should be challenging enough to result in at least a modest degree of muscle fatigue as the last few repetitions of a set are finished. If this does not occur, gains will not be maximized.

## Exercise Sets and Rest Periods

Since the number of training sets is not a critical factor during the first few weeks of strength training, beginners should start with one set on all exercises. Although multiple sets are necessary for long-term strength training gains, multiple sets are not necessary during the first few weeks of training.

Beginners can progress to two or three sets during the second and third months of training, depending on the time available for training as well as individualized training goals. If you are following a multiset protocol, keep in mind that not all exercises need to be performed for the same number of sets. Another important consideration is the rest interval between sets and exercises, because fatigue associated with the previous set or exercise will limit performance on the following set or exercise. In general, a one- to two-minute rest period between sets and exercises is recommended for beginners.

## Exercise Frequency

Beginners should perform a total body workout on two or three alternating days per week. Since only moderate weights are used during this early period, allowing 48 hours between workouts is usually sufficient. Longer recovery periods may be needed during more advanced training programs in which heavier weights are used. Although a training frequency of once per week can be used as an effective maintenance frequency for individuals who have experience in strength training, a higher training frequency is needed to maximize *gains* in muscular fitness.

Beginners should maintain a training frequency of two or three days per week as they progress through the second and third months of training. Although changes may be made to other program variables during this time, an increase in training frequency is not needed for total body training. After successfully completing the beginner program, lifters may use higher training frequencies to perform more specialized training programs. Note that if higher training frequencies are used, specific muscle groups are typically trained only twice per week.

## Program Progression

For continued gains in muscular fitness, the strength training program must be sensibly altered over time so that the body is continually challenged to adapt to the new demands. This does not mean that every workout needs to be harder than the previous workout, but rather that a systematic progression of the exercise

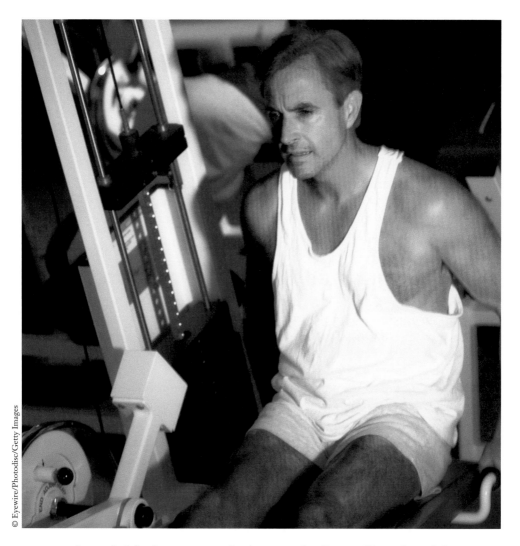

© Eyewire/Photodisc/Getty Images

program is needed for long-term gains in muscular fitness. Even though beginners will improve at a faster rate than more advanced lifters, manipulating the program variables during the first few weeks of training will limit training plateaus. It will also reduce the likelihood that beginners will become bored with their training program and lose their enthusiasm for strength training.

Although it is not possible to improve at the same rate over the long term, a person must gradually place greater demands on the musculoskeletal system if steady gains in muscular fitness are desired. In addition to increasing the amount of weight that is lifted, you can also progress the program by performing additional repetitions with the current weight, adding more sets to the program, altering rest periods between sets, or combining modifications of these variables to provide progressive overload. The key to long-term success in training is to make gradual changes in the exercise program in order to keep the training program effective, challenging, and fun.

For example, beginners can increase the demand of their training program by first performing more repetitions within a training zone and later increasing the weight lifted (by 5 to 10 percent). If one set of 8 repetitions with 50 pounds (22.7 kg) is performed on the chest press exercise, a beginner should work toward performing 12 repetitions with 50 pounds over the next few workouts. Once this is achieved, the weight can be increased to 55 pounds (24.9 kg), and the repetitions should be reduced back to 8. The strength training program can also be advanced by adding additional sets on selected exercises or by adding more challenging exercises to the program. Beginners will likely make gains in muscular fitness from any reasonable strength training program; however, gradually increasing the demands of a beginner workout enables an individual to achieve higher levels of muscular fitness during the intermediate and advanced training periods.

# Suggested Beginner Program

Individual goals, personal preferences, and time available for training will determine the design of more advanced training programs. But for beginners, a total body workout performed two or three days per week on nonconsecutive days is an effective method for improving muscular fitness. The 12-week beginner program gives you time to learn proper exercise technique and develop a fitness base for more advanced training programs as your strength and confidence improve (figure 13.2).

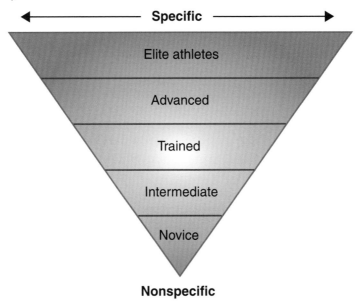

**Figure 13.2**  The design of strength training programs progresses from general programs for beginners to more specific programs for advanced lifters.

Reprinted, by permission, from W. Kraemer and W. Ratamess, 2004, "Fundamentals of resistance training: Progression and exercise prescription," *Medicine & Science in Sports & Exercise* 36(4): 674-688.

Beginners should use a workout card to monitor their training progress. We provide a sample card on pages 288 and 289 that you can photocopy and use. Since there is no optimal combination of sets, repetitions, and exercises that will work for everyone, beginners should assess the effectiveness of the training program every few weeks and make modifications when necessary. In addition, they should be prepared to alter the recommended workout to accommodate their state on a given day. For example, individuals who feel tired or who are sore from a previous workout should decrease the training intensity and number of exercises. This is where the science of designing a strength training workout needs to be combined with the art of developing an exercise program.

## Lower Back Exercises for Beginners

The following three lower back exercises are excellent choices for beginning lifters. They require no more than a floor and a pillow.

### Prone Back Raise

1. Lie face down with both arms extended in front of the head.
2. Use a pillow under the hips to increase comfort and range of motion.
3. With each limb fully extended, simultaneously raise the right arm and left leg two to four inches above the floor.
4. Pause briefly before lowering the arm and leg in the same path as the upward movement.
5. Alternate each side of the body with each repetition.

### Alternating Hip Extension

1. Kneel on the floor and support the body with both hands and both knees.
2. Position the back so that it is flat and neutral.
3. Raise one leg by simultaneously extending at the hip and knee until the extended leg is horizontal.
4. Pause briefly before lowering the leg in the same path used for the upward movement.
5. Alternate the side of the body worked with each repetition.

### Alternating Hip Extension and Shoulder Flexion

1. Kneel on the floor and support the body with both hands and both knees.
2. Position the back so that it is flat and neutral.
3. Simultaneously raise the right arm and left leg until the extended arm and leg are horizontal.
4. Pause briefly before lowering the arm and leg in the same path as the upward movement.
5. Alternate the side of the body worked with each repetition. ∎

## Training Log

Name _____

| Order | Exercise | Reps / Sets | Set | Week # _____ Day 1 | | | Day 2 | | |
|---|---|---|---|---|---|---|---|---|---|
| | | | | 1 | 2 | 3 | 1 | 2 | 3 |
| 1 | | | Wt. | | | | | | |
| | | | Reps | | | | | | |
| 2 | | | Wt. | | | | | | |
| | | | Reps | | | | | | |
| 3 | | | Wt. | | | | | | |
| | | | Reps | | | | | | |
| 4 | | | Wt. | | | | | | |
| | | | Reps | | | | | | |
| 5 | | | Wt. | | | | | | |
| | | | Reps | | | | | | |
| 6 | | | Wt. | | | | | | |
| | | | Reps | | | | | | |
| 7 | | | Wt. | | | | | | |
| | | | Reps | | | | | | |
| 8 | | | Wt. | | | | | | |
| | | | Reps | | | | | | |
| 9 | | | Wt. | | | | | | |
| | | | Reps | | | | | | |
| 10 | | | Wt. | | | | | | |
| | | | Reps | | | | | | |
| 11 | | | Wt. | | | | | | |
| | | | Reps | | | | | | |
| | Body weight | | | | | | | | |
| | Date | | | | | | | | |
| | Comments | | | | | | | | |

# Weeks 1 Through 4

During the first month of strength training, workouts should include one set of each of 8 to 12 different exercises, performed using a moderate weight (see table 13.1). This preparatory period is designed to gradually enhance physical ability and proper technique as you start the process of strength training. Beginners with a very low level of fitness may need to "get in shape" before they can participate in a strength training program that is designed to maximize gains

| Week # _____ | | | | | | | | | | | |
|---|---|---|---|---|---|---|---|---|---|---|---|
| Day 3 | | | Day 1 | | | Day 2 | | | Day 3 | | |
| 1 | 2 | 3 | 1 | 2 | 3 | 1 | 2 | 3 | 1 | 2 | 3 |
| | | | | | | | | | | | |
| | | | | | | | | | | | |
| | | | | | | | | | | | |
| | | | | | | | | | | | |
| | | | | | | | | | | | |
| | | | | | | | | | | | |
| | | | | | | | | | | | |
| | | | | | | | | | | | |
| | | | | | | | | | | | |
| | | | | | | | | | | | |
| | | | | | | | | | | | |
| | | | | | | | | | | | |
| | | | | | | | | | | | |
| | | | | | | | | | | | |
| | | | | | | | | | | | |
| | | | | | | | | | | | |
| | | | | | | | | | | | |
| | | | | | | | | | | | |
| | | | | | | | | | | | |
| | | | | | | | | | | | |
| | | | | | | | | | | | |

From *Strength Training* by the National Strength and Conditioning Association (NSCA), 2007, Champaign, IL: Human Kinetics. Reprinted from W. Westcott and T. Baechle, 1999, *Strength training for seniors: Instructor guide* (Champaign, IL: Human Kinetics), 207. By permission of W. Westcott.

in muscular fitness. In other words, if you have never strength trained before, give your muscles a chance to adapt to strength exercise by making sensible modifications to the beginner program. For example, instead of performing 8 to 12 exercises with a moderate weight, try 4 to 6 different exercises with a light weight. This will give your muscles a chance to gradually adapt to strength exercise while providing you with an opportunity to gain confidence in your ability to strength train.

Table 13.1   **Beginner Strength Training Program: Weeks 1 to 4\***

| Weight machine exercise | Free weight exercise | Sets | Repetitions |
|---|---|---|---|
| Leg extension (p. 224) | Back squat, dumbbell (p. 214) | 1 | 8-12 |
| Seated leg curl (p 223) | – | 1 | 8-12 |
| Machine chest press (p. 184) | Dumbbell bench press (p. 178) | 1 | 8-12 |
| Seated machine row— rear deltoids (p. 195) | One-arm dumbbell row (p 193) | 1 | 8-12 |
| Machine biceps curl (p. 207) | Dumbbell biceps curl (p. 204) | 1 | 8-12 |
| Machine triceps extension (p. 203) | Lying triceps extension (p. 200) | 1 | 8-12 |
| Machine back extension (p. 249) | Prone back raise (p. 287) | 1 | 8-12 |
| Machine abdominal crunch (p. 235) | Abdominal crunch (p. 232) | 1 | 8-12 |

\* Note that a progression of this workout plan is required to maximize gains in muscular fitness after the first few weeks of strength training.

An initial load of 60 to 70 percent of 1RM should allow you to do 8 to 12 repetitions on a variety of upper and lower body exercises that target all the major muscle groups. Of course, you can use lighter loads when learning a new exercise or attempting to correct a flaw in exercise technique. At least one exercise for all the major muscle groups should be performed. A major goal of this training phase is to learn proper form and technique on a variety of upper and lower body exercises while practicing training fundamentals (e.g., proper breathing, controlled movements).

## Weeks 5 Through 8

During weeks 5 to 8, the workout should become more challenging as strength improves. By varying the program variables, you start to accomplish specific goals in health and fitness, and you prevent the boredom and training plateaus that eventually lead to a lack of adherence to the program or to dropping out of the program entirely. This is a good time to think about the physical as well as the psychosocial benefits of strength training. Although positive changes in physical abilities are certainly important, so too are the qualitative changes associated with a more active lifestyle.

During this period, increase the training volume by performing one or two sets of 10 exercises at a training intensity of 60 to 70 percent of 1RM (8 to 12 repetitions). Rest for about one to two minutes between sets (see table 13.2). As additional sets are performed in the training program, continued effort will determine training outcomes. Thus, you should expect and welcome the feelings of exercise exertion. A major goal of this conditioning phase is to gain confidence in your abilities to perform strength-building exercises while maximizing training adaptations.

Table 13.2   **Beginner Strength Training Program: Weeks 5 to 8**

| Weight machine exercise | Free weight exercise | Sets | Repetitions |
|---|---|---|---|
| Leg press (p. 216) | Back squat, dumbbell or barbell (p. 214) | 2 | 8-12 |
| Leg extension (p. 224) | Dumbbell step-up (p. 220) | 2 | 8-12 |
| Seated leg curl (p. 223) | — | 2 | 8-12 |
| Machine chest press (p. 184) | Bench press (p. 176) | 2 | 8-12 |
| Seated machine row—rear deltoids (p. 195) | One-arm dumbbell row (p. 193) | 2 | 8-12 |
| Machine lateral raise (p. 173) | Dumbbell side raise (p. 172) | 2 | 8-12 |
| Machine biceps curl (p. 207) | Dumbbell biceps curl (p. 204) | 2 | 8-12 |
| Triceps pushdown (p. 202) | Lying triceps extension (p. 200) | 2 | 8-12 |
| Machine back extension (p. 249) | Alternating hip extension (p. 287) | 2 | 8-12 |
| Machine abdominal crunch (p. 235) | 90–90 crunch (p. 233) | 2 | 8-12 |

# Weeks 9 Through 12

After the first eight weeks of strength training, improvements in muscular fitness occur at a slower rate. Beginners who started strength training with great enthusiasm may become disappointed when gains in muscle strength become less dramatic during the third month of training. This is where beginners need to

Table 13.3   **Beginner Strength Training Program: Weeks 9 to 12**

| Weight machine exercise | Free weight exercise | Sets | Repetitions |
|---|---|---|---|
| Leg press (p. 216) | Back squat, dumbbell or barbell (p. 214) | 3 | 8-12 |
| Seated hip abduction (p. 226) | Dumbbell step-up (p. 220) | 2 | 8-12 |
| Seated hip adduction (p. 225) | Dumbbell front lunge (p. 217) | 2 | 8-12 |
| Machine chest press (p. 184) | Bench press (p. 176) | 3 | 8-12 |
| Machine chest fly (p. 185) | Dumbbell fly (p. 186) | 2 | 8-12 |
| Assisted chin-up (p. 190) | One-arm dumbbell row (p. 193) | 3 | 8-12 |
| Seated cable row (p. 194) | Dumbbell upright row (p. 171) | 2 | 8-12 |
| Machine shoulder press (p. 170) | Standing military press (p. 166) | 2 | 8-12 |
| Machine biceps curl (p. 207) | Dumbbell biceps curl (p. 204) | 2 | 8-12 |
| Assisted dip (p. 197) | Lying triceps extension (p. 200) | 2 | 8-12 |
| Machine back extension (p. 249) | Alternating hip extension and shoulder flexion ( p. 287) | 2 | 8-12 |
| Machine abdominal crunch (p. 235) | 90–90 alternate touch (p. 242) | 2 | 8-12 |

understand that a strength training workout that was effective during the first few weeks of training may not be effective in the long term. To make continual gains in muscular fitness, and to achieve specific health and fitness goals, harder work and a more challenging training program are required. This is particularly important for people who want to maximize gains in muscle strength or muscle size.

During this phase, perform two or three sets of 12 exercises at a training intensity of 60 to 70 percent of 1RM (8 to 12 repetitions). Rest about one to two minutes between sets (see table 13.3). Although an endless combination of program variables can be used, continued improvement requires that you increase the training weight (and reduce the repetitions to the lower end of the training zone) once you have performed the desired number of repetitions on the last set. As a general recommendation, you should perform more sets on exercises for large muscle groups as compared to exercises for smaller muscle groups.

Beginners can make remarkable gains in muscular fitness by following established strength training guidelines. By starting with a reasonable training weight and gradually progressing from simple to more complex exercises, novices can make strength training a safe, effective, and enjoyable activity that can be performed for a lifetime. Those who successfully complete the beginner program are prepared to move on to more advanced strength training workouts and to achieve even greater gains in muscular fitness.

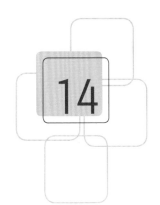

# Intermediate Programs

Jay Hoffman and Avery Faigenbaum

During the first three months of strength training, beginners experience rapid improvements in strength. As discussed in part I of this book, most of these improvements are related to neurological adaptations, although noticeable improvements in muscle size may also be present. However, as the duration of training progresses, the rate of strength improvement slows down. At this point, beginners need to make adjustments to their program in order to provide a new training stimulus to the exercising muscles; what may have been a sufficient stimulus for a beginner may be inadequate for an intermediate lifter (figure 14.1). This chapter discusses how to develop a training program for the intermediate lifter—someone who is currently strength training and has at least three months of regular strength training experience.

## Program Design Considerations

By strength training on a regular basis for three months, a lifter has demonstrated a commitment and a consistency in training that suggest the ability and desire to incorporate a more sophisticated exercise design into his or her training regimen. The workout for the beginner focused on performing a total body workout that involved both single-joint (e.g., machine biceps curl, page 207) and multijoint (e.g., leg press, page 216) exercises. At the intermediate level, it becomes necessary to consider increasing the frequency of training and incorporating a split routine into

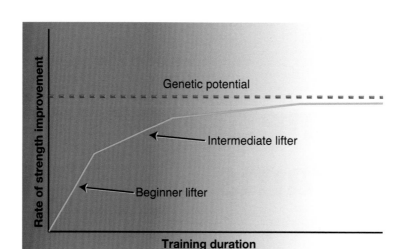

**Figure 14.1**    Rate of strength improvement relative to training duration.

Adapted, by permission, from J. Hoffman, *Physiological aspects of sports training and performance* (Champaign, IL: Human Kinetics), 74.

the training program. As you learned in chapters 3 and 7, a split routine refers to separating your workouts by grouping together exercises that train a certain body part. You then alternate the days that you work on each body part. This allows for the necessary recovery of the muscles while still increasing the number of times you are working out in a given week. For example, you may choose to focus on the chest, shoulders, and triceps for one workout and the legs, back, and biceps for the other workout. Although workouts are performed four days per week, each particular training routine is performed twice per week.

This type of split routine can also be classified as a push-pull routine (see page 142). During one workout, the exercises involve primarily a pushing movement (e.g., exercises for the chest, shoulders, and triceps), whereas in the other workout the exercises involve primarily a pulling movement (e.g., exercises for the legs, back, and biceps). Another benefit of this split routine is that the musculature being recruited for each training session is either the primary mover or an assistant mover for each exercise. For instance, the triceps are recruited as an assistant mover during the bench press (page 176) and shoulder press (page 170) exercises, but they are the primary mover during the triceps pushdown exercise (page 202). If these exercises were performed on consecutive days, the triceps would not receive adequate rest, leading to fatigue and poor performance during the workouts. This is an important reason for splitting the routine in this fashion.

Another benefit of using a split routine is that it allows you to incorporate additional exercises per body part into the training regimen. Including assistance exercises (over and above the core exercises) has been shown to be especially relevant for the intermediate lifter. Apparently, assistance exercises provide the necessary stimulus for generating further physiological adaptations that lead to greater gains in muscle strength and size.

For the beginner who has been lifting consistently for several months, adding assistance exercises to the training regimen may not seem particularly important.

However, in order to further your gains and physiological adaptations, you need to add these types of changes to your training program. Other changes can be accomplished by increasing the number of sets performed per exercise, increasing the intensity of training (using heavier loads), and increasing the number of exercises performed per training session (increasing the volume of training).

## Choice and Order of Exercises

There is no optimum number of exercises to do per body part. The appropriate number depends on the person's experience level, training goals, available time, and ability to adequately recover between sets and workouts. As a beginner, your training program may have included only one exercise per body part, which was sufficient for providing the initial training stimulus. As an intermediate lifter, however, you need to include additional exercises per body part to effectively increase muscle strength and size.

For example, most beginner lifters will use the bench press or chest press exercise as the core exercise for the chest—that is, the exercise that recruits the greatest amount of muscle mass for that body part. But if your goal is to build additional muscle strength or size, then you need to add complementary exercises that move that area of the body through different angles and planes, such as the incline bench press (page 180) or dumbbell fly (page 186).

In general, exercises that recruit the greatest amount of muscle mass are performed before exercises that recruit a smaller muscle mass for any given body part. The primary reason for this is to prevent you from fatiguing the musculature you need to perform the core lifts. This exercise order not only involves performing core before assistance exercises for each body part, but also working the larger muscle groups before the smaller ones. For instance, when exercising the legs, back, and biceps, the legs are the largest muscle group of the three and are therefore trained first, followed by the back, and then the biceps. When training the legs, the exercise that recruits the greatest muscle mass (i.e., the squat; pages 212, 214) is performed before the exercises that recruit a smaller muscle mass (i.e., seated leg curl, page 223; standing calf raise, page 227).

## Exercise Intensity

As you learned in chapter 13, a strength training program for beginners generally requires a moderate training intensity of between 60 and 70 percent of 1RM. As lifters progress and focus on more specific training goals, they can adjust the intensity and vary it to help them meet those goals. For instance, individuals who are interested in maximizing strength improvement will begin to use a higher intensity of training (i.e., greater than 70 percent of 1RM), while individuals whose primary desire is to maximize muscle hypertrophy will use a relatively lower intensity of training. In addition, the rest interval between exercise sets will also vary depending on the specific goals of the training program.

For example, if the exercise prescription was written as "1, 3 × 6-8RM" (the "1" indicates the initial warm-up set) you would choose a weight that you can lift at least six but not more than eight times. For example, if you lift 100 pounds (45.4 kg) for eight repetitions in the first set but feel that you could have easily performed a few more repetitions, then the 100-pound training weight is too light and should be increased. It may take several workouts to find the appropriate weight on all exercises, but once you find it, the progression principle needs to be strictly adhered to. For instance, if a workout requires the intermediate lifter to perform three sets of 6 to 8RM (written as "3 × 6-8RM") in the squat during the first week of training, he or she may be able to squat 140 pounds (63.5 kg) for 8 repetitions in the first set but only six repetitions in the second and third sets. After several weeks of training, this lifter may be able to perform eight repetitions for all three sets, and he or she may feel that it would be possible to perform nine repetitions with proper form. At this point, the lifter needs to add weight to ensure the same relative intensity and performance gains. Obviously, as muscle strength increases, the relative intensity of that particular weight decreases. This is a classic example of the way the progression principle works and how the overload principle leads to strength gains.

## Exercise Sets and Rest Periods

One-set training protocols are effective for beginners, but intermediate lifters will want to use multiple sets per exercise because this provides a better training stimulus for generating even greater gains in muscle strength and size.

The exercise prescription for the intermediate lifter should include a warm-up set followed by the number of work sets to be performed. For instance, an exercise prescription may be written as follows: bench press (1, 3 × 6-8RM). This requires the lifter to perform one warm-up set followed by three sets of 6 to 8 repetitions. The warm-up set usually involves a light to moderate weight that the person can lift comfortably for at least 10 repetitions. It serves to prime the muscle for the greater intensity that will be used in the next sequence of sets.

The number of sets to be performed per exercise will vary. In general, three to five sets per exercise are used for the core lifts (e.g., squats, pages 212, 214; bench press, page 176), while two to four sets are commonly used for assistance exercises (e.g., incline bench press, page 180; leg curls, page 223).

Similar to training intensity, the amount of rest allotted between sets appears to have a significant effect on desired training outcomes. Training programs of high intensity (greater than 80 percent of 1RM) specify rest intervals between sets of at least three minutes in duration. This provides sufficient time for the muscle to replenish used energy from the previous set, maximize recovery, and provide for optimum performance in the next set.

In contrast, when muscle hypertrophy is the goal, the rest interval between sets is shorter (approximately one minute or less). The greater fatigue associated with a low training intensity and short rest intervals appears to be an important factor in stimulating anabolic hormone secretions. This physiological response helps maximize muscle hypertrophy (see chapter 2). Such training programs are common for bodybuilders who want maximal muscle growth. For the lifter who has begun to focus on specific training goals, the proper combination of training intensity and rest intervals provides the opportunity to maximize those goals.

## Exercise Frequency

Similar to the beginner, the intermediate lifter may still exercise two or three days per week using one exercise per body part. This training program may be based on necessity (i.e., time constraints) or desire. The intermediate lifter may add an assistance exercise for the larger or multijoint muscle groups and maintain a single exercise for some of the smaller or single-joint muscle groups. For instance, the intermediate lifter exercising two or three days per week may want to add the incline bench press (page 180) to the upper body or chest routine and add seated leg curls (page 223) to the lower body routine.

## Suggested Intermediate Programs

The remainder of this chapter provides various examples and explanations of intermediate-level strength training programs. Your selection of which program is right for you should be based on several factors. Most notably, you must decide what your goals are for training and how much time you have available to train. The programs listed offer an array of possibilities to choose from.

You'll want to limit the time you spend on any one of these programs (without change) to two to three months. Setting this limit will prevent you from getting too bored with the program, hitting a training plateau, or experiencing chronic fatigue. After two or three months with one program, you'll need to vary things by altering the intensity and volume of training. For example, after two months of general muscular conditioning, the lifter may proceed to a two- to three-month muscular hypertrophy program, followed by two to three months of a muscular strength program. Depending on the goals or needs of the lifter, the training program can continue focusing on strength development, enter an active rest period (during which the lifter does not lift but does participate in other forms of activity), or proceed to a more advanced resistance training program.

## General Muscular Conditioning

The first program (table 14.1*a*) is a three-day-per-week general muscular conditioning program. During each training session, the entire body is trained. The training routines for the first and third training sessions of the week are the same, but the second session uses different exercises per body part. This is intended to provide a change of exercises that can relieve the potential monotony of performing the same exercise routine every workout. In addition, the change of exercises provides a different stimulus to the musculature. The rest period between sets should be from two to three minutes, and at least 48 hours of rest should be allowed between each workout. Notice that the intensity of training is prescribed as 8 to 10RM, which requires the lifter to select a resistance that he or she can do at least 8 but not more than 10 times.

For individuals who are interested in general conditioning but want to exercise four days per week, table 14.1*b* provides an example of a split routine. The legs, back, and biceps are trained on days 1 (Monday) and 3 (Thursday) of the week. The chest, shoulders, and triceps are trained on days 2 (Tuesday) and 4 (Friday) of the week. In contrast to the three-day-per-week training model, this four-day split routine allows you to include additional assistance exercises in the program. Although the workouts are performed on some consecutive days, there is always at least 72 hours of rest for the specific body parts that are trained in order to ensure adequate recovery between workouts. The rest period between sets should be from two to three minutes.

You can perform this four-day workout with variable resistance machines or free weights. (If you use free weights, you can easily substitute squats or lunges for the leg press exercise. Similarly, the supine bench press (page 176 and seated shoulder press can replace the chest press and shoulder press machines, respectively.)

Determining whether to use machines or free weights is an important decision. In terms of comfort and ease of use, variable resistance machines are often recommended. However, people who want to increase the chances of gaining

Table 14.1*a*   **General Muscular Conditioning Program (3 days per week)**

| Exercise | Sets × repetitions |
|---|---|
| **Monday** | |
| Leg press (p. 216) | 3 × 8-10RM |
| Machine chest press (p. 184) | 3 × 8-10RM |
| Machine shoulder press (p. 170) | 3 × 8-10RM |
| Lat pulldown (p. 191) | 3 × 8-10RM |
| Machine back extension (p. 249) | 3 × 8-10RM |
| Seated leg curl (p. 223) | 3 × 8-10RM |
| Triceps pushdown (p. 202) | 3 × 8-10RM |
| Dumbbell biceps curl (p. 204) | 3 × 8-10RM |
| Abdominal crunch (p. 232) | 3 × 20 |
| **Wednesday** | |
| Dumbbell front lunge (p. 217) | 3 × 8-10RM |
| Incline bench press (p. 180) | 3 × 8-10RM |
| Dumbbell upright row (p. 171) | 3 × 8-10RM |
| Seated cable row (p. 194) | 3 × 8-10RM |
| Machine back extension (p. 249) | 3 × 8-10RM |
| Leg extension (p. 224) | 3 × 8-10RM |
| Lying triceps extension (p. 200) | 3 × 8-10RM |
| Dumbbell biceps curl (p. 204) | 3 × 8-10RM |
| Abdominal crunch (p. 232) | 3 × 20 |
| **Friday** | |
| Leg press (p. 216) | 3 × 8-10RM |
| Machine chest press (p. 184) | 3 × 8-10RM |
| Machine shoulder press (p. 170) | 3 × 8-10RM |
| Lat pulldown (p. 191) | 3 × 8-10RM |
| Machine back extension (p. 249) | 3 × 8-10RM |
| Seated leg curl (p. 223) | 3 × 8-10RM |
| Triceps pushdown (p. 202) | 3 × 8-10RM |
| Dumbbell biceps curl (p. 204) | 3 × 8-10RM |
| Abdominal crunch (p. 232) | 3 × 20 |

"carryover" strength may want to include as many free weight exercises as possible. *Carryover strength* refers to the degree of strength improvement achieved during exercise that is reflected in improved performance in another activity (i.e., activities

Table 14.1*b*   **General Muscular Conditioning Program (4 days per week)**

| Exercise | Sets × repetitions |
|---|---|
| **Monday and Thursday** | |
| Leg press (p. 216) | 1, 4 × 8-10RM |
| Leg extension (p. 224) | 3 × 8-10RM |
| Seated leg curl (p. 223) | 1, 3 × 8-10RM |
| Standing calf raise (p. 227) | 3 × 8-10RM |
| Lat pulldown (p. 191) | 1, 4 × 8-10RM |
| Machine back extension (p. 249) | 3 × 8-10RM |
| Dumbbell biceps curl (p. 204) | 4 × 8-10RM |
| Abdominal crunch (p. 232) | 3 × 20 |
| **Tuesday and Friday** | |
| Machine chest press (p. 184) | 1, 4 × 8-10RM |
| Incline bench press (p. 180) | 3 × 8-10RM |
| Machine shoulder press (p. 170) | 1, 4 × 8-10RM |
| Dumbbell upright row (p. 171) | 4 × 8-10RM |
| Triceps pushdown (p. 202) | 4 × 8-10RM |
| Lying triceps extension (p. 200) | 3 × 8-10RM |
| Abdominal crunch (p. 232) | 3 × 20 |

The "1" before the number of sets and repetitions of select exercises indicates that one warm-up set should be performed prior to the main set.

of daily living or sporting events). For instance, if an athlete (competitive or recreational) improves his or her squat performance by 20 percent, this does not necessarily translate into a 20-percent improvement in athletic performance. To ensure the greatest degree of carryover strength, the exercise chosen should simulate the activity as closely as possible. In most sporting activities, the athlete performs in an upright position; thus, the best way to improve leg strength that will carry over to sport would be to incorporate the squat exercise (pages 212, 214) into training for the lower body.

## Circuit Training

Table 14.2 shows a circuit training program that can be performed either two or three days per week. (Note that there should be at least 48 hours of rest between each workout.) This program is designed to develop general muscle fitness, enhance local muscle endurance, and improve cardiovascular fitness. It provides a well-rounded program, especially for individuals who are limited in the time they have to devote to physical activity. Although it does not impart the magnitude of cardiovascular benefit that strict endurance exercise (e.g., jogging or cycling)

## Table 14.2    Circuit Training Program (2 or 3 days per week)

| Exercise | Sets × repetitions |
|---|---|
| Leg press (p. 216) | 1 × 12-15RM |
| Machine chest press (p. 184) | 1 × 12-15RM |
| Seated leg curl (p. 223) | 1 × 12-15RM |
| Machine shoulder press (p. 170) | 1 × 12-15RM |
| Leg extension (p. 224) | 1 × 12-15RM |
| Lat pulldown (p. 191) | 1 × 12-15RM |
| Triceps pushdown (p. 202) | 1 × 12-15RM |
| Machine back extension (p. 249) | 1 × 12-15RM |
| Dumbbell biceps curl (p. 204) | 1 × 12-15RM |
| Machine abdominal crunch (p. 235) | 1 × 12-15 |
| Cycle ergometer | 5 minutes |

provides, this program has been shown to improve aerobic capacity by five to eight percent.

Circuit training requires that you perform one set per exercise, alternating between an upper body exercise and a lower body exercise, with minimal rest between exercises (about 30 seconds). Then you repeat the circuit if desired. To maximize caloric expenditure during exercise, incorporate as many multijoint exercises as possible. To maintain the rotation between upper and lower body exercises and ensure constant blood flow between body parts, several assistance exercises need to be included. At the end of each circuit is a cardiovascular station where you perform three to five minutes of exercise on a cycle ergometer or a treadmill.

Circuit training may be an ideal training program for people who have limited time to exercise. This is the basis for many franchise fitness centers that are designed for individuals who want to perform a quick circuit of strength exercises. Depending on their available time and level of conditioning, individuals can perform up to two or three circuits in one workout. This type of training will enhance the aerobic conditioning effect.

# Maximal Strength Training

For people whose training goal is to maximize strength improvement, the resistance training programs outlined in tables 14.3a and 14.3b may be the best options. Table 14.3a is a three-day-per-week program designed to maximize strength improvement in the intermediate lifter. Table 14.3b provides a four-day-per-week training program for strength improvement in these individuals. The three-day-per-week program allows 48 hours of rest between each training session (similar to all such programs). The four-day program is a split routine that requires at least 72 hours of rest for the body parts being worked; however, you perform the workouts for

## Table 14.3a  Strength Development Program (3 days per week)

| Exercise | Sets × repetitions |
|---|---|
| **Monday** | |
| Squat (front or back; p. 212 or 214) | 1, 3 × 6-8RM |
| Bench press (p. 176) | 1, 3 × 6-8RM |
| Machine shoulder press (p. 170) | 1, 3 × 6-8RM |
| Lat pulldown (p. 191) | 1, 3 × 6-8RM |
| Seated leg curl (p. 223) | 1, 3 × 6-8RM |
| Triceps pushdown (p. 202) | 3 × 6-8RM |
| Dumbbell biceps curl (p. 204) | 3 × 6-8RM |
| Abdominal crunch (p. 232) | 3 × 20 |
| **Wednesday** | |
| Dumbbell lunge (side, front, or reverse; p. 219, 217, or 218) | 3 × 6-8RM |
| Incline bench press (p. 180) | 3 × 6-8RM |
| Dumbbell upright row (p. 171) | 3 × 6-8RM |
| Seated cable row (p. 194) | 3 × 6-8RM |
| Leg extension (p. 224) | 3 × 6-8RM |
| Lying triceps extension (p. 200) | 3 × 6-8RM |
| Biceps curl, barbell (p. 204) | 3 × 6-8RM |
| Abdominal crunch (p. 232) | 3 × 20 |
| **Friday** | |
| Squat (front or back; p. 212 or 214) | 1, 3 × 6-8RM |
| Bench press (p. 176) | 1, 3 × 6-8RM |
| Machine shoulder press (p. 170) | 1, 3 × 6-8RM |
| Lat pulldown (p. 191) | 1, 3 × 6-8RM |
| Seated leg curl (p. 223) | 1, 3 × 6-8RM |
| Triceps pushdown (p. 202) | 3 × 6-8RM |
| Dumbbell biceps curl (p. 204) | 3 × 6-8RM |
| Abdominal crunch (p. 232) | 3 × 20 |

The "1" before the number of sets and repetitions of select exercises indicates that one warm-up set should be performed prior to the main set.

days 1 and 2 on consecutive days and the workouts for days 3 and 4 on consecutive days. Since strength development is the primary goal, you should take at least three minutes of rest between each set for either of these training programs.

As discussed earlier, maintaining the proper training intensity is critical for developing maximum strength. If the training program requires three sets of 6 to 8RM, you need to select a resistance that you can lift for at least 6 but not more than 8 repetitions. Once you get to the point that you can perform three sets of 8

### Table 14.3*b*   Strength Development Program (4 days per week)

| Exercise | Sets × repetitions |
|---|:---:|
| **Monday and Thursday** | |
| Squat (front or back, p. 212 or 214) | 1, 4 × 6-8RM |
| Leg extension (p. 224) | 3 × 6-8RM |
| Seated leg curl (p. 223) | 3 × 6-8RM |
| Standing calf raise (p. 227) | 3 × 6-8RM |
| Lat pulldown (p. 191) | 1, 4 × 6-8RM |
| Seated cable row (p. 194) | 4 × 6-8RM |
| Dumbbell biceps curl (p. 204) | 4 × 6-8RM |
| Machine back extension (p. 249) | 3 × 10 |
| **Tuesday and Friday** | |
| Bench press (p. 176) | 1, 4 × 6-8RM |
| Incline bench press (p. 180) | 3 × 6-8RM |
| Machine shoulder press (p. 170) | 1, 4 × 6-8RM |
| Dumbbell upright row (p. 171) | 4 × 6-8RM |
| Triceps pushdown (p. 202) | 4 × 6-8RM |
| Abdominal crunch (p. 232) | 3 × 20 |

The "1" before the number of sets and repetitions of select exercises indicates that one warm-up set should be performed prior to the main set.

repetitions, in order to maintain the appropriate training intensity and overload, you will need to add resistance to the exercise for the next session. Most intermediate strength programs focus on using free weight exercises. This is seen in both of the provided programs. The primary difference between the two programs is that you can include more assistance exercises in the four-day program.

## Hypertrophy Training

Table 14.4 depicts a program for people who are interested in maximizing muscle growth. This is a split routine training regimen that should be performed four days per week. To maximize muscle hypertrophy, assistance exercises must be incorporated into the training routine, hence the recommendation for a split routine program. The rest period used between sets is another important factor for training programs that focus on muscle growth. For these programs, lifters will generally reduce the rest period between sets to no more than one minute. The reason for this is primarily to increase the fatigue rate, which as discussed earlier has been demonstrated to be a potent stimulator of anabolic hormone secretion rates.

The overload principle is still an important concept for increasing muscle growth even though the intensity of exercise is much lower than that of the strength program. The lifter who is interested in maximizing muscle growth still needs to

## Table 14.4  Muscle Hypertrophy Program (4 days per week)

| Exercise | Sets × repetitions |
|---|---|
| **Monday and Thursday** | |
| Back squat (p. 214) | 1, 4 × 10-12RM |
| Leg extension (p. 224) | 3 × 10-12RM |
| Seated leg curl (p. 223) | 3 × 10-12RM |
| Standing calf raise (p. 227) | 3 × 10-12RM |
| Lat pulldown (p. 191) | 1, 4 × 10-12RM |
| Seated cable row (p. 194) | 4 × 10-12RM |
| EZ bar curl (p. 205) | 3 × 10-12RM |
| Dumbbell biceps curl (p. 204) | 3 × 10-12RM |
| Machine back extension (p. 249) | 3 × 10 |
| **Tuesday and Friday** | |
| Bench press (p. 176) | 1, 4 × 10-12RM |
| Incline bench press (p. 180) | 3 × 10-12RM |
| Dumbbell fly, incline  (p. 186) | 3 × 10-12RM |
| Machine shoulder press (p. 170) | 1, 4 × 10-12RM |
| Dumbbell upright row (p. 171) | 4 × 10-12RM |
| Dumbbell side raise (p. 172) | 3 × 10-12RM |
| Triceps pushdown (p. 202) | 4 × 10-12RM |
| Lying triceps extension (p. 200) | 3 × 12-15 |
| Abdominal crunch (p. 232) | 3 × 20 |

The "1" before the number of sets and repetitions of select exercises indicates that one warm-up set should be performed prior to the main set.

exercise the muscle at a level that provides the required stimulus. Therefore, it is just as important for this type of lifter to increase the resistance when he or she has met a given training protocol—three sets of 10 to 12RM, for example—as it is for a lifter who is focusing on maximal strength development to do so.

An important difference between the two training paradigms (muscle hypertrophy and muscle strength development) is the relationship between training intensity and training volume. Training volume is typically defined as the number of sets times the number of repetitions performed per set. For the person interested in maximizing muscle hypertrophy, the focus of the workout is on high volume and low intensity (typical of a bodybuilder's resistance training program); on the other hand, the lifter interested in maximal strength development focuses on low volume and high intensity. Interestingly, there is a natural inverse relationship between training intensity and training volume. As the intensity of exercise increases, the number of repetitions that can be performed is reduced (training

**Table14.5    Comparison of Training Paradigms for the Intermediate Lifter**

| Training paradigm | Training intensity (RM) | Training volume (sets) | Rest interval between sets (minutes) |
|---|---|---|---|
| General muscular conditioning | 8-10 | 2-3 | 1-2 |
| Muscle hypertrophy | 10-12 | 3-4 | 0-1 |
| Muscle strength | 6-8 | 3-4 | 3 |

volume is decreased); likewise, as the intensity of exercise is reduced, the number of repetitions is increased (training volume is increased). In addition to exercise intensity and training volume, the rest interval used between sets is also important in eliciting the desired training adaptations. Table 14.5 provides a brief overview of the intensity, volume, and rest intervals used for the various training paradigms.

□■■■

The intermediate lifter can begin to maximize gains in muscle strength and muscle size. As a result, specific training paradigms can be designed to assist the intermediate lifter in achieving his or her training objectives. This chapter highlighted training program variables that need to be addressed when developing these specific training programs and provided examples of various exercise protocols for the intermediate lifter.

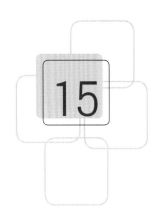

# Advanced Programs

Jay Hoffman and Avery Faigenbaum

As the intermediate lifter becomes more experienced, his or her ability to stimulate further physiological change is reduced. Without further modification to the training stimulus, the program becomes stale, and performance improvements begin to wane. For some intermediate lifters, the reduced rate of improvement may be acceptable, yet for others, it may lead to frustration.

This chapter discusses the design and development of advanced resistance training programs. It describes how to further manipulate training variables in order to maximize your desired gains while peaking your strength performance at the appropriate time.

## Chronic Program Adaptations

The strength training program for the lifter who progresses from an intermediate to a more advanced level may begin to resemble that of a competitive athlete. The fundamental difference between the training of an advanced lifter versus a competitive athlete is that the competitive athlete has a defined period of competition. The advanced lifter who is not a competitive athlete may train toward reaching peak physical condition at a time of his or her own choosing rather than a predetermined period related to a competition schedule.

For advanced lifters (or competitive athletes), the primary goal of training is to maximize athletic potential and reach optimal physical condition at the

307

appropriate time period. However, it is difficult to maintain peak physical condition for a prolonged period of time without becoming fatigued. But by systematically manipulating both training volume and intensity, an advanced lifter can make the necessary physiological adaptations while reaching peak condition at the appropriate time. In addition, by altering the volume and intensity of training with appropriately timed short unloading phases (of one to two weeks), the advanced lifter will minimize his or her risk of becoming fatigued or stale. Feelings of fatigue and staleness are often associated with a syndrome called *overtraining*, which can occur when training intensity and volume are increased without periods of rest and recovery interspersed within the training cycle. This eventually results in a decrease in performance, and in some cases, illness and injury.

It is well known that athletes are unable to maintain a high intensity of training stimulus for a prolonged duration without suffering some sort of performance or physiological detriment. To reduce the risk of this occurring, sport scientists have developed *periodized* training programs that separate a training year, known as a macrocycle, into four different training phases (see also chapters 3 and 7 for more discussion of periodization). These different phases are referred to as *mesocycles*. The duration of each mesocycle is approximately two to three months depending on the individual lifter and his or her specific training goals.

As you'll recall from chapter 3, periodization is partially based on principles related to the general adaptation syndrome (GAS) developed by Dr. Hans Selye, a Czech-trained endocrinologist who became well known for his work on the study of stress. The GAS principle (figure 15.1) suggests that there are three distinct phases that the body experiences in response to the stressful demands that are placed on it. The first phase is known as the *alarm phase*, and it is the body's initial response to a stimulus (e.g., exercise). This phase consists of both shock and soreness, and in response to a new exercise stimulus, it frequently results in a reduction in performance. The second phase is an *adaptation* to this new stimulus. During this

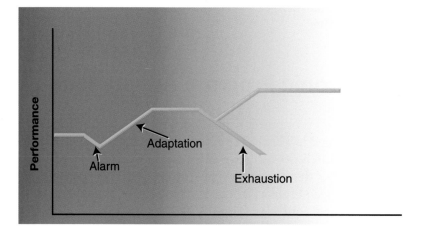

**Figure 15.1** A diagrammatic representation of Selye's General Adaptation Syndrome (GAS).

Adapted, from H. Selye, 1956, *The stress of life* (New York: McGraw-Hill Companies). By permission of McGraw-Hill Companies.

phase, the body has adapted to the training stimulus, resulting in an observable improvement in performance. The third phase is one of *exhaustion*. During this phase, the body is unable to make any further adaptation to the training stimulus. Unless this stimulus is reduced, a situation leading to chronic fatigue (overtraining) may occur. On the other hand, if the body is allowed sufficient recovery, it can then make further adaptations, and performance may increase even more. The purpose of periodization is to maintain an effective training stimulus that leads to long-term gains in performance while minimizing the risk of illness, injury, or burnout.

Periodization is based on the manipulation of both training volume and training intensity. During the first mesocycle, often referred to as the *preparatory* or *hypertrophy* phase, training volume (total number of repetitions) is high and training intensity (percentage of the individual's maximal lifting ability in a particular exercise) is low. For the advanced lifter, this phase of the training cycle is designed to focus on increasing muscle mass and muscle endurance. A secondary objective is to help prepare the lifter for the more intense training cycles that will occur later in the training program. During the next two mesocycles—referred to as *strength* and *strength-power*—intensity of training is elevated, while the volume of training is reduced. During these two mesocycles, the advanced lifter is primarily concerned with strength and power development. The final mesocycle of the training year is the *peaking* phase. This phase is specifically geared for the competitive athlete who wants to attain peak conditioning for a specific competition or the most important competitions of the year. During this mesocycle, training volume is again reduced, while training intensity is at its highest level. The volume and intensity typically seen during the various mesocycles in a training cycle are shown in table 15.1.

Although the basis for a periodized training program is to prepare an athlete to reach peak condition for a specific event during the year, many advanced lifters (specifically competitive athletes) participate in sports that place importance on an entire season of competition. For these athletes, peak strength must be achieved by the onset of the competitive year and maintained throughout the competitive season. The peaking phase for these athletes generally occurs several weeks before the preseason period. However, once the competitive season begins, the athlete performs an additional mesocycle known as the *maintenance* phase, which is designed to maintain the strength and size gains made during the off-season strength and conditioning program. During this phase of training, the exercise intensity is reduced to the levels used during the strength mesocycle, while training volume is lowered by reducing the number of assistance exercises performed during each workout.

It is not uncommon for the advanced lifter to use short training cycles known as *microcycles* to transition from mesocycle to mesocycle. The purpose of the microcycles is to provide the lifter with an opportunity to recover before beginning a new training phase. These microcycles can last between one and two weeks, and they allow lifters to feel refreshed and energized for the next training phase.

Table 15.1 **Typical Intensities and Volumes of Training for a Periodized Training Program Designed for an Advanced Strength or Power Athlete**

| | Phase of training | | | |
|---|---|---|---|---|
| | **Hypertrophy** | **Strength** | **Strength-power** | **Peaking** |
| Sets | 3-5 | 3-5 | 3-5 | 3-5 |
| Repetitions | 8-12 | 6-8 | 4-6 | 2-4 |
| Intensity (% 1RM) | 60-75 | 80-85 | 85-90 | >90 |

# Periodized Programs

The basic model of periodization focuses on uniform changes in training intensity and volume between each mesocycle, but these training variables remain relatively constant during each mesocycle. This periodization model, sometimes referred to as a *linear* model, is the traditional or classical form used for designing most periodized training programs. However, nonlinear or undulating models of periodization are also becoming popular. In this type of periodization scheme, the volume and intensity of training vary from workout to workout. Table 15.2 provides an example of a nonlinear training model. The intensity of the workouts varies between a light, moderate, and heavy training intensity.

This nonlinear training model may be appropriate for advanced lifters who participate in sports that involve a varied schedule—such as basketball, hockey, baseball, or soccer—with several games or competitions in a given week, or sports that have a schedule of games and travel that does not permit a regularly scheduled strength maintenance program during the season. Some coaches and athletes may prefer to use relatively light intensities of training before or on days of competition. In the undulating periodized program, the athlete can still train at a high intensity but at a more appropriate time of the week given his or her competition schedule.

**Table 15.2   Example of a Nonlinear Periodized Training Program**

|       | Program | Sets | Repetitions (RM) | Rest between sets (min) |
|-------|---------|------|------------------|-------------------------|
| Day 1 | Strength-power | 3-4 | 3-5 | 2-3 |
| Day 2 | Strength | 3-4 | 6-8 | 3-4 |
| Day 3 | Hypertrophy | 3-4 | 10-12 | 1 |

## General Muscular Conditioning

For the advanced lifter whose primary training goal is to improve general muscular conditioning, an undulating program may be the most appropriate training program. For these individuals, the primary purpose is general fitness. They are not preparing for a specific competition or a season of competition, so a program that is designed to have them peak for a specific time frame is irrelevant. Thus, for these people, the potential danger in using a training program that is not manipulated is an increased risk of staleness, monotony, and possible injury. A program that provides a different stimulus during each workout of the week may provide the greatest benefit and enjoyment for these people. Table 15.3 depicts an undulating program for an advanced lifter interested in general muscular fitness.

On careful examination of this program, it appears quite similar to the three-day-per-week general muscular fitness program for the intermediate lifter (see table 14.1a). It is unlikely that a person can maintain that training program for a prolonged time period without suffering some form of staleness or other symptom associated with overtraining syndrome. Thus, as these individuals move on to the advanced lifting program, they need to manipulate their weekly training sessions. On Monday, the lifter focuses on basic strength. Each exercise should be performed with a resistance that can be performed for at least 6 but not more than 8 repetitions, with three minutes of rest between each set. On Wednesday,

### Table 15.3    Undulating Program for General Muscular Conditioning

| Exercise | Sets × repetitions |
|---|---|
| **Monday** | |
| Leg press (p. 216) | 1, 3 × 6-8RM |
| Machine chest press (p. 184) | 1, 3 × 6-8RM |
| Seated barbell overhead press (p. 168) | 3 × 6-8RM |
| Lat pulldown (p. 191) | 1, 3 × 6-8RM |
| Seated leg curl (p. 223) | 3 × 6-8RM |
| Machine back extension (p. 249) | 3 × 6-8RM |
| Triceps pushdown (p. 202) | 3 × 6-8RM |
| Dumbbell biceps curl (p. 204) | 3 × 6-8RM |
| Sit-up (p. 232) | 3 × 20 |
| **Wednesday** | |
| Dumbbell lunge (front, reverse, or side; p. 217, 218, or 219) | 3 × 10-12RM |
| Incline bench press (p. 180) | 3 × 10-12RM |
| Dumbbell upright row (p. 171) | 3 × 10-12RM |
| Seated cable row (p. 194) | 3 × 10-12RM |
| Leg extension (p. 224) | 3 × 10-12RM |
| Lying triceps extension (p. 200) | 3 × 10-12RM |
| Dumbbell biceps curl (p. 204) | 3 × 10-12RM |
| Abdominal crunch (p. 232) | 3 × 20 |
| **Friday** | |
| Leg press (p. 216) | 3 × 8-10RM |
| Machine chest press (p. 184) | 3 × 8-10RM |
| Seated barbell overhead press (p. 168) | 3 × 8-10RM |
| Lat pulldown (p. 191) | 3 × 8-10RM |
| Seated leg curl (p. 223) | 3 × 8-10RM |
| Machine back extension (p. 249) | 3 × 8-10RM |
| Triceps pushdown (p. 202) | 3 × 8-10RM |
| Dumbbell biceps curl (p. 204) | 3 × 8-10RM |
| Sit-up (p. 232) | 3 × 20 |

The "1" before the number of sets and repetitions of select exercises indicates that one warm-up set should be performed prior to the main set.

the workout focuses on muscle hypertrophy by requiring a lighter resistance that allows the lifter to perform a greater number of repetitions (10 to 12) per set, with one minute between sets. On Friday, the workout involves a moderate intensity and volume (8 to 10RM), with a two- to three-minute rest between each set. Advanced lifters should rest at least 48 hours between each training session.

## Strength and Power Training

Table 15.4 depicts a three-day-per-week undulating (nonlinear) training program for the competitive strength or power athlete. During each training session, a whole body workout is performed. The difference between each workout is in the

**Table 15.4    Undulating Program for the Competitive Athlete**

| Exercise | Sets × repetitions |
|---|---|
| **Monday** | |
| Back squat (p. 214) | 1, 4 × 3-5RM |
| Bench press (p. 176) | 1, 4 × 3-5RM |
| Push press (p. 266) | 1, 4 × 3-5RM |
| High pull (p. 257) | 3 × 3-5 RM |
| Lat pulldown (p. 191) | 3 × 3-5RM |
| Triceps pushdown (p. 202) | 3 × 6-8RM |
| Biceps curl, barbell (p. 204) | 3 × 3-5RM |
| **Wednesday** | |
| Front squat (p. 212) | 1, 4 × 6-8RM |
| Incline bench press (p. 180) | 1, 4 × 6-8RM |
| Seated barbell overhead press (p. 168) | 1, 4 × 6-8RM |
| Dumbbell upright row (p. 171) | 3 × 6-8RM |
| Seated cable row (p. 194) | 3 × 6-8RM |
| Lying triceps extension (p. 200) | 3 × 6-8RM |
| Dumbbell biceps curl (p. 204) | 3 × 6-8RM |
| **Friday** | |
| Dumbbell lunge (front, reverse, or side; p. 217, 218, or 219) | 1, 3 × 10-12RM |
| Dumbbell bench press (p. 178) | 3 × 10-12RM |
| Seated barbell overhead press (p. 168) | 3 × 10-12RM |
| Compound set:   Barbell shrug (p. 165) | 3 × 10-12RM |
|                 Dumbbell side raise (p. 172) | 3 × 10-12RM |
| Bent-over row (p. 192) | 3 × 10-12RM |
| Assisted dip (p. 197) | 3 × 10-12RM |
| Dumbbell hammer curl (p. 206) | 3 × 10-12RM |

The "1" before the number of sets and repetitions of select exercises indicates that one warm-up set should be performed prior to the main set.

variety of exercises, the intensity and volume of the training session, and the rest period. These acute program variables will correspond to the goal of the training session. The first workout of the week focuses on strength and power, whereas the second and third workouts emphasize muscle strength and muscle hypertrophy, respectively. Rest periods between sets should be approximately three minutes during the first two training sessions, and approximately one minute during the muscle hypertrophy workout. At least 48 hours of rest should be included between each training session. As discussed earlier in this chapter, this training program may be used by athletes who are involved in a season of competition.

Table 15.5 provides an example of a periodized (linear) yearly training program for advanced lifters who are interested in maximizing strength and power development. This program would be appropriate for a strength or power athlete such as a powerlifter, football player, or basketball player. It would not be the ideal training program for the recreational athlete who is not attempting to reach a peak performance for a specific time of the year. This program uses a four-day-per-week split routine. Similar to other four-day split routines that have been described, the workouts on days 1 and 2 are performed consecutively, as are the training sessions on days 3 and 4. However, there are at least 72 hours of rest between workouts 1 and 3 and between workouts 2 and 4 in order to provide adequate rest for the specific muscle groups. The rest interval between sets is determined by the mesocycle in which the individual is training. During the hypertrophy (or preparatory) phase, the rest between sets is approximately one minute. During the strength, strength-power, and peaking phases, the rest interval is three minutes between sets.

In the linear program, each phase of training should last from six to eight weeks, with a one-week unloading period between each phase during which the individual does not perform any resistance training but may be recreationally active (e.g., playing racket sports, jogging). The peaking phase may be shorter in duration, lasting approximately four to six weeks. Some advanced lifters may repeat these cycles to provide greater variability in their yearly training program. For instance, football players may perform these cycles before spring football and then repeat the same training paradigm following spring football and leading into preseason training camp.

## Muscle Growth (Hypertrophy) Training

For the advanced lifter who is interested in maximizing muscle growth, the primary change from the intermediate-level hypertrophy program is the number and type of exercises. Since lifters who are interested in maximizing muscle hypertrophy generally use high volume, low intensity, and short rest (less than one minute between sets) in their training programs, the variability you can introduce in these acute program variables is limited. Although some individuals who train in this manner may incorporate several higher-intensity exercise routines, for the most part, these training protocols (in regard to volume, intensity, and rest) are often similar.

# Table 15.5 Periodized Training for Strength and Power

| Phase I: Preparatory or hypertrophy | Phase II: Basic strength | Phase III: Strength-power | Phase IV: Peaking |
|---|---|---|---|
| **Days 1 and 3** | | | |
| Back squat (p. 214) (1, 4 × 8-10RM) | Back squat (p. 214) (1, 4 × 6-8RM) | Back squat (p. 214) (1, 5 × 4-6RM) | Back squat (p. 214) (1, 5 × 1-3RM) |
| Leg extension (p. 224) (3 ×8-10RM) | Deadlift (p. 222) (3 × 6-8RM) | Deadlift (p. 222) (4 × 4-6RM) | Deadlift (p. 222) (4 × 1-3RM) |
| Seated leg curl (p. 223) (3 × 8-10RM) | Seated leg curl (p. 223) (3 × 6-8RM) | Seated leg curl (p. 223) (3 × 4-6RM) | Seated leg curl (p. 223) (3 × 4-6RM) |
| Standing calf raise (p. 227) (3 × 8-10RM) | Standing calf raise (p. 227) (3 × 8-10RM) | Lat pulldown (p. 191) (5 × 4-6RM) | Lat pulldown (p. 191) (5 × 4-6RM) |
| Lat pulldown (p. 191) (1, 4 × 8-10RM) | Lat pulldown (p. 191) (1, 4 × 6-8RM) | Seated cable row (p. 194) (5 × 4-6RM) | Seated cable row (p. 194) (5 × 4-6RM) |
| Seated cable row (p. 194) (1, 4 × 8-10RM) | Seated cable row (p. 194) (1, 4 × 6-8RM) | Dumbbell biceps curl (p. 204) (3 × 4-6RM) | Dumbbell biceps curl (p. 204) (3 × 4-6RM) |
| Dumbbell biceps curl (p. 204) (3 × 8-10RM) | Dumbbell biceps curl (p. 204) (3 × 6-8RM) | Biceps curl, barbell (p. 204) (3 × 4-6RM) | Back extension and hyper-extension (p. 250) (3 × 30) |
| Biceps curl, barbell (p. 204) (3 × 8-10RM) | Biceps curl, barbell (p. 204) (3 × 6-8RM) | Back extension and hyper-extension (p. 250) (3 × 25) | Abdominal crunch (p. 232) (3 × 35) |
| Back extension and hyper-extension (p. 250) (3 × 15) | Back extension and hyper-extension (p. 250) (3 × 20) | Abdominal crunch (p. 232) (3 × 30) | – |
| Abdominal crunch (p. 232) (3 × 20) | Abdominal crunch (p. 232) (3 × 25) | – | – |
| **Days 2 and 4** | | | |
| Bench press (p. 176) (1, 4 × 8-10RM) | High pull (p. 257) (1, 4 × 6-8RM) | Power clean (p. 252) (1, 4 × 3-6RM) | Power clean (p. 252) (1, 4 × 1-3RM) |
| Incline bench press (p. 180) (3 × 8-10RM) | Bench press (p. 176) (1, 4 × 6-8RM) | Bench press (p. 176) (1, 4 × 4-6RM) | Bench press (p. 176) (1, 4 × 1-3RM) |
| Dumbbell fly, incline (p. 186) (3 × 8-10RM) | Incline bench press (p. 180) (3 × 6-8RM) | Incline bench press (p. 180) (5 × 4-6RM) | Incline bench press (p. 180) (5 × 1-3RM) |
| Seated barbell overhead press (p. 168) (1, 4 × 8-10RM) | Dumbbell fly, incline (p. 186) (3 × 6-8RM) | Push press (p. 266) (5 × 4-6RM) | Push press (p. 266) (5 × 1-3RM) |
| Dumbbell upright row (p. 171) (3 × 8-10RM) | Seated barbell overhead press (p. 168) (4 × 6-8RM) | Dumbbell upright row (p. 171) (4 × 4-6RM) | Dumbbell upright row (p. 171) (4 × 4-6RM) |
| Dumbbell side raise (p. 172) (3 × 8-10RM) | Dumbbell front raise (p. 174) (3 × 6-8RM) | Lying triceps extension (p. 200) (3 × 4-6RM) | Lying triceps extension (p. 200) (3 × 4-6RM) |
| Triceps pushdown (p. 202) (3 × 8-10RM) | Lying triceps extension (p. 200) (3 × 6-8RM) | Assisted dips (p. 197) (3 × 4-6RM) | Assisted dips (p. 197) (3 × 4-6RM) |
| Lying triceps extension (p. 200) (3 × 8-10RM) | Triceps pushdown (p. 202) (3 × 6-8RM) | Sit-up (p. 232) (3 × 30) | Sit-up (p. 232) (3 × 30) |
| Sit-up (p. 232) (3 × 20) | Sit-up (p. 232) (3 × 25) | – | – |

315

What the advanced lifter may do is vary the selection and order of exercises in the program. For instance, some bodybuilders will change the order of exercise so that instead of performing the exercises that recruit the larger muscle mass first, they first perform the assistance exercises to "prefatigue" the muscle. Although this may seem to contradict what has been said in earlier chapters, the focus for these lifters is not to maximize strength gains but to maximize muscle growth. By prefatiguing the muscle fibers these lifters are trying to achieve a greater anabolic effect on the muscle. Exercise order can also be manipulated through super setting and compound setting. You'll recall from chapter 3 that super setting involves

### Table 15.6   Advanced Program for Muscle Hypertrophy (4 days per week)

| Exercise | Sets × repetitions |
|---|---|
| **Monday and Thursday** | |
| Back squat (p. 214) | 1, 4 × 10-12RM |
| Front squat (p. 212) (Mon)<br>Leg press (p. 216) (Thurs) | 1, 3 × 10-12RM |
| Compound set:   Leg extension (p. 224)<br>Seated leg curl (p. 223) | 3 × 10-12RM |
| Calf raise, seated (p. 227) | 3 × 10-12RM |
| Standing calf raise (p. 227) | 3 × 10-12RM |
| Lat pulldown (p. 191) | 4 × 10-12RM |
| Seated cable row (p. 194) | 4 × 10-12RM |
| Back extension and hyperextension (p. 250) | 4 × 20 |
| Biceps curl, barbell (p. 204) | 4 × 10-12RM |
| Dumbbell biceps curl (p. 204) | 4 × 10-12RM |
| Sit-up (p. 232) | 4 × 20 |
| **Tuesday and Friday** | |
| Bench press (p. 176) | 1, 4 × 10-12RM |
| Dumbbell incline bench press (p. 182) | 3 × 10-12RM |
| Incline bench press (p. 180) | 3 × 10-12RM |
| Dumbbell fly, incline (p. 186) | 3 × 10-12RM |
| Seated barbell overhead press (p. 168) | 1, 4 × 10-12RM |
| Compound set:   Dumbbell upright row (p. 171)<br>Dumbbell side raise (p. 172) | 3 × 10-12RM |
| Barbell shrug (p. 165) | 3 × 10-12RM |
| Triceps pushdown (p. 202) | 4 × 10-12RM |
| Lying triceps extension (p. 200) | 4 × 10-12 |
| Abdominal crunch (p. 232) | 4 × 20 |

alternating exercises for agonist and antagonist muscle groups, with little or no rest between exercises (e.g., biceps curl on page 204 and triceps pushdown on page 202). Compound setting involves performing different exercises for the same muscle group in an alternating fashion, with little or no rest between exercises (e.g., incline bench press on page 180 and dumbbell fly on page 186).

For many advanced lifters interested in body sculpting, a four- or six-day-per-week split routine may be employed. Tables 15.6 and 15.7 provide examples of both of these options.

**Table 15.7 Advanced Program for Muscle Hypertrophy (6 days per week)**

| Exercise | Sets × repetitions |
|---|---|
| **Days 1 and 4 (chest and triceps)** | |
| Bench press (p. 176) | 4 × 10-12RM |
| Incline dumbbell bench press (p. 182) | 4 × 10-12RM |
| Dumbbell fly, incline (p. 186) | 4 × 10-12RM |
| Assisted dip (p. 197) | 3 × 10-12RM |
| Triceps pushdown (p. 202) | 4 × 10-12RM |
| Lying triceps extension (p. 200) | 3 × 6-8RM |
| Sit-up (p. 232) | 3 × 20 |
| **Days 2 and 5 (back and shoulders)** | |
| Machine shoulder press (p. 170) | 4 × 10-12RM |
| Dumbbell upright row (p. 171) | 4 × 10-12RM |
| Compound set: Dumbbell side raise (p. 172) | 3 × 10-12RM |
| Dumbbell front raise (p. 174) | 3 × 10-12RM |
| Assisted chin-up (p. 190) | 3 × 10-12RM |
| Lat pulldown (p. 191) | 4 × 10-12RM |
| Bent-over row (p. 192) | 4 × 10-12RM |
| Back extension and hyperextension (p. 250) | 3 × 10-12RM |
| **Days 3 and 6 (legs and biceps)** | |
| Back squat (p. 214) | 4 × 10-12RM |
| Dumbbell step-up (p. 220) | 3 × 10-12RM |
| Super set: Leg extension (p. 224) | 3 × 10-12RM |
| Seated leg curl (p. 223) | 3 × 10-12RM |
| Compound set: Standing calf raise (p. 227) | 3 × 10-12RM |
| Calf raise, seated (p. 227) | 3 × 10-12RM |
| Biceps curl, barbell (p. 204) | 3 × 10-12RM |
| Compound set: Dumbbell biceps curl (p. 204) | 3 × 10-12RM |
| Dumbbell hammer curl (p. 206) | 3 × 10-12RM |

The primary reason some advanced lifters prefer a six-day-per-week training program is that it provides a greater opportunity to focus on a single muscle group, or perhaps two muscle groups, per workout session and to add additional assistance exercises for the selected group or groups. However, it is difficult for most individuals, even advanced lifters, to maintain a six-day-per-week training program for more than a month. Such training protocols often pose problems when it comes to providing adequate recovery.

Another feature of the six-day training program is the increased number of compound and super sets that can be incorporated, allowing for greater fatigue to occur during each training session.

Similar to other split routine training programs, both sample programs include at least 72 hours of rest between workouts of the same body part. For the six-day program, workouts on days 1, 2, and 3 can be performed on consecutive days so that there is one day of complete rest before day 4. Although not necessary, you may consider interchanging different exercises for those listed in the training program to help reduce potential monotony.

The advanced lifting programs are geared toward individuals who are committed to resistance training. Although the goals described in the previous chapter on intermediate lifting are still relevant, they are addressed and maintained by the advanced lifter via the manipulation of acute program variables over the course of a yearly training program. The systematic manipulation of these acute program variables to develop the yearly training protocol is known as *periodization*.

A periodized training program for a recreational athlete who is gearing for peak performance at a specific time period may resemble that of a competitive athlete. A recreational lifter who is primarily interested in general muscular fitness, on the other hand, may put together a different periodized program or may decide that the move from an intermediate-level program to advanced program is not necessary. This chapter focused on how the acute training program variables can be manipulated during a training year to meet the individual weightlifting goals of experienced lifters.

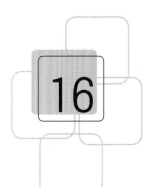

# Youth Programs

Avery Faigenbaum and Jay Hoffman

Children and teenagers have traditionally been encouraged to participate regularly in aerobic activities—such as swimming and bicycling—to enhance and maintain their cardiovascular fitness. However, a compelling body of evidence indicates that strength training can also be a safe, effective, and fun method of exercise for boys and girls as young as seven years of age, provided that appropriate training guidelines are followed. Over the past decade, strength training has become a popular conditioning tool with proven benefits for children and teenagers who want to improve their health, fitness, and sports performance. Today, boys and girls are strength training as part of a general fitness workout in physical education classes, in after-school programs, at recreation centers, and at sport camps.

Despite the previously held belief that strength training was inappropriate or unsafe for children, the qualified acceptance of youth strength training by professional organizations has become universal. In fact, public health objectives discussed in the surgeon general's report, *Physical Activity and Health* (1996), aimed to increase the number of children who regularly participate in physical activities that enhance and maintain muscular fitness. Indeed, a strong musculoskeletal system is now recognized as an important component of health-related physical fitness (along with aerobic fitness, flexibility, and appropriate body composition). Like riding a bike and playing basketball, participation in a youth strength training program provides boys and girls with yet another opportunity to improve their health, fitness, and quality of life.

Even though a growing number of boys and girls now participate in strength training programs in schools, camps, YMCAs, and fitness centers, some parents and coaches have lingering concerns about the safety of youth strength training. Others are unsure if the potential benefits of youth strength training outweigh the risks.

## Dispelling the Myths

Many myths surrounding youth strength training still persist; the most prevalent myths and the facts that refute them include the following:

**Myth:** Strength training stunts the growth of children.

**Fact:** No scientific evidence supports the belief that strength training stunts the growth of children. Despite traditional concerns associated with this type of training, properly performed strength training exercises do not put too much pressure on the developing growth plates of young lifters. Since physical activity is essential for normal growth and development, regular participation in strength training activities will likely have a favorable influence on growth during childhood and adolescence. Additional concerns associated with this myth are discussed later in this chapter.

**Myth:** Children cannot increase muscle strength because they do not have enough testosterone.

**Fact:** Testosterone is not essential for achieving strength gains, as evidenced by women who experience impressive gains in strength even though they have little testosterone. When compared on a relative or percent basis, training-induced strength gains during childhood are comparable to those of adults.

**Myth:** Strength training is unsafe for children.

**Fact:** The risks associated with strength training are not greater than those associated with other physical activities in which children regularly participate. The key is to provide qualified supervision, age-specific instruction, and a safe training environment. However, as with all types of physical activity, accidents can happen if children do not follow established training guidelines and adhere to safety rules.

**Myth:** Strength training is only for fit young athletes.

**Fact:** Regular participation in a youth strength training program can be a safe, effective, and worthwhile experience for boys and girls of all abilities. Strength training can certainly make young athletes faster and stronger, but it may also spark an interest in physical activity in sedentary or overweight youth who tend to dislike prolonged periods of continuous aerobic exercise.

**Myth:** Strength training will make kids "muscle bound" and inflexible.

**Fact:** Performing strength-building exercises throughout the full range of motion will not result in a loss of flexibility. In fact, strength training combined with stretching exercises may actually improve flexibility in children and teenagers. ■

# Benefits of Strength Training for Youths

When appropriately designed and competently supervised, youth strength training programs can offer observable health and fitness value to boys and girls such as the following:

- Increases in muscle strength and power
- Increases in local muscle endurance
- Increases in bone mineral density
- Improvements in blood lipid profile
- Improvements in body composition
- Increases in motor skill performance (jumping, throwing, and sprinting)
- Improvements in athletic ability
- Increases in resistance to sport-related injuries
- Improvements in body image and self-confidence
- A more positive attitude toward lifetime physical activity

In addition to increasing muscular strength and power, strength training has the potential to positively influence local muscular endurance (ability to perform more repetitions at a given weight), body composition, bone mineral density, and motor performance skills such as sprinting, jumping, and throwing. Furthermore, aspiring young athletes who participate in a preseason conditioning program that includes strength training tend to suffer fewer sport-related injuries during practice and competition than kids who don't strength train.

In the United States, about 30 million children participate in competitive organized sports and community-based programs. But along with this remarkable interest in youth sport, there has been an accompanying increase in the number of sport-related injuries because of poorly prepared or improperly trained young athletes. Although factors such as improper footwear and hard playing surfaces have been implicated as risk factors for overuse injuries (such as stress fractures and tendinitis), we must also consider the current physical activity level of boys and girls who want to play competitive sports. Generally, today's youth spend less time being physically active and more time with sedentary pursuits such as watching television or playing video games. Parents need to recognize that participation in physical activity should not begin with competitive sports; instead, it should evolve out of preparatory conditioning that includes strength training. To obtain the specific benefits from strength training, boys and girls need to participate regularly in a strength training program.

If children and teenagers spend more time developing fundamental physical abilities (such as muscular fitness) before participating in sports, their musculoskeletal system will be better prepared for the demands of sport practice and competition. By strengthening the supporting structures (ligaments, tendons, and bones), by enhancing muscle fitness, and by developing muscle balance around a joint, strength training may help to decrease the incidence of injuries in youth sport. Although the total elimination of sport-related injuries is an unrealistic goal, aspiring young athletes should be advised to participate in at least six weeks of preparatory conditioning (including strength, aerobic, and flexibility training) before competitive sport participation (figure 16.1). Not only will this type of conditioning better prepare boys and girls for the demands of practice and competition, but it may also decrease the likelihood that some will drop out of sport because of frustration, embarrassment, failure, or injury.

In addition to helping young athletes, strength training may also be beneficial for boys and girls who are overweight. Although aerobic exercise is typically prescribed for decreasing body fat, it appears that regular participation in a strength training program can have a favorable influence on the body composition of overweight youth. In addition, youngsters who are not accustomed to physical activity tend to enjoy strength training because it is not aerobically taxing and it gives all participants—regardless of body size and fitness ability—a chance to experience success and feel good about their performance. Along with support from family and friends, regular participation in a physical activity program that includes strength training may be part of the solution for long-term fat loss and weight management in overweight boys and girls. But to be effective, youth strength training programs need to be properly designed. Inappropriate training programs can be ineffective or unsafe.

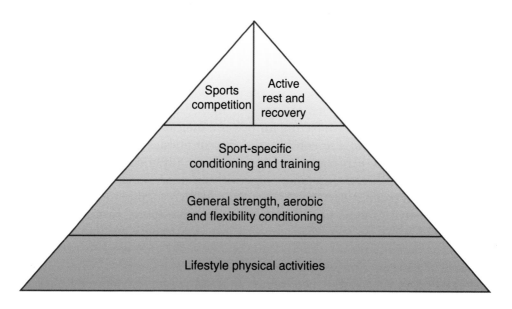

**Figure 16.1**  Physical activity pyramid.

Reprinted, by permission, from A. Faigenbaum, 2001, "Progression conditioning for high school athletes," *Strength and Conditioning* 23(1): 70-72.

# Risks and Concerns

In general, the risk of injury associated with strength training is similar for children and adults. However, one of the unique concerns associated with youth strength training involves the potential for injury to the epiphyses, or growth plates, of the long bones (such as the radius in the arms and the femur in the legs). The growth of the long bones in a child is initiated from a section of cartilage, known as a *growth plate*, at the end of each long bone (figure 16.2). This area is the weak link in the developing skeleton because growth cartilage is not as strong as bone. Although children and teenagers are susceptible to growth plate fractures, this type of injury has not been reported in any research study of youth strength training involving programs that were properly designed and supervised by qualified adults. It appears that the risk of a growth plate fracture is minimal if boys and girls are taught how to strength train properly and use appropriate training loads.

The greatest concern for children and teenagers who strength train is the risk of repetitive or overuse injuries to the soft tissue of the muscles, tendons, and ligaments. Although the incidence of this type of injury is difficult to determine since it does not always result in a visit to a physician, limited evidence suggests that the risk of developing this kind of injury is worth mentioning. In studies involving teenage athletes, about half of the reported injuries from strength training were to the lower back region. Although these young athletes presumably trained with very heavy weights, similar injuries could occur in boys and girls who participate in school-based or recreational programs. These findings highlight the importance of following safety standards (e.g., adult supervision, safe equipment) and using appropriate weights as well as proper exercise technique.

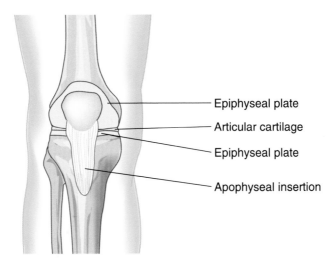

**Figure 16.2**   Growth plate cartilage in the knee.

Reprinted, by permission, from W. Kraemer and S. Fleck, 2005, *Strength training for young athletes,* 2nd ed. (Champaign, IL: Human Kinetics), 37.

No justifiable safety reasons exist to preclude children and adolescents from participating in strength-building activities; however, youth strength training programs need to be carefully designed and appropriately progressed because serious accidents can happen if safety guidelines are not followed. In addition, since some youth spend too much time training their so-called "mirror muscles" (e.g., chest and biceps) and not enough time (or no time at all) strengthening their abdominal and lower back muscles, additional guidance is often needed to help youth develop a balanced strength training program. In fact, because of the potential for lower back injuries noted previously, it makes sense for all boys and girls, as well as adults, to include abdominal and lower back strengthening exercises in their general fitness program.

# Program Design Considerations

There is no minimum age requirement for participating in a youth strength training program. However, all children who participate should have the emotional maturity to accept and follow directions and should understand the benefits and risks associated with this type of training. In general, if a child is ready for participation in sport, then he or she may be ready for some type of strength training. Although children as young as age seven or eight have participated in supervised youth strength training programs, cautionary measures need to be taken when children of any age want to participate in strength training. In addition, strength training should be just one part of a total physical activity program for children and teenagers, a program that also include free play and recreational physical activities.

Since there is no major difference in relative strength between prepubescent boys and girls (generally under age 13), strength training programs for both genders can be similar in design. In only a short period of time (about 8 to 12 weeks), untrained boys and girls can increase their strength by about 40 percent. Even though most of this increase is because of neuromuscular adaptations, this relative gain is similar to the relative gains made by adolescents and adults. Although boys and girls will get stronger on their own simply because of normal growth and development, a well-designed strength training program helps to optimize training-induced strength gains in youth.

No matter how big or strong a child is, adult training philosophies (e.g., "No pain, no gain") should not be imposed on boys and girls who are physically and psychologically less mature. When designing strength training programs for children, it is always better to underestimate their physical abilities—and gradually increase the intensity or weight—than to overestimate their abilities and risk an injury. Some beginners may want to see how much weight they can lift on the first day of the program; if this occurs, you should try to redirect their enthusiasm and interest in lifting heavy weights toward the development of proper form and

© Human Kinetics

technique on a variety of strength-building exercises using lighter loads. In any case, children should always learn proper form and technique with a light weight (or even a wooden dowel) before adding weight to the bar.

Tangible outcome measures such as increasing muscle strength are important, but they are not the only benefits associated with a youth strength training program. When instructing children, focus on intrinsic rewards such as skill improvement, personal success, and having fun. Throughout the program, teach children and teenagers about proper lifting techniques and safe training procedures (e.g., controlled movements and proper breathing). Furthermore, do not overlook the importance of children developing a more positive attitude toward strength training and other types of physical activity. Rather than compete against each other in the weight room, with appropriate guidance and supervision, boys and girls can learn to embrace self-improvement and feel good about their own accomplishments. Using individualized workout cards can help focus each child's attention on his or her own performance.

Other issues to address in designing an effective strength training program for children and teenagers include the quality of instruction, mode of training, choice and order of exercises, and rate of progression as well as those provided on page 326.

# Youth Strength Training Guidelines

☐ Provide qualified supervision and instruction.

☐ Ensure that the exercise environment is safe and free of hazards.

☐ Begin each session with a 5- to 10-minute warm-up period.

☐ Start with one light set of 10 to 15 repetitions on a variety of exercises.

☐ Progress to two or three sets of 6 to 15 repetitions depending on individual needs and goals.

☐ Perform 8 to 12 exercises for the upper body, lower body, and midsection.

☐ Increase the resistance gradually as strength improves (e.g., 5 to 10 percent).

☐ Focus on the correct exercise technique instead of the amount of weight lifted.

☐ Strength train two or three times per week on nonconsecutive days.

☐ Use individualized workout logs to monitor progress.

☐ Provide proper spotting, when necessary, to actively assist a child in the event of a failed repetition.

☐ Keep the program fresh and challenging by systematically varying the training program. ■

## Quality of Instruction

Children and teenagers should strength train only when under the watchful eye of a qualified adult. Although the efforts of inexperienced adults are appreciated, it is unlikely that they will be able to provide the quality of instruction that is needed for safe and effective training. Parents, youth coaches, and fitness trainers should have a thorough understanding of youth strength training guidelines and safety procedures. They should speak to children and teenagers at a level they understand. They should also keep the program fun and challenging while recognizing the importance of adhering to safe training procedures. All exercises must be clearly explained and properly demonstrated to all participants. Easy-to-follow explanations and verbal learning cues (e.g., "back flat," "head up") can facilitate the learning of a desired skill or movement.

Unsafe behavior in the strength training area should not be tolerated under any circumstances. In that regard, we do not recommend strength training at home for youth unless a competent adult is willing to provide supervision and instruction to ensure that proper training guidelines and exercise technique are followed. Some home exercise equipment, such as that used for the bench press, can result in serious injury if used inappropriately without a spotter.

With competent instruction and quality practice time, children and teenagers can learn the skills needed for successful and enjoyable participation in a youth strength training program. The first step is to get boys and girls interested in strength training so it becomes a regular part of their weekly routine.

When introducing young people to strength training, keep in mind that they are active in different ways than adults and for different reasons. Attempting to sell strength training to kids on the basis that it will enhance their quality of life is a losing proposition. Boys and girls should be aware of the potential health- and fitness-related benefits associated with regular strength training, but enthusiastic leadership, positive reinforcement, and effective teaching are more likely to get youth energized about participating in a strength training program. Provide an environment in which children and teenagers can have fun, socialize with friends, listen to music, and interact with adults who are positive and can provide age-appropriate training tips. It may be appropriate for adults to tell children why they strength train and how they stay healthy, fit, and strong. The following list provides additional tips for teaching youth.

- Listen to each child's concerns and answer any questions.
- Speak to children using words they understand.
- Demonstrate proper form on each exercise.
- Provide constructive feedback when necessary.
- Focus on proper exercise technique, not the amount of weight lifted.
- Highlight personal successes and value the importance of having fun.
- Remind children that it takes time to learn a new exercise and to get in shape.
- Offer a variety of activities and avoid regimentation.

## Mode of Training

Different modes of training can be effective in youth strength training programs, including performing exercises using body weight as resistance and using rubber tubing, medicine balls, free weights, and child-size weight machines. When evaluating strength training equipment for boys and girls, consider factors such as the cost, quality of instruction, adjustability, proper fit, and weight stack increments.

Most children are too small to use adult-size weight machines, but many teenagers can fit into these machines if extra pads are used. Note that a common problem with adult weight machines is that the increments on the weight stacks are often too large—10 to 20 pounds (4.5 to 9.0 kg)—for most youth, who typically increase the weight by increments of 2 to 5 pounds (.9 to 2.3 kg). Child-size weight machines are a viable alternative and have proven to be safe and effective for youth, but the cost is relatively expensive when compared to most other modes of training. Free weights, rubber tubing, and medicine balls are relatively inexpensive types of equipment that can be used with children and teenagers of all ages and abilities.

If equipment is not available, you can also develop a circuit of body weight exercises; however, this type of training may be too challenging for sedentary

© Human Kinetics

or overweight boys and girls who may not have the muscular strength and local muscular endurance to perform exercises such as push-ups or pull-ups. If available, weight-assisted machines that reduce body weight by using a counterweight system can be used to perform chin-ups and dips.

The best training results are likely to occur when children and teenagers have an opportunity to participate in different strength training programs and develop proper form and technique on a variety of exercises. However, young people also need to warm up properly (see page 150) and begin strength training with appropriate weights and exercises that are consistent with each individual's needs and abilities. The idea is for children to understand the concept of a fitness workout while enhancing their strength and gaining confidence in their abilities to perform strength exercise.

## Choice and Order of Exercises

Both single-joint (e.g., biceps curl) and multijoint (e.g., dumbbell squats) exercises can be incorporated into a youth strength training program. Although single-joint exercises are relatively easy to perform and are appropriate for beginners when the activation of a specific muscle group is desired, multijoint exercises require the coordinated action of many muscle groups. When preparing young athletes for sport participation, you should include multijoint exercises in the workout program. This type of exercise requires more balance and stabilization, and it promotes the coordinated use of multijoint movements that an athlete will use in his or her sport. In addition, the variety of exercises in a program should focus on the upper body, lower body, and midsection.

The sequence of exercises in a training session can be arranged in many ways. Traditionally, experts recommend performing exercises for large muscle groups before those for smaller muscle groups and performing multijoint exercises before single-joint exercises. Following this exercise order allows heavier weights to be used on the multijoint exercises because the muscles are not fatigued by previous exercises. It is also helpful to perform more challenging exercises earlier in the workout when the neuromuscular system is less fatigued.

## Training Intensity

Most experts recommend that children perform somewhere between 6 and 15 repetitions on each exercise. However, when introducing boys and girls to strength training, have them begin with a light to moderate weight that they can lift for 10 to 15 repetitions. This not only allows for positive changes in muscular performance, but it also provides an opportunity for children to feel good about their performance. The best approach may be to first establish the repetition training range (e.g., 10 to 15) and then by trial and error determine the appropriate load that the child can handle for that repetition range.

Of course, when learning a multijoint exercise such as the squat, it is a good idea for young weight trainers to start with a long wooden dowel instead of a loaded barbell. Not only is this safer, but it also helps children learn how to perform an exercise correctly the first time, which is easier than trying to break bad habits later on.

Another issue to note here is training speed. Although various speeds of movement can be effective for strength development, fast lifting speeds are not recommended for general strength training exercises by young people. Controlled lifting speeds with a consistent application of force are recommended for children and teenagers. Controlled lifting speeds are especially important during the lifting and lowering phase of each repetition.

## Training Sets and Rest

Children should perform one to three sets on a variety of exercises. However, they do not need to perform all exercises for the same number of sets. A good strategy is to begin strength training with a single set on each exercise, and then add additional sets on selected exercises depending on the needs, goals, and time available for training.

In general, youth should rest about one minute between sets and exercises. Although longer rest periods (about two to three minutes) may be appropriate for some young athletes who are following an advanced strength training program, youth have shorter attention spans than adults and will likely get bored if they have to "stand around" and wait for an extended period before doing the next exercise.

## Training Frequency

A strength training frequency of two or three nonconsecutive days per week is recommended for boys and girls who are participating in an introductory strength training program. This allows for adequate recovery between workouts, which is essential for maximizing training adaptations. Children and teenagers who perform more advanced strength training programs may increase the training frequency, but specific muscle groups should only be trained two or three times per week.

## Rate of Progression

A fundamental principle of strength training is that as the muscle adapts to the strength training stimulus, the demands placed on it need to become more challenging in order to maintain the same relative training intensity. As you learned in previous chapters, this does not mean that every strength training session needs to be more intense than the previous session. But over a period of weeks, the training stimulus needs to be advanced by gradually increasing the resistance, the number of repetitions, or the number of sets.

Youth should start with a basic workout for the first four weeks using relatively light weights and with an emphasis on learning proper technique. This introductory period is an important phase that gives a child's muscles, tendons, and ligaments time to adapt to the demands of strength exercise. A common mistake is for youth to begin strength training with a relatively heavy weight instead of mastering correct exercise technique. This misguided approach to strength training can result in injury and burnout.

On average, a 5- to 10-percent increase in training load is an appropriate increment for increasing the intensity of most exercises. Thus, a teenager performing two sets of 15 repetitions with 20 pounds (9 kg) on the dumbbell bench press exercise (page 178) can probably progress to 22 pounds (10 kg) and reduce the number of repetitions to 10 to allow for continual gains. Remember that young lifters should always develop proper form and technique before the weight is increased.

Once children develop proper form and technique on a variety of exercises and understand the concept of progression, they can advance to more challenging workouts. This may include heavier weights, extra sets, or the addition of new exercises to the workout plan. As long as qualified instruction is available and age-appropriate weights are used, children who successfully complete a beginner program can progress to the more advanced programs discussed in this book. However, because of individual differences in the ability of children to tolerate advanced strength training workouts, each child must be treated as an individual and carefully observed for signs of burnout or overfatigue that would require a modification in the frequency, intensity, or volume of training.

# Youth Program

Since strength training should be only one part of a youngster's weekly physical activity routine, a total body conditioning workout performed two or three nonconsecutive days per week is recommended for boys and girls who have no experience strength training. Children and young athletes who have experience strength training may perform more advanced training programs outlined in this book; however, they should first learn proper form and technique on a variety of upper and lower body exercises before progressing to more complex training programs. In addition, children need to genuinely appreciate the potential benefits and concerns associated with strength training if this type of exercise is to become a lifelong physical activity.

The beginner workout for youth shown in table 16.1 is designed to strengthen all the major muscle groups. Youth should use an initial weight that allows for 10 to 15 repetitions. Once 15 repetitions can be performed with proper form, the weight should be increased by about 5 to 10 percent (about 2 to 5 pounds [.9 to 2.3 kg]) and the repetitions cut back to 10. Children and young athletes who have experience strength training can perform additional sets with heavier weights. However, all participants, regardless of age or strength training experience, should use a light weight when learning how to perform a new exercise.

### Table 16.1   Beginner Workout for Youth

| Exercise | Sets | Repetitions |
| --- | --- | --- |
| Back squat, dumbbell (p. 214) | 1 | 10-15 |
| Standing calf raise (p. 227) | 1 | 10-15 |
| Dumbbell bench press (p. 178) | 1 | 10-15 |
| One-arm dumbbell row (p. 193) | 1 | 10-15 |
| Dumbbell side raise (p. 172) | 1 | 10-15 |
| Dumbbell biceps curl (p. 204) | 1 | 10-15 |
| Lying triceps extension (p. 200) | 1 | 10-15 |
| Prone back raise (p. 287) | 1 | 10-15 |
| Abdominal crunch (p. 232) | 1 | 10-15 |

Note that progressing to heavier weights and additional sets is required to maximize gains in muscular fitness after the first 8 to 12 weeks of strength training.

After six to eight weeks of general strength training, add new exercises and change the number of sets and repetitions in order to keep the program effective and fun. For example, lifters may perform two sets of exercises for large muscle groups (legs, chest, and back) and gradually increase the training weight so that they can only perform 8 to 10 repetitions. The importance of program progression is discussed in more detail in chapters 13, 14, and 15 (sample workouts are also provided in those chapters). Just remember that strength training should be only one component of a youngster's exercise plan, which should also include free play and other fun physical activities.

Keep in mind that no matter how big or strong a child is, that child is still growing and may be experiencing a game or activity for the first time. When introducing boys and girls to strength-building exercises, you must respect children's feelings and appreciate the fact that their thinking is different from yours. Remember that the primary reason children engage in physical activity is to have fun and feel successful. If boys and girls have a positive experience while strength training, they will likely become adults who regularly strength train.

Despite outdated concerns associated with youth strength training, qualified professional organizations now recommend strength training for boys and girls provided that age-specific training guidelines are followed. With qualified supervision and an appropriate progression of the training program, boys and girls of all abilities—from the inactive child to the young athlete—can benefit from regular participation in a strength training program. Along with other types of physical activity, strength training provides boys and girls with yet another opportunity to enhance their health, fitness, and quality of life.

# Senior Programs

Avery Faigenbaum and Jay Hoffman

Americans now live nearly twice as long as they did only a hundred years ago. The number of men and women over the age of 65 continues to increase, and by the year 2040, the number of Americans over age 65 will likely reach 70 million. The aging of our population has resulted in the development of interventions that are designed to optimize health and reduce health care costs.

Although aerobic exercise such as walking and swimming has long been recognized as an important recommendation for seniors, recent research studies and clinical observations indicate that strength training can also offer numerous health and fitness benefits for this segment of our population. These benefits can offset the declines in musculoskeletal health that occur with aging.

Since physical inactivity can lead to a deterioration in general health and the ability to perform activities of daily life (such as climbing stairs and carrying groceries), it is not surprising that regular strength training can help maintain and enhance musculoskeletal health. Of particular importance to seniors is the observation that regular participation in a well-designed strength training program can reduce the risk of falls and hip fractures. Given the potential long-term loss of function or even death associated with hip fractures, this reduced risk is an important benefit.

Despite outdated concerns that strength training is unnecessary or ineffective for seniors, current research clearly indicates that seniors have a significant ability to benefit from strength-building exercises. In fact, even individuals over the age of 90 can enhance their muscular fitness by strength training. Major health and fitness organizations, including the National Strength and Conditioning

Association, recommend strength training for seniors to help maintain and enhance musculoskeletal health and fitness. When incorporated into a comprehensive exercise program that includes aerobic exercise and stretching, strength training can help to offset the age-related declines in bone, muscle mass, and strength that often make activities of daily life more difficult.

# Benefits of Strength Training for Seniors

It is well established that aerobic exercise such as walking and swimming is effective for burning calories and improving cardiovascular fitness. However, the benefits of strength exercise are equally impressive, especially for senior men and women. Strength training is well known for enhancing sport-specific fitness, but it can also have profound effects on an individual's health and functional capacity. In addition to enhancing muscle strength and preserving muscle mass, regular participation in a strength training program can reduce body fat, increase metabolic rate, decrease resting blood pressure, lower cholesterol, improve glucose tolerance, and reduce lower back pain and the risk of developing osteoporosis and colon cancer. Collectively, these benefits can help to maintain long-term independence and enhance self-confidence as muscle strength and function improve. As such, these potential benefits are important incentives for seniors to initiate an exercise program that includes safe and proper strength training.

Advancing age is associated with a number of changes that are detrimental to health and performance. Referred to as *sarcopenia*, the age-related loss of muscle mass in seniors results in weakness, reduced physical activity, and an increased risk of falls or injury. Research studies indicate that muscle strength declines by about 15 percent per decade in the sixth and seventh decades of life, and by about 30 percent thereafter. Decreased muscular strength and mass not only makes activities such as walking and standing up from a chair more difficult, this age-related loss of muscle can also result in physical disability and a loss of independence. Moreover, the loss of muscle that occurs with aging is accompanied by a decline in resting metabolic rate, which can lead to unwanted fat gain if declining caloric needs are not matched with an appropriate decline in caloric intake.

Since muscle is metabolically active (and therefore burns calories), regular participation in muscle-building activities can increase resting metabolic rate. This in turn helps to maintain a desirable body weight. These potential benefits are particularly important for seniors because advancing age is typically associated with a loss of muscle and a gain of fat (figure 17.1).

Is it possible to rebuild muscles that have already atrophied from lack of physical activity and lack of regular strength exercise? Yes, and the rate of muscle development is quite impressive in seniors. Research studies have shown that the age-related declines in muscle structure and function are not an inevitable consequence of aging, but rather a result of a sedentary lifestyle. Seniors can

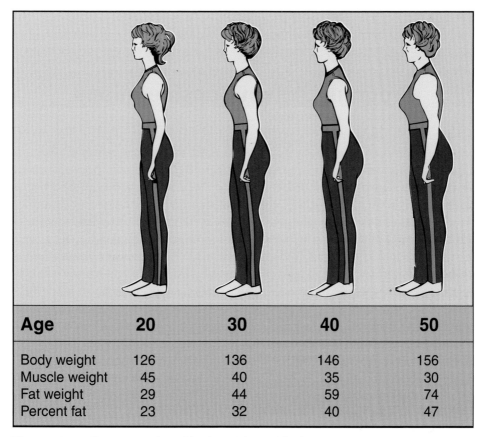

| Age | 20 | 30 | 40 | 50 |
|---|---|---|---|---|
| Body weight | 126 | 136 | 146 | 156 |
| Muscle weight | 45 | 40 | 35 | 30 |
| Fat weight | 29 | 44 | 59 | 74 |
| Percent fat | 23 | 32 | 40 | 47 |

**Figure 17.1**    Some examples of body weight and body composition changes over four decades.

Reprinted, by permission, from W. Westcott, 2003, *Building strength and stamina*, 2nd ed. (Champaign, IL: Human Kinetics), 9.

respond favorably to a strength training program that is appropriately designed and properly progressed. Therefore, strength-building exercises may be warranted to enhance muscle strength, muscle mass, and muscle performance in seniors. In fact, since muscle weakness is a problem for many seniors, seniors who increase their muscle strength may also be more likely to participate in aerobic activities such as swimming and tennis.

Another major issue related to musculoskeletal health is the loss of bone (osteoporosis). The prevalence of osteoporosis increases with aging. Osteoporosis is associated with fractures in the hip, back, and forearm. For seniors, fractures are a serious medical concern. Since bone strength decreases markedly with age, the enhancement or even maintenance of bone strength is a desirable result of regular strength training for seniors. Although any type of weight-bearing physical activity can have a favorable impact on bone strength, a total body strength training workout can be designed to enhance or maintain bone strength in the upper body, lower body, and midsection. Thus, strength training should be considered an essential component of a well-rounded exercise program for seniors who want to enhance their musculoskeletal health and quality of life.

# Program Design Considerations

To maximize the benefits of strength training, the fundamental principles of overload, progression, and specificity must be followed, and the program variables must be manipulated over time to keep the program effective. Furthermore, training-induced improvements in health and performance will depend on the program design as well as an individual's training status or level of fitness. For example, a previously untrained senior will make remarkable gains in muscle strength and performance during the first eight weeks of strength training, whereas a senior who has been strength training for several months or even years will show a much slower rate of improvement. These differences highlight the importance of proper program design, sensible progression, and realistic expectations. In some cases, seniors who have attained a certain level of fitness may want to maintain that level and may not want to progress to higher levels. In any case, in addition to the guidelines provided on this page, the next section details recommendations to consider when designing strength training programs for seniors.

## Senior Strength Training Guidelines

- ☐ Undergo health screening by a physician or health care provider before participating.
- ☐ Use a 5- to 10-minute warm-up period before each strength training workout.
- ☐ Begin with one set of 10 to 15 repetitions of 8 to 10 exercises.
- ☐ Strength train two or three days per week on nonconsecutive days.
- ☐ Perform each repetition through a pain-free range of motion.
- ☐ Focus on proper breathing patterns while strength training.
- ☐ Seek guidance from a qualified fitness professional if needed. ■

## Safety Considerations

Some seniors have physical or mental conditions that make it difficult for them to participate in a traditional strength training program. Thus, the first step is to check with your physician or health care provider for specific exercise recommendations and training modifications. Seniors must be especially observant if they have any preexisting medical condition (such as heart disease, high blood pressure, or diabetes) that may require close supervision or some type of modification in their exercise program. Any undesirable responses to exercise—such as light-headedness, chest pain, or joint discomfort—should be addressed with a medical professional.

To ensure a safe and productive strength training experience, seniors should also adhere to the following safety recommendations:

- Make sure the exercise area is well lit, adequately ventilated, and spacious, with plenty of room between equipment and machines.
- Avoid exercising in areas with a cluttered floor because this will increase the risk of tripping and falling.
- Wear comfortable, lightweight clothing that allows for freedom of movement.
- Wear athletic shoes that will provide adequate support and good traction to prevent slipping.

Above all, use common sense when strength training and always respect your body. For example, be sure the correct weight load is selected on a weight machine, and have a spotter nearby to assist you if performing a free weight exercise such as the bench press. If you're feeling tired or if your muscles are still sore from your last exercise session, modify the training session by using lighter weights or simply skip the workout altogether.

Since advancing age is associated with increased muscle stiffness and reduced elasticity of supporting structures, seniors must perform a proper warm-up before each strength training session. This can reduce the risk of injury and may even enhance performance. A 5- to 10-minute warm-up consisting of low-intensity aerobic exercise, such as walking (at a level you can maintain a conversation) or calisthenics, followed by static stretching is sufficient. Be sure to cool down after each strength training session too. End your workout with several minutes of slow walking and more static stretching. Since your body will have warmed up from the workout, postexercise stretching will be more effective because your muscles, tendons, and ligaments will be more elastic.

## Training Technique

The key to safe and successful strength training is to perform each exercise with proper form and technique. In addition to the technical guidelines discussed in part III, seniors need to pay particular attention to their movement speed, movement range, and exercise breathing.

Strength training exercises should be performed at a controlled movement speed (about two seconds for the lifting phase and two to three seconds for the lowering phase). Although different movement speeds may be acceptable, seniors should perform each repetition under control.

Furthermore, the goal is to perform each repetition through a pain-free range of motion. Although seniors should attempt to perform each repetition through

© Human Kinetics

the full range of joint motion whenever possible, some seniors may be limited because of arthritis or other physical limitations. Therefore, seniors should perform strength exercises throughout a range of motion that does not exceed normal joint limits or result in pain. For example, if you cannot perform a squat exercise through the full range of motion, modify the exercise by bending your knees and hips only slightly. As you continue to perform the modified squat exercise and your strength and flexibility improve, you may be able to gradually increase the range of motion.

Seniors must also avoid the Valsalva maneuver (holding your breath during exertion). Practicing proper breathing during each repetition is important for seniors because breath holding may result in high blood pressure responses. Common practice is to exhale when you lift the weight and inhale when you lower the weight.

## Choice and Order of Exercises

Seniors can use different types of exercise equipment, including weight machines, free weights (barbells and dumbbells), and simple devices such as ankle bags filled with sand or household objects such as plastic milk jugs filled with water. Whatever type of equipment is used, the training program should address all the major muscle groups that are used in everyday activities, paying particular attention to developing muscle balance. For example, if you perform an exercise for your chest muscles, you should also perform an exercise using your back muscles. If you do not give equal attention to opposing muscle groups on your upper body, midsection, and lower body, you may develop poor posture and increase your risk of developing an injury.

You can incorporate both single-joint (e.g., dumbbell biceps curl, page 204) and multijoint (e.g., squats, pages 212, 214) exercises into the training program. Keep in mind that on some weight machines, the lightest weight may be too heavy and the increments may be too large (e.g., 10 pounds [4.5 kg]). Furthermore, linear movements on weight machines may not address some common daily movement patterns that require balance and coordination. Nevertheless, if you have access to weight machines, you may want to start strength training on weight machines and then gradually progress to free weight exercises that require more balance, skill, and coordination.

Most seniors find it preferable to exercise large muscle groups first and then progress to smaller muscle groups. Since heavier weights are typically used on leg exercises as compared to arm exercises, this exercise order allows you to work with heavy weights early in the workout and to exercise your leg muscles at the start of your workout when they are fresh. After training the legs, you can do exercises for the chest, back, shoulders, and arms. Near the end of your workout, train the abdominal and lower back muscles around the midsection.

Of course, you don't have to follow the same exercise order every workout. Sometimes it makes sense to strengthen the weaker muscle groups early in the workout when you are less fatigued. Just keep in mind that altering the exercise order may change the number of repetitions that you can perform.

If a workout consists of both strength and aerobic exercise, begin with aerobic activity and then do strength training. If the workout only involves strength training, perform 5 to 10 minutes of light aerobic activity or calisthenics, followed by stretching exercises, before strength training.

# Training Intensity

A variety of different strength training programs have proven to be effective for seniors. The key is to start with a weight that will allow you to lift the prescribed number of repetitions using proper form and then gradually increase the demands placed on the exercising muscles. In short, the goal of the exercise program should be to challenge your muscles so they adapt to the training program and get stronger.

Seniors should begin strength training with 10 to 15 repetitions per set of 8 to 10 exercises that use all the major muscle groups. It is always prudent to err on the side of safety when starting a strength training program, and the higher repetition range represents relatively lower exercise resistance (approximately 60 to 75 percent of 1RM).

However, as strength increases, you may progress to higher exercise resistance and fewer repetitions per set. This is done because the intensity of the strength training workout is what determines the magnitude of the gains in strength and muscle size. An acceptable resistance range may extend from 60 to 90 percent of maximum, with a corresponding repetition range of 4 to 15 repetitions. If the intensity of the exercise is too low (a weight that can be lifted for more than 20 repetitions), gains in local muscular endurance are likely, but gains in muscle strength or muscle mass will be limited.

As a general guideline, beginning seniors may train with 60 to 75 percent of maximum resistance (10 to 15 repetitions); seniors with several months of strength training experience may train with 75 to 90 percent of maximum resistance (4 to 10 repetitions) on selected exercises for large muscle groups in order to enhance strength development. Training variety enhances strength development and reduces the risk of overtraining; therefore, the best approach for advanced seniors may be to periodically vary the training intensity by performing fewer repetitions with a relatively heavy weight and more repetitions with a relatively light weight.

# Training Sets and Rest

Seniors should begin strength training with a single set on each exercise. This is an efficient and effective means for enhancing muscle strength during the first six to eight weeks of training. However, as you become more advanced, you may want to perform a second or third set on selected exercises in order to keep the training program effective. If multiple sets are performed, be sure to maintain a balanced training program. For example, if you perform two sets of a chest exercise, you should also perform two sets of a back exercise.

Keep in mind that not all exercises need to be performed for the same number of sets. If time permits, you may want to progress to two or three sets on exercises for large muscle groups and stay with only one set on exercises for smaller muscle groups. If you perform multiple sets, you can use the same weight, or you can change the weight and the repetitions on the second and third sets. For example, advanced seniors could perform a set of 10 repetitions on the leg press exercise (page 216) with 100 pounds (45.4 kg), a second set of 8 repetitions with 120 pounds (54.4 kg), and a third set of 6 repetitions with 140 pounds (63.5 kg). If you perform multiple sets with a heavier weight, you should rest about two minutes between each set to allow yourself to recover.

## Training Frequency

For best results, seniors should strength train two or three nonconsecutive days per week using a full body workout (most major muscle groups) each exercise session. After each strength training session, your muscles need about 48 to 72 hours to rebuild in order to get stronger; therefore, strength training the same muscle group on two consecutive days can be counterproductive. For seniors, strength training every other day is a reasonable recommendation that will result in larger and stronger muscles. This training frequency also ensures training consistency, which is essential for long-term gains. Short-term programs may increase muscle strength; however, long-term (lifetime) training is necessary to ensure lasting improvements in muscle strength and other physical factors that reduce the risk of various diseases and physical ailments associated with aging.

# Senior Program

Regular participation in strength training workouts is essential for enhancing and maintaining muscular fitness so that seniors can live a physically independent lifestyle. Although the training overload must be adequate and the training program must be progressive, seniors also need to learn how to strength train properly right from the start. Poor exercise technique and haphazard programming not only increase the risk of injury but also undermine the purpose of strength training. In short, it is always better to develop good habits right from the start than try to break bad habits later on.

Seniors should start with the home program outlined in table 17.1 or the beginner program discussed in chapter 13. The goal should be to develop proper exercise technique on a variety of exercises that use all the major muscle groups. Beginning with one set of 10 to 15 repetitions, seniors should first increase the number of repetitions (up to 15) and then gradually increase the weight as strength improves. As seniors progress from one exercise to the next, they may need a little extra time to adjust to postural changes such as moving from a supine position to a standing position. With these considerations in mind, seniors may find it worthwhile to learn proper exercise technique from a qualified fitness trainer who understands their individual needs, goals, and medical history.

A growing number of recreation centers and fitness facilities now offer supervised strength training workouts for seniors. In these settings, fitness trainers can

Table 17.1   **Sample Home Strength Training Program**

| Exercise | Sets | Repetitions |
|---|---|---|
| Back squat, dumbbell (p. 214) | 1 | 10-15 |
| Dumbbell bench press (p. 178) | 1 | 10-15 |
| Dumbbell upright row (p. 171) | 1 | 10-15 |
| Dumbbell side raise (p. 172) | 1 | 10-15 |
| Dumbbell biceps curl (p. 204) | 1 | 10-15 |
| Lying triceps extension (p. 200) | 1 | 10-15 |
| Alternating hip extension (p. 287) | 1 | 10-15 |
| Abdominal crunch (p. 232) | 1 | 10-15 |

provide positive reinforcement for correct technique and specific suggestions for improved performance. Since it is often more enjoyable to exercise with someone else, strength training with a fitness trainer or a friend not only makes the workout more enjoyable, but it also increases the likelihood that you will stick with the exercise program.

Strength training with friends and family members is a perfect opportunity to stay healthy and strong while having fun. We also recommend that you keep careful records of your strength training workouts. This information provides you with important material for future program design and can serve as a powerful motivational tool.

It is clear that men and women of all ages retain the capacity to adapt to strength training. Since muscle weakness is a common characteristic of advancing age, seniors can benefit from physical activity programs that preserve or enhance muscular fitness and bone strength. Regular strength training can improve muscle function, increase bone strength, and have a meaningful impact on the ability of seniors to maintain a high-quality lifestyle. Although the fundamental principles of strength training are similar for individuals of all ages and abilities, there are unique considerations specific to seniors that must be considered when designing strength training programs. Perhaps the best recommendation for seniors who want to optimize their current and future health is to begin a sensible strength training program that is consistent with their current needs, abilities, and medical history.

# References

American College of Sports Medicine (ACSM). 2002. American College of Sports Medicine position stand. Progression models in resistance training for healthy adults. *Medicine and Science in Sports and Exercise* 34(2):364-380.

Biolo, G., S.P. Maggi, B.D. Williams, K.D. Tipton, and R.R. Wolfe. 1995. Increased rates of muscle protein turnover and amino acid transport after resistance exercise in humans. *American Journal of Physiology* 268:E514-E520.

Cramer, J.T., T.J. Housh, G.L. Johnson, J.M. Miller, J.W. Coburn, and T.W. Beck. 2004. Acute effects of static stretching on peak torque in women. *Journal of Strength and Conditioning Research* 18(2):236-241.

Drought, J.H. 1992. Program design: Personal training program design and periodization. *National Strength and Conditioning Association Journal* 14(5):31-34.

Dudley, G.A., P.A. Tesch, B.J. Miller, and P. Buchanan. 1991. Importance of eccentric actions in performance adaptations to resistance training. *Aviation and Space Environmental Medicine* 62:543-550.

Fleck, S.J., and W.J. Kraemer. 2004. *Designing resistance training programs.* 3rd ed. Champaign, IL: Human Kinetics.

Gotshalk, L.A., R.A. Berger, and W.J. Kraemer. 2004. Cardiovascular responses to a high-volume continuous circuit resistance training protocol. *Journal of Strength and Conditioning Research* 18(4):760-764.

Greenhaff, P.L. 1995. Creatine and its application as an ergogenic aid. *International Journal of Sports Nutrition* 5(suppl.):S100-S110.

Haff, G.G., M.H. Stone, B.J. Warren, R. Keith, R.L. Johnson, D.C. Nieman, F. Williams, and B. Kirksey. 1999. The effect of carbohydrate supplementation on multiple sessions and bouts of resistance exercise. *Journal of Strength and Conditioning Research* 13:111-117.

Hansen, S., T. Kvornign, M. Kajaer, and G. Sjogaard. 2001. The effect of short-term strength training on human skeletal muscle: The importance of physiologically elevated hormone levels. *Scandinavian Journal of Medicine and Science in Sports* 11:347-354.

Hather, B.M., P.A. Tesch, P. Buchanan, and G.A. Dudley. 1991. Influence of eccentric actions on skeletal muscle adaptations to resistance training. *Acta Physiologica Scandinavica* 143:177-185.

Hawke, T.L. 2005. Muscle stem cells and exercise training. *Exercise Sport Science Review* 33:63-68.

Hoeger, W.W.K., S.L. Barette, D.F. Hale, and D.R. Hopkins. 1990. Relationship between repetitions and selected percentages of one repetition maximum. *Journal of Applied Sport Science Research* 4(2):47-54.

Horton, T.J., M.J. Pagliassotti, K. Hobbs, and J.O. Hill. 1998. Fuel metabolism in men and women during and after long-duration exercise. *Journal of Applied Physiology* 85:1823-1832.

Huxley, H.E. 2004. Fifty years of muscle and the sliding filament hypothesis. *European Journal of Biochemistry* 271(8):1403-1415.

Jones, K., P. Bishop, G. Hunter, and G. Fleisig. 2001. The effects of varying resistance-training loads on intermediate- and high-velocity-specific adaptations. *Journal of Strength and Conditioning Research* 15(3):349-356.

Kadi, F., and L.E. Thornell. 2000. Concomitant increases in myonuclear and satellite cell content in female trapezius muscle following strength training. *Histochemical Cell Biology* 113:99-103.

Knuttgen, H.G., and W.J. Kraemer. 1987. Terminology and measurement in exercise performance. *Journal of Applied Sport Science Research* 1(1):1-10.

Kraemer, W.J., S.E. Gordon, S.J. Fleck, L.J. Marchitelli, R. Mello, J.E. Dziados, K. Friedl, E. Harman, C. Maresh, and A.C. Fry. 1991. Endogenous anabolic hormonal and growth factor responses to heavy resistance exercise in males and females. *International Journal of Sports Medicine* 12:228-235.

Kraemer, W.J., L. Marchitelli, S.E. Gordon, E. Harman, J.E. Dziados, R. Mello, P. Frykman, D. McCurry, and S.J. Fleck. 1990. Hormonal and growth factor responses to heavy resistance exercise protocols. *Journal of Applied Physiology* 69:1442-1450.

Kraemer, W.J., and N.A. Ratamess. 2004. Fundamentals of resistance training: Progression and exercise prescription. *Medicine and Science in Sports and Exercise* 36(4):674-688.

Kraemer, W.J., and N.A. Ratamess. 2005. Hormonal responses and adaptations to resistance exercise and training. *Sports Medicine* 35:336-361.

Kraemer, W.J., N. Ratamess, A.C. Fry, T. Triplett-McBride, L.P. Koziris, J.A. Bauer, J.M. Lynch, and S.J. Fleck. 2000. Influence of resistance training volume and periodization on physiological and performance adaptations in collegiate women tennis players. *American Journal of Sports Medicine* 28(5):626-633.

Kraemer, W.J., and J.S. Volek. 2000. L-Carnitine supplementation for the athlete: A new perspective. *Annals of Nutrition and Metabolism* 44:88-89.

Malliaropolous, N., S. Papalexandris, A. Papalada, and E. Papacostas. 2004. The role of stretching in rehabilitation of hamstring injuries: 80 athletes follow-up. *Medicine and Science in Sports and Exercise* 36(5):756-759.

Maynard, J., and W.P. Ebben. 2003. The effects of antagonist prefatigue on agonist torque and electromyography. *Journal of Strength and Conditioning Research* 17(3):469-474.

McBride, J.M., and W.J. Kraemer. 1999. Free radicals, exercise, and antioxidants. *Journal of Strength and Conditioning Research* 13:175-183.

McBride, J.M., T. Triplett-McBride, A. Davie, and R.U. Newton. 2002. The effect of heavy- vs. light-load jump squats on the development of strength, power, and speed. *Journal of Strength and Conditioning Research* 16(1):75-82.

Montain, S.J., S.A. Smith, R.P. Mattot, G.P. Zientara, F.A. Jolesz, and M.N. Sawka. 1998. Hypohydration effects on skeletal muscle performance and metabolism: A 31P-MRS study. *Journal of Applied Physiology* 84(6):1889-1894.

Moritani, T., and H.A. deVries. 1979. Neural factors versus hypertrophy in the time course of muscle strength gains. *American Journal of Physical Medicine* 58(3):115-130.

Peterson, M.D., M.R. Rhea, and B.A. Alvar. 2004. Maximizing strength development in athletes: A meta-analysis to determine the dose-response relationship. *Journal of Strength and Conditioning Research* 18(2):377-382.

Phillips, S.M., K.D. Tipton, A. Aarsland, S.E. Wolf, and R.R. Wolfe. 1997. Mixed muscle protein synthesis and breakdown after resistance exercise in humans. *American Journal of Physiology* 273:E99-E107.

Rasmussen, B.B., K.D. Tipton, S.L. Miller, S.E. Wolf, and R.R. Wolfe. 2000. An oral amino acid-carbohydrate supplement enhances muscle protein anabolism after resistance exercise. *Journal of Applied Physiology* 88:386-392.

Ratamess, N.A., W.J. Kraemer, J.S. Volek, M.R. Rubin, A.L. Gomez, D.N. French, M.J. Sharman, M.M. McGuigan, T. Scheett, K. Häkkinen, R.U. Newton, and F. Dioguardi. 2003. The effects of amino acid supplementation on muscular performance during resistance training overreaching. *Journal of Strength and Conditioning Research* 17(2):250-258.

Rhea, M.R., S.D. Ball, W.T. Phillips, and L.N. Burkett. 2002. A comparison of linear and daily undulating periodized programs with equated volume and intensity for strength. *Journal of Strength and Conditioning Research* 16(2):250-255.

Staron, R.S., D.L. Karapondo, W.J. Kraemer, A.C. Fry, S.E. Gordon, J.E. Falkel, F.C. Hagerman, and R.S. Hikida. 1994. Skeletal muscle adaptations during early phase of heavy resistance training in men and women. *Journal of Applied Physiology* 76:1247-1255.

Tan, B. 1999. Manipulating resistance training program variables to optimize maximum strength in men: A review. *Journal of Strength and Conditioning Research* 13(3):289-304.

Tipton, K.D., B.E. Gurkin, S. Martin, and R.R. Wolfe. 1999. Nonessential amino acids are not necessary to stimulate net muscle protein synthesis in healthy volunteers. *Journal of Nutritional Biochemistry* 10:89-95.

Tipton, K.D., B.B. Rasmussen, S.L. Miller, S.E. Wolf, S.K. Owens-Stovall, B.E. Petrini, and R.R. Wolfe. 2001. Timing of amino acid-carbohydrate ingestion alters anabolic response of muscle to resistance exercise. *American Journal of Physiology* 281:E197-E206.

Volek, J.S. 2000. General nutritional considerations for strength athletes. In C. Jackson, *Nutrition and the strength athlete*. Boca Raton, FL: CRC, pp. 31-51.

Volek, J.S. 2004. Influence of nutrition on responses to resistance training. *Medicine and Science in Sports and Exercise* 53436(4):689-696.

Volek, J.S., N.D. Duncan, S.A. Mazzetti, R.S. Staron, M. Putukian, A.L. Gomez, D.R. Pearson, W.J. Fink, and W.J. Kraemer. 1999. Performance and muscle fiber adaptations to creatine supplementation and heavy resistance training. *Medicine and Science in Sports and Exercise* 31(8):1147-1156.

Volek, J.S., W.J. Kraemer, M.R. Rubin, A.L. Gómez, N.A. Ratamess, and P. Gaynor. 2002. L-carnitine L-tartrate supplementation favorably affects markers of recovery from exercise stress. *American Journal of Physiology* 282:E474-E482.

Weiss, L.W. 1991. The obtuse nature of muscular strength: The contribution of rest to its development and expression. *Journal of Applied Sport Science Research* 5(4):219-227.

Wilson, G.J., R.U. Newton, A.J. Murphy, and B.J. Humphries. 1993. The optimal training load for the development of dynamic athletic performance. *Medicine and Science in Sports and Exercise* 25(11):1279-1286.

# Index

Note: The italicized *f* and *t* following page numbers refer to figures and tables, respectively.

# About the Editor

**Lee E. Brown, EdD, CSCS*D, FACSM,** is a certified strength and conditioning specialist (CSCS) through the National Strength and Conditioning Association (NSCA) and the current president of the NSCA. He is also a certified health fitness instructor through the American College of Sports Medicine (ACSM) and a certified club coach by USA Weightlifting (USAW). In 2003 Brown received the NSCA Outstanding Young Investigator award for his research in high-velocity exercise.

Brown holds both a master's degree in exercise science and a doctorate in educational leadership from Florida Atlantic University. He has published more than 75 articles, books, and book chapters on strength and conditioning. Formerly a high school physical education teacher and coach of many sports, Brown is now an associate professor of kinesiology in the department of kinesiology at California State University at Fullerton.

# About the Contributors

**Michael Barnes, MEd, CSCS*D, NSCA-CPT**, earned his master's degree in human performance from Auburn University. Mike is currently the education director for the National Strength and Conditioning Association (NSCA) and is certified with distinction as an NSCA strength and conditioning specialist and as an NSCA personal trainer. Previously he worked as a strength and conditioning coach at the Division I collegiate level and for USA Rugby, and he was the strength development coordinator for the San Francisco 49ers for seven years. Mike is a popular national speaker on strength and conditioning and has authored numerous publications.

**Sagir G. Bera, MS, ATC, CSCS**, is pursuing a career in medicine while teaching physics, mathematics, and critical thinking for Princeton Review. He is a certified athletic trainer and NSCA-certified strength and conditioning specialist. He obtained his master's degree in kinesiology from California State University at Fullerton, where he studied the effects of high-velocity resistance training.

**Keith E. Cinea, MA, CSCS*D, NSCA-CPT*D**, earned his bachelor's and master's degrees from the University of Northern Colorado. Currently he is the senior education coordinator for the NSCA, where he works as the editor of the *NSCA's Performance Training Journal* and editorial assistant for the *Strength and Conditioning Journal*. Before taking this position, he was the strength training coordinator for the YMCA of Metro Denver Downtown branch and worked as an adjunct faculty member at Front Range Community College in Westminster, Colorado. In addition, Keith currently serves on the advisor board for *Maximum Fitness*.

**Avery Faigenbaum, EdD, CSCS, FACSM**, is an associate professor in the department of health and exercise science at the College of New Jersey. He is a fellow of the ACSM and served as vice president of the NSCA. He is a leading researcher and practitioner in the area of strength training and has authored five books and more than 100 articles on fitness and conditioning. Faigenbaum resides in Newtown, Pennsylvania.

**Brian W. Findley, MEd, CSCS*D**, is a professor and department chair of health and wellness at Palm Beach Community College in Boca Raton, Florida. An NSCA-certified strength and conditioning specialist, Findley earned his MEd in exercise science and wellness education and is pursing his PhD in educational leadership, both from Florida Atlantic University. His research interests include occupational physiology and rehabilitative strength training. Findley resides in Royal Palm Beach, Florida.

**Steven J. Fleck, PhD, CSCS**, is currently professor and chair of the sport science department at Colorado College in Colorado Springs. Dr. Fleck's main research interests relate to physiological adaptations to resistance training and using sport science information to optimize the design of resistance training programs. He is an internationally known scientist and author in the area of resistance training and has authored numerous research articles as well as several books.

**Maren S. Fragala, MS**, is currently a doctoral fellow in the department of kinesiology working in the Human Performance Laboratory at the University of Connecticut. Ms. Fragala earned her master's degree in exercise science from the University of Massachusetts at Amherst and returned to graduate school from a research position at the Harvard School of Public Health in Boston. Her research interests are in the area of exercise endocrinology.

**Disa L. Hatfield, MA, MA**, is currently a doctoral fellow in the department of kinesiology working in the Human Performance Laboratory at the University of Connecticut at Storrs, where she earned a master's degree in exercise physiology. Ms. Hatfield has an additional master's degree in health psychology from Antioch University in Santa Barbara. Her major focus of research is exercise endocrinology and resistance training.

**Jay Hoffman, PhD, FACSM, CSCS\*D**, is the chair of the department of health and exercise science at the College of New Jersey. He holds the rank of full professor. Dr. Hoffman has served on the board of directors of the NSCA and served as vice president of that organization. He has published more than 80 articles and chapters in peer-reviewed journals. His books include *Physiological Aspects of Sport Training and Performance*; *Norms for Fitness, Performance, and Health* (Human Kinetics); and *Practical Guide to Designing Resistance Training Programs* (Coaches Choice).

**William J. Kraemer, PhD, CSCS**, is a full professor in the department of kinesiology in the Neag School of Education working in the Human Performance Laboratory at the University of Connecticut at Storrs. He also holds an appointment as a full professor in the department of physiology and neurobiology. In addition, he has an appointment as a full professor of medicine at the UCONN Health Center and School of Medicine. He has published more than 300 scientific manuscripts in the areas of exercise endocrinology, sports medicine, nutritional supplements, and resistance training.

**Daniel P. Murray, MS, PT, CSCS**, is a physical therapist specializing in the treatment of orthopedic and sport-related injuries. He is an adjunct faculty member of the physical therapy department at Northeastern University and works in private practice in Boston. He obtained his master's degree in kinesiology from California State University at Fullerton, where he studied the effects of high-velocity resistance training.

**Barry A. Spiering, MS, CSCS**, is currently a doctoral fellow in the department of kinesiology working in the Human Performance Laboratory at the University of

Connecticut at Storrs. He earned a master's degree from Ithaca College. He has also worked as a research assistant in the sports physiology division at the U.S. Olympic Committee's Olympic Training Center in Lake Placid. His research interests are in the area of exercise endocrinology and the molecular biology of resistance exercise and training.

**Jakob L. Vingren, MS**, is a doctoral fellow in the Human Performance Laboratory, Department of Kinesiology at the University of Connecticut at Storrs. He earned a master's degree in kinesiology from the University of North Texas. His major research interests are in the areas of exercise endocrinology and resistance training physiology.

**Jeff S. Volek, PhD, RD**, is an assistant professor in the department of kinesiology with an adjunct appointment in nutritional sciences at the University of Connecticut at Storrs. Dr. Volek is also a registered dietitian and has conducted several prospective research studies investigating a variety of dietary and exercise interventions in the area of diabetes, cardiovascular disease, and sport performance. He has authored and coauthored more than 100 scientific manuscripts as well as several book chapters, conference proceedings, technical reports, and editorials.